URBAN ENVIRONMENTS IN AFRICA

A critical analysis of environmental politics

Garth Myers

D1615532

First published in Great Britain in 2016 by

Policy Press
University of Bristol
1-9 Old Park Hill
Bristol
BS2 8BB
UK
t: +44 (0)117 954 5940
pp-info@bristol.ac.uk
www.policypress.co.uk

North America office:
Policy Press
c/o The University of Chicago Press
1427 East 60th Street
Chicago, IL 60637, USA
t: +1 773 702 7700
f: +1 773-702-9756
sales@press.uchicago.edu
www.press.uchicago.edu

British Library Cataloguing in Publication Data
A catalogue record for this book is available from the British Library

Library of Congress Cataloging-in-Publication Data
A catalog record for this book has been requested

ISBN 978-1-4473-2292-4 paperback
ISBN 978-1-4473-2291-7 hardcover
ISBN 978-1-4473-2295-5 ePub
ISBN 978-1-4473-2296-2 Mobi

Cover design by Hayes Design
Printed and bound in Great Britain by CMP, Poole
Policy Press uses environmentally responsible print partners

To all of God's bits of wood

Contents

List of figures and tables

Figures

Tables

List of abbreviations

CADD	Cooperative of development non-governmental organizations in Pikine
CCM	*Chama cha Mapinduzi*, or Revolutionary Party, Tanzania's ruling party
CCVI	Climate Change Vulnerability Index
CFA	*Communauté Financière d'Afrique* (Financial Community of Africa), which produces the CFA franc, the currency of former French colonies of West Africa
CFRS	Cape Flats Renewal Strategy
CUF	Civic United Front, Zanzibar-based opposition party in Tanzania
DRC	Democratic Republic of Congo
EIU	Economist Intelligence Unit
FEDUP	Federation for the Urban Poor, South Africa
IDP	internally displaced persons
IPCC	Intergovernmental Panel on Climate Change
KDI	Kounkuey Design Initiative
LECZs	low-elevation coastal zones
MoNMeD	Ministry for Nairobi Metropolitan Development (2008–13)
MOVE	invented acronym of the group, Socio-Ecological Movements in Urban Ecosystems
NGO	non-governmental organization
PD	People's Dialogue, a collaborative movement group in South Africa
SAHPF	South African Homeless People's Federation
SUPE	situated urban political ecologies
UN	United Nations
UPE	urban political ecology
VM	Victoria Mxenge Housing Development Association
VPUU	Violence Prevention through Urban Upgrading, a Cape Town program
ZATI	Zanzibar Association of Tourism Investors

Glossary of foreign terms

Abahlali baseMjondolo
(people who live in shacks), the radical shack-dwellers' movement in South Africa (Zulu)

Arrondissement
urban administrative level in Senegal; smaller units within each *arrondissement* are called *communes d'arrondissement* (French)

Banlieue
suburb; in Africa, the term often has negative connotations (French)

Bidonville
tin-can town, a term sometimes used for informal settlements (French)

Citimene
rotational bush-fallow agriculture of Zambia (Bemba)

Dambo
a seasonally flooded grassy depression (Chinyanja-Chichewa)

Eka tatu
three acres (Swahili)

Esprits
spirits; local branch units in the *Y'en a Marre* movement in Senegal (French)

Fitina
discord (Swahili)

Fynbos
Sclerophyllous Mediterranean scrub biome of the Western Cape, South Africa (Afrikaans)

Giningi
the Swahili spirit world in Zanzibar

Kibuki
ritual spirit group in Zanzibar

Glossary of foreign terms

Kusadikika
to make-believe or imagine (Swahili)

Mabonde
lowland wetlands (Zanzibari Swahili)

Matatu
term used for mini-bus in Nairobi

Maweni
stony coral bushlands in Unguja (Zanzibari Swahili)

Miombo
Central African woodland dominated by *Brachystegia Isoberlinia* and *Julbernardia*

Mjini
in the city (Swahili)

Munga
Central African woodland dominated by *Acacia*, *Combretum*, and *Afrormosia*

Ngoma
drum or dance; also rituals of affliction (Swahili)

Set/Setal
Be Clean/Make Clean; a Senegalese youth environmental group (Wolof)

Shamba
Zanzibari Swahili term for plantation, farm, or countryside

Uwaba
(from: *Umma wa Wapanda Baisekeli*, or Bicycle Riders' Society), a bicycling and environmental activist group in Dar es Salaam.

Uwanda
grassland and low bush country of Unguja (Zanzibari Swahili)

Y'en a Marre
Enough Is Enough; We Are Sick of It; a Senegalese movement (French)

Note on the author

Garth Myers is the Paul E. Raether Distinguished Professor of Urban International Studies at Trinity College, Hartford, CT, USA. He is director of the urban studies program and a member of the international studies program. He is the author of three other books on urban Africa and co-editor of two other volumes; he has also published more than 60 articles and book chapters.

Acknowledgments

When I began to think about and write this book in 2012, I called it my "tree book." I felt that not enough had been written about trees, and nature more broadly, in cities of sub-Saharan Africa. I would jokingly tell people that I wanted to get away from always writing about political things in urban Africa. I could have chapters on "dirt," "water," "air," and "animals" to go along with the trees (And I thank Morten Nielsen for that idea!). But of course, I knew, from the beginning, even the trees—along with the dirt, water, air, and animals—are political in the cities of Africa, as they are anywhere, even (or maybe especially) in the cities of Connecticut, where I live, or Pennsylvania ("Penn's Woods," after all), where I grew up. I also became steadily humbled by the staggering productivity of my world of colleagues studying urban Africa and its environments. Carlos Nunez Silva at the University of Lisbon, creator of the African Urban Planning Research Network (AUPRN), deserves specific mention in this regard. AUPRN has proved an invaluable source of information on the growing wealth of research relevant to urban environments in Africa. The African Centre for Cities at the University of Cape Town should also be highlighted in this same regard as arguably the continent's finest center for urban research, along with the Langaa Research & Publishing Common Initiative Group in Bamenda, Cameroon, whose publications have been quite inspirational.

Parts of the book have been presented at the Universities of Virginia, Wisconsin, Miami, Connecticut, Kentucky, Cape Town, Kansas, Stanford, and Oxford, along with Hong Kong Baptist University, Massachusetts Institute of Technology, Clark University, and conferences of the Association of American Geographers, African Studies Association, Institute of British Geographers, Dimensions of Political Ecology, and European Conference on African Studies. Zarina Patel, Sophie Oldfield, Gordon Pirie, Edgar Pieterse, Nancy Odendaal, Warren Smit, Liza Cirolia, Henrietta Nyamnjoh, Jenny Mbaye, Antonio Tomas, Sue Parnell, Vanessa Watson, Owen Crankshaw, Jenny Robinson, James McCarthy, Jim Murphy, Deborah Martin, Ellen Foley, Gabriella Carolini, Larry Vale, David Baker, Richard Grant, Miguel Kanai, Ellen Bassett, Guoping Huang, Mary Lawhon, Henrik Ernstson, Sarah Smiley, Hilary Hungerford, Jon Silver, Colin McFarlane, Rozy Fredericks, Maliq Simone, Rick Schroeder, Jacqueline Klopp, Morten Nielsen, Filip de Boeck, Laura Fair, Martin Murray, Anne Pitcher, Jim Delehanty, Tom Spear, Phebe Myers, Ken Foote, Carol

Atkinson-Palombo, Jeff Osleeb, George Bentley, Jonathan Highfield, David Hoegberg, Anthony Vital, Simon Lewis, Liz MacGonagle, Glenn Adams, Byron Santangelo, John Janzen, Ebenezer Obadare, Jamie Shinn, Leonie Newhouse, Jim Ferguson, Malini Ranganathan, Anne Rademacher, Jia-Ching Chen, Jeremia Njeru, Jesse McClendon, Idalina Baptista, Margret Frenz, Claire Mercer, Wing-Shing Tang, Christina West, Don Mitchell, Lisa Kim-Davis, Steve Commins, Ilda Lindell, Nik Heynan, Maria Kaika, Erik Swyngedouw and Dick Walker, and many others have given constructive comments as the project has progressed. Anthony Vital, Mary Lawhon, Byron Santangelo, Kjersti Larsen, John Janzen, Jenny Mbaye, and Jenny Robinson, in particular, have helped me through a number of key issues in the book at fairly obvious places that intersect with their expertise, though they bear no responsibility for any shortcomings in my interpretation of their works.

A nine-page segment of Chapter One is reprinted with permission, in a reformulated manner, from my 2015 article "A world-class city region? Envisioning the Nairobi of 2030," *American Behavioral Scientist* 59(3): 328–46. A five-page portion of Chapter Two is reprinted with permission, in a reformulated manner, from my "Remaking the edges: surveillance and flows in sub-Saharan Africa's new suburbs," in A. Luescher and C. Loeb (eds) *The design of frontier spaces: control and ambiguity* (Farnham: Ashgate, 2015), pp 45–63. The maps have all been produced for this book by Darin Grauberger at the Kansas Cartographic Services offices.

I have been blessed with a terrific set of colleagues at Trinity College, including Xiangming Chen, Vijay Prashad, Zayde Antrim, Pablo Delano, Dario Euraque, Maurice Wade, Luis Figueroa, David Cruz-Uribe, Jeff Bayliss, Janet Bauer, Donna Marcano, Tom Wickman, Sonia Cardenas, Tony Messina, Isaac Kamola, Serena Laws, Stefanie Chambers, Tanetta Andersson, Davarian Baldwin, Cheryl Greenberg, Andy Flibbert, Renny Fulco, Ralph Moyer, Anne-Marie Hanson, Gary Reger, Joan Morrison, Seth Markle, Kent Dunlap, Christoph Geiss, Jon Gourley, Mary Pelletier, Anne Lambright, Andrea Dyrness, Johnny Williams, Leslie Desmangles, Michael Lestz, Terry Romero, Marilyn Murphy, Jason Rojas, Carlos Espinosa, Robert Cotto, Anne Lundberg, Fakhmiddin Fazilov, Mustafa Ibraheem, Abbas Kazemi, and more. The unofficial happy hour *batos* (you know who you are) deserve my deepest gratitude for including me in their allegedly misbegotten circle and keeping me sane.

My students and former students at Trinity and Kansas have also kept me thinking about many of the issues in this book: many thanks to Ang Gray Subulwa, Dustin Crowley, Hilary Hungerford, Sarah Smiley, Josh Long, Emmanuel Birdling, Makame Muhajir, Megan Holroyd, Jamie Shinn, Aaron Gilbreath, Mary Lawhon, Shimantini Shome, Nouri Elfarnouk, Almokhtar Attwairi, Cort Miller, Shoki Mapokgole, George Denkey, Salima Etoka, Shaun McGann, Alex Gray, Chloe Shiras, Amanda Gurren, Nicole Schwartz, Billy Burchill, Seth Browner, Pierce Classen, Ned Mandel, Jarred Jones, and more.

The fieldwork for this book project occurred in more fits and starts than for any of my other books, for a variety of reasons. The extent to which my research in and explorations of Nairobi, Lusaka, Zanzibar, Dakar, and Cape Town since 2006 have been successful owes a great deal to those who have been my guides and colleagues in these cities: Peter Ojiambo, Peter Ngau, Laura Petrella, Patricia Kameri-Mbote, Wilma Nchito, Evaristo Kapungwe, Imasiku Nyambe, Mushe Subulwa, Ang Gray Subulwa, Hassan Sachedina, Danielle Monty-Mara, Alasse El-Hadji Diop, Birame Diop, Tom Hanlon, Makame Muhajir, Ali Hasan Ali, Ismail Jussa, Aboud Jumbe, Sheha Mjaja Juma, Hamza Rijal, Jenny Robinson, and all of the University of Cape Town and African Centre for Cities colleagues named earlier. I am thankful to Tom and Muhajir for including me in the crazy, unlikely scheme at the US Military Academy through which Tom and I led a study-abroad course for four cadets in Dakar in 2012–13. Some of the fieldwork has been in the field of literature, and my understanding of African ecocriticism has been shaped by Anthony Vital, Jonathan Highfield, Rob Nixon, and overwhelmingly, especially, Byron Santangelo. Byron, you would have had a million-seller with just a tweak of your latest book's title, to *Fifty shades of green*, but even so, thanks to you, I have been able to think in new ways about some of my favorite books, perhaps most of all *God's bits of wood*.

I have always cared about cities and their environments, and I have been obsessed with Africa since I was very young. This book is about *Africa's* urban environments, but my interests in urban environments and in urban political ecology have roots in my childhood in the Endless Mountains and the Wyoming Valley of Pennsylvania. I spent a lot of my younger years in the greater Scranton/Wilkes-Barre metropolitan area *outside*—playing, camping, canoeing, hiking, fishing, or bird-watching in those much-disturbed secondary-growth forests, or the tattered ribbons of riparian woodland along the Susquehanna River.

The greatest disturbance of my life came when that river flooded the valley, on June 23, 1972. Our home was destroyed along with those of thousands of our neighbors. It was only in a hydrology course in graduate school when I learned that the floods associated with Tropical

Storm Agnes in the Susquehanna watershed were not 'natural' acts of God, but the result of poor flood control and a lack of investment in prevention measures, alongside the peculiar climatological event called a 100-year flood—and its geography. The disaster could only be understood any more, for me, as a part of what I would now call an interactionist urban political ecology (If that phrase does not make sense yet, well, read on!) that took account of the political, cultural, historical, and economic dimensions alongside the environmental, and that understood the multiple perspectives and voices of a panoply of Pennsylvanians on Agnes. I remembered these voices a lot while I was writing this book—from the aptly named, corrupt congressman Daniel J. Flood, whose offices secured a trailer for my family, to the rumors that whirled around the city about bodies from the cemetery strewn in backyards or about my own family's disappearance. I remembered the solidarity of the young neighbors, including my oldest brother, organizing (unsuccessfully) to sandbag the dikes on the Susquehanna. I remembered the taste of the powdered eggs at the Army emergency field kitchen in the park up the street. I remembered the graffiti about a valley with a heart on abandoned homes.

Even as a nine year old, I had wondered why some Wilkes-Barre people suffered and others did not from the flood and its aftermath. The flood marked the crescendo, or the coda, of the valley's economic decline. Deep mining had died with another flood, the 1959 Knox Mine Disaster, and strip mining had stalled as concerns arose over the environmental costs of the valley's "dirty" anthracite coal. However, I also realized that many of greater Wilkes-Barre's wealthiest folks lived by the river, while many of its poorest lived, literally, in The Heights. There was no one single, simple way to read the map of environmental justice and injustice through fate, class, race, ethnicity, gender, or topography.

Now that the traumas and tragedies of Agnes are fleeting memories, hydraulic fracking brings a new boom and new political-environmental crisis points to Northeastern Pennsylvania. I read Tom Bauman's great novel set in the Endless Mountains amid this latest boom, *Dry bones in the valley*, and I would like to thank Tom for unknowingly helping me along to the recognition that I have written this "critical analysis of environmental politics" in Africa's cities in part because of those dry bones, if you will, in my own home city and valley. Also, I thank Melanie Hepburn for buying me that novel! I thank Melanie for everything else in our life together, and Atlee and Phebe for coaxing me along through the writing.

Urban environments in Africa

Introduction

Urban studies as a field is on the rise in Africa, environmental studies is a mainstay of scholarship on or about the continent, and urban environments are increasingly central to urban studies as a field. Yet, it is still rare to find works that offer political-environmental analyses of urban issues or urban analyses of environmental issues for Africa. This is beginning to change, but thus far, most of the works produced target one issue—for example, water or solid waste—and usually for one city. Many of the few broader analyses of urban environments come in rather dry policy documents or superficial observations from Western journalists, meaning that key aspects of political, economic, and cultural dimensions are shortchanged. In the study of Africa's urban environments, there is need for works that cover an array of environmental issues in a range of cities, and from a variety of political and scholarly perspectives, to provide readers—whether scholars, policymakers, students, or the interested public—with a fuller picture of urban Africa's multi-vocality and its complexities.

To try to meet that need, I first face several conceptual challenges. The biggest of these challenges concerns how to "read" Africa's urban environments. Are they an utter mess caused by incompetent governance and an absence of environmental consciousness? Are they manifestations of the "environmentalism of the poor" (Martinez-Alier, 2003; Nixon, 2011a, 2011b), as churning sites of devastation and contestation? Are they a combination of these two? Or are they fundamentally impossible to uniformly characterize in the first place given the incredible diversity of the continent's cities? There are no neat answers to these questions. Instead, in this book, I offer a range of readings of, or ways of reading, the diverse and complex environments of cities on the continent.

I begin by acknowledging the obvious reality that it is impossible to cover all aspects of urban environments for all cities of Africa. In this Introduction's next section, I make note of the book's geographical and methodological parameters and work to begin setting the limits of what I am examining in terms of urban environments. After that, I lay out my conceptual framework for this examination in the book.

Africa's cities: geographical scope

While I understand that it can be a problem to make claims for anything "African," given the long history of overgeneralizations about the continent, it is also the case that Africa is taken as a region, addressed in policy terms as a region, and conceived of as a coherent region by scholars, practitioners, and most residents of the region. One need only think of the hysteria across Europe and North America in 2014 surrounding the devastating outbreak of the Ebola virus in Guinea, Sierra Leone, and Liberia, when many Westerners associated the virus with "Africa" rather than with merely the three small countries within West Africa that experienced the overwhelming share of this epidemic. I had immigration officials and intelligent professional colleagues sincerely concerned for my welfare in traveling to Cape Town, South Africa, far from any genuine risk zones, because Ebola had struck "Africa." It is therefore imperative to examine how the urban environments of this region, this reality, this "Africa-in-the-world" (Ferguson, 2006: 6) can be characterized and represented, to confront such geographic illiteracy head-on. My approach is to concentrate on cities of varied sizes in different regions and physical settings of Africa to give at least some sense of the diversity of urban environments on the continent. In each chapter, I have extended analysis of one city— Nairobi, Lusaka, Zanzibar, Dakar, and Cape Town, respectively—based around my fieldwork and study in them, as well as in-depth analysis of secondary sources for them. However, beyond these cities, there is material, scattered through the chapters, on the urban environments of a wider variety of cities in Africa. Data for those five cities are in Table I.1, which contains basic environmental data on cities that figure in my argument somewhere along the way.

According to the UN Habitat's (2014) most recent estimates, there are now 70 cities with more than 750,000 people on the African continent (see Table I.2 and Figure I.1). These cities manifest diversity in size, shape, biophysical environment, boundaries, climatic features, planning systems, politics, and sociocultural dynamics. Let us just consider diversity in population size. Over 50 of these cities contain populations above 1 million, with almost 20 more just below this. Yet, these range from the megacities of Lagos, Cairo, or Kinshasa (with populations that the UN has conservatively estimated will exceed 15 million, 13 million, and 12 million, respectively, by 2020) to the cities

Table I.1: Environmental facets of cities discussed in the book

CITY NAME	COUNTRY	Biome	2011 Pop.[a]	2010-20 Growth[e]	Climate Threat	Green City Index	Climate[c]
Cairo	Egypt	Mediterranean N Africa	13254	1.84	sea level rise	average	Bwh
Lagos	Nigeria	Guinea Forest	11223	3.83	sea level rise	average	Aw
Kinshasa	DR Congo	Congo Forest	8798	3.81	flooding	N/A	Aw
Dar es Salaam	Tanzania	East African coastal	3588	5.08	sea level rise	well below average	Aw
Cape Town	South Africa	Fynbos	3492	1.6	sea level rise	above average	Csb
Nairobi	Kenya	Somali-Maasai steppe	3363	4.23	flooding	below average	Bsh
Casablanca	Morocco	Mediterranean N Africa	3046	1.74	sea level rise	above average	Csa
Dakar	Senegal	Sahel	3035	3.68	sea level rise	N/A	Bsh
Accra	Ghana	Guinea savanna	2573	4.59	sea level rise	above average	Aw
Bamako	Mali	Sahel	1932	4.39	drought	N/A	Bsh
Lusaka	Zambia	Zambezian	1719	4.75	drought	N/A	Cwa
Mogadishu	Somalia	Somali-Maasai steppe	1554	6.36	sea level rise	N/A	Bsh
Harare	Zimbabwe	Zambezian	1526	2.66	drought	N/A	Cwa
Kigali	Rwanda	East African highland	961	4.45	flooding	N/A	Aw
Bosaso	Somalia	Somali-Maasai steppe	700[d]	a	sea level rise	N/A	Bwh
Thiés	Senegal	Sahel	636[e]	2.66	drought	N/A	Bsh
Zanzibar	Tanzania	East African coastal	593[f]	3.41	sea level rise	N/A	Aw

Notes: [a] Population in thousands. [b] Estimated annual percentage growth.

[c] According to the Köppen-Geiger Classification System: Aw = Tropical wet-and-dry savanna; Bsh = Hot steppe; BWh = Hot desert; Csa = Mediterranean with hot summer; Csb = Mediterranean with warm summers; Cwa: Humid Sub-Tropical Climates with warm summers

[d] Estimate of Bosaso Municipality (http://bosasomunicipality.com/726/urbanization-process.html) as of 2011. The city had only 50,000 people in 1990, so the rate of growth has probably been higher for Bosaso than for any city on the chart.

[e] Urban-West Region – metropolitan Zanzibar in the 2012 Tanzania census.

[f] Thies Departement in the 2013 Senegal census. All other population data from UN Habitat (2014).

3

Table I.2: Largest urban areas in Africa

CITY	COUNTRY	2020 POPULATION (IN MILLIONS, PROJECTED)
Lagos	Nigeria	15.8
Cairo	Egypt	13.3
Kinshasa	DR Congo	12.3
Luanda	Angola	7.6
Khartoum	Sudan	6
Abidjan	Cote d'Ivoire	5.9
Dar es Salaam	Tanzania	5.7
Alexandria	Egypt	5.5
Nairobi	Kenya	4.9
Kano	Nigeria	4.7
Johannesburg	South Africa	4.4
Dakar	Senegal	4.2
Ibadan	Nigeria	4.2
Cape Town	South Africa	4.1
Addis Ababa	Ethiopia	3.9
Ekurhuleni (E Rand)	South Africa	3.9
Ouagadougou	Burkina Faso	3.7
Algiers	Algeria	3.6
Casablanca	Morocco	3.6
Durban	South Africa	3.5
Yaounde	Cameroon	3.4
Douala	Cameroon	3.4
Abuja	Nigeria	3.3
Antananarivo	Madagascar	3.1
Bamako	Mali	3

Note: Based on UN Habitat (2014) projections for 2020.

whose populations will have exceeded 750,000 but not yet reached a million by 2020. Indeed, most of Africa's major cities will still have less than 2 million people by 2020, by the UN's data, including nearly half (34) of the 70 that they included in their 2014 Statistical Annex. It is just as important to an overall understanding of urban environments, then, to study these smaller or medium-sized cities as well as the largest ones. Indeed, many cities with *less than* 750,000 people matter greatly to a robust understanding of urban-environmental geographies on the continent given how rapidly many of these small cities are growing or how significant they are becoming to the political economies

Figure I.1: Map of cities of Africa

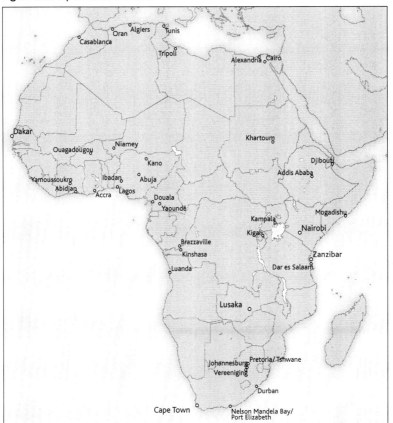

of Africa. Tanzania, for instance, has been among the world's most rapidly urbanizing countries for a half-century, and to study Tanzanian urbanization by only studying its only city greater than 750,000 people (Dar es Salaam) would be to miss the dynamics behind the growth for at least a dozen other substantial cities (Mwanza, Zanzibar, Arusha, Moshi, Tanga, Dodoma, and others). In 2010, government economic data identified the little-studied town of Mafinga (with a 2012 census population of 51,902) as Tanzania's second-most productive town (by gross domestic product [GDP] per capita) to Dar es Salaam, mostly because of a boom in tea, timber, and furniture manufacturing.

Most scholars and policymakers have highlighted the rapid rates of population growth for African cities for a half-century, and although the rates are generally slowing, it remains the case that the continent's urban populations are increasing rather steadily (by more than 4% per year). The most rapidly growing cities in percentage terms are often the smaller major cities rather than the megacities; these rapidly growing cities tend to be in countries with modest or even poor economic growth and development, while cities in countries with higher rates of human and economic development actually tend to have slower rates of population growth. The UN's estimated rates of growth for 2010–20 for major cities vary from the small group with rates of more than 5% per year (Dar es Salaam, Tanzania; Kampala, Uganda; Mogadishu, Somalia; Niamey, Niger; Ouagadougou, Burkina Faso; and Yamoussoukro, Cote d'Ivoire), to those below 2%—all of which are in North Africa (Cairo, Egypt; Casablanca, Morocco; Oran, Algeria; Tripoli, Libya; and Tunis, Tunisia) or the Republic of South Africa (Cape Town, Durban, Ekurhuleni, Johannesburg, Port Elizabeth, Pretoria/Tshwane, and Vereeniging). The North African countries (despite their recent political turmoil) and South Africa have larger urban-industrial economies and GDP numbers (for total production and per capita) than all but a handful of oil- or diamond-producing sub-Saharan states. By contrast, Somalia, Niger, Burkina Faso, and Cote d'Ivoire have all had rather dismal economies for much of the last quarter-century, and even with recent positive developments, Tanzania and Uganda remain among the world's poorest countries. Moreover, the population growth rates for Kampala and Dar es Salaam have actually *slowed* during the period of positive economic growth, reversing a long trend of even more rapid population growth that came with little to no economic growth.

This book discusses several of these most- and least-rapidly growing cities, as well as a larger set of cities in between. Beyond these varied rates of population growth and economic development, the urban areas discussed in the book vary in size from just over 500,000 (Thiés, Senegal and Zanzibar, Tanzania) to the megacities of Cairo and Lagos (both with populations of more than 12 million in the UN's 2014 projection). Not only are the cities spread throughout much of the continent, but they also vary in terms of the biophysical environments in which they are set, from deserts to rainforests, coastlines to mountains or plateaus. Through such a broad and diverse sample, it is possible to gain a glimpse of the extensive variation found among urban environments on the continent, and yet still see the extent to which some themes may be held in common—or common enough for comparability.

Analyzing Africa's urban environments

Too often, when people think of the environment or environmental issues, they conceive of natural processes, absent of humans or human causation. While natural, biophysical processes are certainly at work in the transformation of urban environments, it is perhaps a little easier to understand that in cities—which, after all, are first and foremost dense concentrations of human beings along with their built environments—we need to address political, economic, and cultural dynamics along with the biophysical ones to comprehend environmental problems. This is quite pertinent to cities in Africa since, historically, indigenous African conceptions of the environment often did not make a distinct break between nature and society (Mamabolo, 2012; Mawere, 2014a, 2014b). This factor figures into a common perception that seemingly irreconcilable differences exist between Western/outsider environmentalist/scientific perspectives and those of many ordinary Africans. This then carries over into the debate in African *urban* studies over the question of the "clash of rationalities," which appears in the planning dynamics of the continent's cities—where rational, Western planning mindsets clash with the vision of ordinary urban majorities who often reside in poorer, informal settlements in cities (eg Watson, 2003, 2009a; Harrison, 2006; Robins, 2006; Myers, 2011). This conceptualization of the clash of rationalities has yet to be extended into the realm of urban environmental studies, but at first pass, such an extension is an easy one, probably too easy. There is, to be sure, an evident clash between the visions of the environment that one sees in most planning documents or Western scholarship and in the voices of Africa's urban majorities. Yet, all manner of variety in perspectives and possibilities for dialogue also appear in between.

Nearly 20 years ago, I conducted an interview with the head of an informal women's gravel miners' union in Zanzibar, Tanzania, and I asked her how she felt when someone like me, a white, Western outsider, told her that she was destroying the environment through this illegal mining for building materials on the city's expanding edge. Her pitched reply lingers in my head many years later:

> These people, they keep hearing announcements on the radio, some people have been fired from their jobs, so where are they going to find work? The rocks. Let me tell you something, you listen here. My children eat because of these rocks, they have clothes on their backs because of these rocks. The Forestry Department comes and tells us we are destroying the environment. Whose environment? (Myers, 1999: 105)

What I tried to show in that publication was that neither the Forestry Department nor the union had uniform answers to the question of whose environment the peri-urban fringe was. Certainly, there was this clash between the rational planner mindset and the impassioned informal activist mindset at the grassroots. However, there were spaces of ambivalence for both sides, and there were many nuanced locations in between in that clash (Myers, 1999).

A similar story emerges with urban Africa's solid waste management. It is typically seen as disastrous across much of the continent from the rational Western planning side of things, but urban Africans often see waste issues far differently from planners and scholars. In a January 2013 focus group discussion during my collaborative fieldwork with geographer Tom Hanlon and the non-governmental organization (NGO) Partners Senegal, the president of a scavengers' union on the (in)famous "Trash Mountain" of Mbeubeuss in the municipality of Pikine in Dakar made a pun with the French word for waste, *ordure*, breaking it in two to note the French words for gold (*or*) and solid/hard (*dure*): "waste," he said, is "solid gold." Yet, waste is solid misery for other urban Africans, even in Mbeubeuss (Cissé, 2012), who may protest at the decrepit state of sanitation and waste services in their neighborhoods—or they may have too many other concerns weighing them down to bother with any protest over waste issues.

One way to break the apparent impasse between Western modernist planning perspectives and ordinary people's views of the environment in Africa's cities would be to force-feed the outside lenses or Western environmentalist perspectives on to the continent. A similar way would be to fall back on the rather tired pattern of concluding that African cities do not work, or are not cities in the right way, and have to be refashioned and corrected. One might also simply champion the indigenous urban poor majority's views of urban environments— "Waste is solid gold!"—as a part of creating "Afropolitan" urbanism (Nuttall and Mbembe, 2008). To me, other possibilities present themselves that can articulate a broader set of African views of urban environments, and these have yet to be explored to any great extent, especially in one volume, on the continent. In this book, I highlight five of these possibilities, through what I term the readings of: (1) "the experts"—analyzing the pronouncements and findings of policymakers, planners, and scholars on Africa's urban environmental problems; (2) "the past"—excavating and interrogating pre-colonial and colonial urban environmental histories and their post-colonial legacies; (3) "the cityscape"—thoroughly engaging with the physical-material settings but also cultural beliefs and practices surrounding them, such as in place-naming and in the spiritual/symbolic worlds of urban Africans; (4) "the artists"—recovering the political-environmental urban visions of African writers, poets, photographers, painters, or musicians; and (5) "the grassroots"—building from everyday community environmental activism in cities. This book is about getting at these varied possibilities and alternative readings of Africa's urban environments. My primary practical, policy, and planning-oriented argument is rather simple: any efforts to "improve" urban environments in Africa will fail without engagement with and (re)building from the reality of the diverse and complex perspectives on those urban environments.

My argument here fits more broadly with the global discussion of re-centering urban studies. Over the last decade, a considerable critique has arisen that challenges universal understandings of and policy prescriptions for urbanism emanating from European and North American cities (Robinson, 2006; Pieterse and Simone, 2013; Parnell and Oldfield, 2014). Many scholars of Global South and African cities like me now demand "that the cities [we] study deserve wider consideration in theoretical analysis" (Robinson, 2011: 4). Some of us even want to see "the center of theory-making move to the Global South" in urban studies (Roy, 2009: 820; see also Simone, 2010, 2012; Myers, 2014). An invigorated focus on cities in Africa in this regard has already brought to the fore the endogenous creativity, inventiveness, and artistry of the continent's urbanites in crafting their everyday worlds and environments as a potentially inspirational avenue for research across the globe rather than just in Africa (Förster, 2013; Macamo, 2013; Vierke and Siegert, 2013; Quayson, 2014).

To some extent, this shifting landscape of urban studies could connect up well with the broader effort in African studies beyond just urban studies, the aims of which are best captured in the title of the recent two-volume edited book from Ghana, *Reclaiming the human sciences and humanities through African perspectives* (Lauer and Anyidoho, 2012). One key step in the "reclaiming" is to work in ways that "more effectively involve not only African scholars but also local experts and communities … in the research design and implementation," with the aim of "increased endogeneity in knowledge production and dissemination" (Olukoshi and Nyamnjoh, 2011: 25). That is definitely a key goal of my book: to foreground the perspectives of local experts, artists, and communities in urban Africa from the beginning. However, in any attempt to meet such a goal, we come to the question of building a conceptual framework that will allow for this reclaiming, which is my task in the next section.

A theoretical framework for Africa's urban environments

This book contributes to the expanding literature of *urban political ecology* (UPE) in relation to Africa. UPE scholars seek to understand urban environmental change in political, historical, cultural, and economic terms, as well as ecological, and to see causal factors in that change at multiple scales. UPE scholars are currently grappling with what to do with cities in Africa, and I seek to offer my perspective here, with nuance, such that the need for the broader range of perspectives discussed in the previous section can be accounted for in the framework.

Political ecology has a strong tradition in rural Africa, critiquing the prevailing wisdom in environmental decline discourse and its colonial origins. The literature of explicitly *urban* political ecology, though, emerged largely outside of the continent, and particularly in reference to the West's cities. Scholars have yet to build much dialogue between approaches commonly found in this UPE with the critical analyses in Africa-based political ecology that have focused around what are typically conceived of as rural environmental issues like desertification, deforestation, soil erosion, or wildlife conservation. Furthermore, although there are exceptions (eg Njeru, 2006; Bjerkli, 2015), most work explicitly labeled as UPE in Africa is still based on South African cities. I am working to further expand UPE's geography of operation and establish stronger links with that longer tradition of rural political ecology. In later chapters, this comes with material on cities in a variety of different African countries, the critique of policymakers, analyses of colonial legacies, and attention to a diversity of voices, artists, and cultural practices in African cityscapes. For an Africa-based UPE to thrive, it needs to find roots for urban environmental voices from Africa, outside of the expected cases in South Africa, and outside of both the "experts" or a simplistically rendered voice of the urban poor. Later chapters of the book seek to do these things, too. Here, let me suggest how UPE can be broadened to strengthen critical scholarship on African urban environments.

Urban political ecologists seek to "disrupt the idea of the city as the anti-thesis of nature," building on Marxist urban theory to see cities as ecosystems that are *socio-naturally* produced in the power relationships of capitalism (Loftus, 2012: 3; see also Harvey, 1996; Swyngedouw, 1996, 2003; Keil, 2003, 2005; Kaika, 2005; Heynan et al, 2006; Kaika and Swyngedouw, 2011). UPE's "historical materialist roots are much more evident" than those of the other, rural-focused political ecology in Africa (Loftus, 2012: 5; see also Lawhon, 2012; Robbins, 2012;

Lawhon et al, 2014) or those of many contemporary political ecologists in anthropology (Biersack, 2006: 4–5). A UPE that builds specifically from African theoretical or conceptual bases, outside of South Africa, is thin on the ground, and African voices of UPE are rarely heard (Njeru, 2006, 2010; Myers, 1999, 2005a; Nzeadibe and Mbah, 2015). Despite a modestly expanding number of exceptions, the small volume of UPE in urban Africa is made particularly striking by the evident potential for scholarly work examining urban environments from a variety of perspectives and building from African conceptualizations given the magnitude of urban environmental-political challenges and conflicts.

It is difficult to generalize across a region comprising more than 50 countries and, as noted previously, more than 50 cities with populations in excess of 1 million people. Yet, I believe that some thinness of UPE research in this zone results from the potentially alienating starting places of Western urban theory as it travels to Africa. Its conceptual emphasis "tends to overlook the situated understandings of the environment, knowledge and power that form the core of other political ecological understandings as well as recent work in Southern urbanism" (Lawhon et al, 2014: 498).

For one specific example of the problems of theory transfer, water infrastructure networks do not provide the flows—literally (of water) or figuratively (of power)—in cities of the region in the same manner as they may in Western cities, where they have been perhaps the central empirical focus of urban political ecologists. Hilary Hungerford (2012) found that the map of the water supply network of Niamey, Niger, for instance, obscures more than it reveals about either the flow of water or the flow of power: many pipes do not have any water flowing in them, and many areas off the grid are more likely to have the best quality and cheapest water (see also Bontianti et al, 2014).

Similarly, Western-oriented UPE's stronger political-economy orientation does not always fit neatly into African urban contexts. Since significant proportions of the urban economy occur informally in many sub-Saharan cities, and since much of the urban population expansion has occurred without large-scale manufacturing growth, multiple sources of sociocultural identity, such as religion, political party affiliation, or ethnicity, will rival or even transcend class bases for organizing and activism. The urban neoliberalism—market-based management of the urban environment, enabled by pro-free market states—that is the linchpin around which UPE scholars often build research on urban environmental governance in the West takes on very different meanings in urban Africa (Pieterse, 2008; Robinson and Parnell, 2011; Bekker and Fourchard, 2013).

Given those challenges, it might be encouraging for African urban political ecologists that UPE is increasingly turning to post-structuralist theoretical approaches, which can lead to very intriguing research results (Keil and Ali, 2011; Gabriel, 2014). Roger Keil (2011: 29) has recently highlighted "the squatter settlements of the global South" as "the frontiers of urban political ecology," arguing that it is there where we find "the new reality in which strategies of sustainability are being negotiated." However, "Global South" researchers can struggle with the applicability of post-structuralist UPE as much as they struggle with Marxist UPE (Rademacher, 2011; Shillington, 2012; Green, 2013). African conceptualizations of nature–society relations rarely seem to leave room for the same sort of valuing of non-human agency that one finds in post-structuralist UPE; pets, for one, are remarkably different in many cities in Africa than they are in Western cities. I have my doubts as to whether Erik Swyngedouw's (2009b: 63) inspiring notion of a "cyborg urbanization" that results in a "socio-natural network combining circulations and metabolisms of human and nonhuman" was intended for contemplating the widely prevalent spiritual and supernatural consciousness of urban spaces in Africa (eg De Boeck, 2011, 2012; see also Gandy, 2008). I am reminded of an overfilled trash slab in Zanzibar, from which municipal trash workers were reluctant to remove the waste because the slab was a local portal to the Zanzibari Swahili spirit world, Giningi, and they had absolute confirmation of this in the form of evil spirits embodied as Indian house crows eating at the trash slab in a substantial unkindness. "Cyborg" just does not suffice, to me, as a means of interpreting *that* intersection of "human and non-human" metabolisms. There might be room for some sort of post-structuralist thinking in an Africa-centered UPE, but complexities like that abound.

In his *Everyday environmentalism: creating an urban political ecology*, Alex Loftus (2012) offers tantalizing potential building blocks for a new UPE that might account for African urban realities. The everyday life of South Africa's urban poor serves as his inspiration for seeking out new ways of thinking, and he offers "the postapartheid political project of ensuring access to services" and the work of "artists and activists to transform our cities into laboratories for radical experimentation" as "concrete" examples (Loftus, 2012: xi, xiii). He offers a healthy dose of caution about the potential for the onslaught of Western alarmist rhetoric on global climate change to "disempower" the urban poor and "depoliticize the processes and relationships out of which climate change is produced" (Loftus, 2012: xvi), an effective argument very much in line with that of the urban geographer David Harvey (2012), whose works inspired most of what is called "urban political ecology." Furthermore, the book has a careful, close reading of both the (Western) literature of UPE and a slew of radical urban theorists for their attention to the environment, or lack thereof. He builds chapters around the works of Harvey, Neil Smith, Georg Lukacs, Antonio Gramsci, and Henri Lefebvre.

Yet, as that last list may suggest, the book is surprisingly limited in terms of its appreciation of *African* urban voices and the diverse and complex readings of urban environments that emerge from them. One loses track of what "the everyday" means in the book's dense thicket of abstract, non-African radical philosophy. Only in the 17 pages that deal with a portion of the city of Durban, Inanda, do we read much about what urban Africans think, feel, or do about the environment of their city. That segment is where Loftus (2012: 78) is "more directly concerned with how the radical ideas of subaltern peoples come to cohere within and between specific historical and geographical contexts." Even in this portion, though, I am less sanguine than Loftus about the oppositional potential or radical unity of the urban poor, whom he characterizes, following Gramsci, as the subaltern. Power relationships within apartheid-era (1948–94) South African townships were much more complicated and fractured than Marxist class analysis can express, to say nothing of how much more fractious and complex these have become in post-apartheid South Africa, or of how vastly different urban South African race and class dynamics are from those of generally less-industrialized cities in the rest of Africa. We need a messier theoretical lens to see "everyday" environmentalism and UPE in Africa.

To some extent, Loftus wants the messier lens, too. He introduces some post-structuralist or feminist ideas in several chapters. The material on Inanda, too, contains an empathetic understanding of politicized cultural practice, as in the post-apartheid efforts to shape a consumer mentality out of a "culture of non-payment" for water. We still do not hear enough from Inanda's people, and certainly not from any broad cross-section. In Inanda, as in many similar townships or informal settlements in Africa, it is rarely possible to categorize and simplify historical blocs of society into neat revolutionary packages.

Consider the following two anecdotes about a different urban environment in Africa, next to a fish market in Dakar. Looking out at the Atlantic ocean coastline from a bridge over the mouth of a canal laden with garbage, reeking of human waste and clogged by the rotting headless carcass of a goat, my US research colleague, Tom Hanlon, asked our Senegalese research assistant, Alasse El-Hadji

Diop, what Dakar residents like him thought of when they looked at the ocean: "It's the place where we get fish," he replied. A few feet from us, in the space occupied by the Theatre of the Beach in Soumbedioune, in December 2012, activists had placed two copies of a makeshift billboard, emblazoned with the words *"President merci pour le repos biologique marin mais les ordures constituent une bombe ecologique"* ("President thanks for the marine biological rest period [temporary fishing ban] but waste comprises an ecological bomb") (see Figure I.2).

Figure I.2: Protest sign on the Theatre of the Beach, Soumbedioune, Dakar

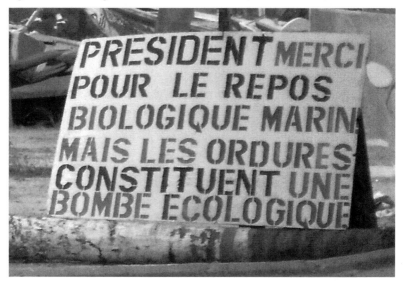

The first anecdote suggests that Dakarois are only concerned about the environment for the immediate material benefits that they might obtain from it, with no consciousness of the waste and rot enveloping them or broader appreciation of the geographical scale of environmental dynamics. The second suggests something like the opposite—that Dakar's fisherfolk are extremely aware of, and directly and negatively impacted by, the environmental decline of Dakar's waters due to the dumping of untreated waste and sewage, as well as the implications of national policies and global forces. Both statements and the movements and processes behind them are far more complex than this, of course. My point here is to highlight that African urban environmental consciousness is not a linear unified concept readily translatable into Marxist language or post-structuralist thinking. Any time I am compelled to contemplate the "flows of urbanized nature in the community," let alone the "more than human" or the "post-human" in urban Africa (ie using some lingo often found in Western UPE), I am compelled to contemplate, together, that headless goat carcass and that protest sign in Soumbedioune. The realities of "everyday environmentalism" in urban Africa are myriad and varied (see Figure I.3).

Figure I.3: Fishing boats at Soumbedioune, Dakar

If we are to build UPE from African perspectives, we need to begin from being "situated" somewhere other than in the heads of Western theorists alone, even if we accept that Marxist or post-structuralist thought can still be helpful to our analysis. Perhaps this is where the long and deep bench of more rurally based political-ecology research from Africa may offer a way forward—in its substantial commitment to the multi-vocality of the everyday environmental consciousness of the continent's ordinary people. As an overarching framework, it seems quite plausible to return to the political ecology offered by Piers Blaikie (1995) in his succinct, cogent, 20-year-old essay "Changing environments or changing views? A political ecology for developing countries." Blaikie (1995: 204, emphasis added) laid out what he termed an "interactionist" approach to environmental problems, "in which there is not an objective reality, *but many subjective ones* which are provided by different people who see their 'real' landscape in their own ways."

We can see these many subjective realities of different people come to life in works like Richard Schroeder's (1999, 2012) books, the careful, richly theoretical studies of Donald Moore (1993), the collaborative publications from Thomas Bassett (Bassett and Koli Bi, 2000; Bassett and Crummey, 2003), and, crucially for me, the rigorously empirical, gendered, and textured studies of pastoralism (livestock-raising) done long ago by Gudrun Dahl, often in collaboration with Anders Hjort (Dahl and Hjort, 1976, 1979; Dahl, 1979). These scholars are just a small sample of (rural) political ecologists working on Africa—a comprehensive list would have to include Judith Carney, Dianne Rocheleau, Alice Hovorka (2006), and Michael Watts, among many others. All bring a critical eye to the historical and cultural dimensions of landscape change, in classic political-ecology fashion. Schroeder brings alive the varied perspectives and agendas of women and men in Gambian horticultural and arboricultural development schemes, and then, more recently, in spaces of interaction between white South Africans and their Tanzanian hosts in mining, ranching, hunting, and wildlife tourism; Moore creates a multilayered, multi-sided, and thoroughly peopled understanding of "the state" in Zimbabwe embedded in nuances of cultural practice; and Bassett and colleagues juxtapose and test a broad range of discourses for the veracity of their claims on land degradation in Ivory Coast.

One of the greatest shortcomings that stems from the lack of dialogue as yet between UPE scholarship and the supposedly more rural focus of "older" political ecology in Africa is the missed opportunity of highlighting both the specific spatiality of peri-urban contexts in between the rural and urban settings and the inextricability of rural and urban political-ecological dynamics in the first place. UPE has recently been critiqued for its failure to interrogate linkages that urbanization has beyond cities despite its supposed claims for rejecting the urban–rural binary, and for its "metrocentricity" that maps poorly onto cityness in Africa and other parts of the developing world (Bunnell and Maringanti, 2010; Angelo and Wachsmuth, 2015)—and this has long been a frustration of mine. My own initial understanding of political ecology was virtually entirely formed from reading Dahl's and Hjort's works from the 1970s, together and apart, based on studies in northern Kenya—studies I have never seen cited by urban political ecologists, to say nothing of the under-appreciation of their groundbreaking work even by other "rural" political ecologists. Dahl and Hjort not only integrated non-human agency explicitly into their scientifically ecological analysis years ahead of its trendiness (*Having herds* [Dahl and Hjort, 1976] is an incredibly detailed study of the relationship of north

Kenya herds with herders), but, more significantly for my interests, they also made the boundaries of rural and urban irreparably fuzzy in their work. Dahl (1979: 12), especially, in *Suffering grass*, laid out the purpose of a *political* ecology because, she argued, a natural science "ecology can only provide partial answers to our questions. There is already considerable evidence that it is not so much ecological change in itself that causes crisis ... but that political and economic changes frequently express themselves in ecological effects." Crucial among the political and economic changes that Dahl examined for the Borana of north-central Kenya's Isiolo district was *urbanization*, where towns formed a major center of dis-integration between pastoral lifestyles and the global capitalist marketplace. For Dahl, it was as impossible to differentiate between rural and urban as it was to differentiate between ecological and political processes as part of the same political ecology, explicitly situated in Isiolo as a complex and cosmopolitan place. Isiolo Borana everyday cultural-environmental practices, and the differentiation within the society along political, economic, and ideological lines, were her central themes.

Of course, in hearkening back to these rural political ecologies, I might run the risk of perpetuating the undue reliance on Western knowledge or theory derived from the work of outsiders. Even if all that I am doing is essentially nodding toward these non-Africans' political ecology for my framework or approach, it is imperative to likewise build from African-based theory. I do so through examination of the multidisciplinary literatures of African urban studies, African indigenous ideas of the urban and of nature, Africa-based or Africa-centered theorization on cities, and African voices on urban environments. This encompasses or at least touches upon African history, literature, performing and visual arts, grassroots activist organizations, and everyday sociocultural beliefs and practices. I have taken particular inspiration from the Zimbabwean philosopher-anthropologist Munyaradzi Mawere (2014a, 2014b; Mawere and Mubaya, 2014), who has pioneered new routes and roots for the conceptualization of Africa's urban environments through an incredibly fruitful burst of recent scholarship.

In line with African studies scholars arguing that UPE can be greatly enhanced by becoming "situated" in Africa (Lawhon et al, 2014), Mawere provides some significant possibilities for that situatedness, as I seek to show in Chapters Three and Five as well. Even if, like much of the outsider political ecology I have discussed, he has rural Africa in mind as he develops his philosophy, Mawere (2014a: 4) notes that in Africa, "all communities—whether rural, urban or semi-urban—have certain traditional knowing innovations, norms and values" that can be at the base of indigenous knowledge of socio-environmental solutions. Mawere (2014a: 23) seeks to revalorize this African indigenous knowledge of the environment, which has been "unjustifiably and unfairly despised and relegated as superstitious, primitive, illegitimate, irrational and unscientific." At the same time, he is wary of "fundamentalism of all kinds including African IK [indigenous knowledge] fundamentalism," and cautious about the unthinking adaptation of belief in the "homogeneity of cultures" across such a vast continent.

While recognizing that indigenous knowledge systems on the environment vary in the region, and are "never static, but always dynamic," Mawere situates most of his wide-ranging arguments in Zimbabwean (and occasionally Cameroonian, Mozambican, or Tanzanian) everyday socio-ecological realities (Mawere, 2014a, 2014b). He seeks direct, practical applications of indigenous environmental knowledge in the rebuilding of people-centered conservation and development in Africa, in fact, also drawing inspiration from the works of outsider political ecologists, precisely for their openness to dialogue and multi-vocality (Mawere, 2014a; Sigauke et al, 2014). Other recent work in African environmental philosophy (Okoyea, 2014: 139) also points us to avenues of tension within African conceptions of the environment: Western modernization and urbanization often warp indigenous environmental consciousness such that "nature loses value," and creeping anthropocentrism leads to careless exploitation. Much as Dahl and Hjort (1979) recognized how capitalist political economy and colonial–origin social relations led to platforms for the destruction of northern Kenya pastoralists' environmental strategies, Mawere and Okoyea remind us of the diversity, elasticity, and mutability of indigenous environmental conceptions in multiplex urban areas.

There is much to be gained by the adaptation of an interactionist framework along the lines of the studies from Dahl, Dahl and Hjort, and the others mentioned earlier (whose works, admittedly, vary from one another, of course) for reading urban environments in Africa if we keep in mind the grounded, situated socio-ecological philosophy of Mawere and other like-minded African philosophers. Chiefly, these are the central features that I believe can be produced from an interactionist lens on an Africa-centered UPE: (1) an appreciation of the multi-vocality that surrounds urban-environmental conflicts; (2) a valorization of the wide range of African voices in that multi-vocality, including but not limited to the voices of intellectuals and marginalized indigenous people; (3) the vitality of an everyday environmentalism that foregrounds that multi-vocality; and (4) a problematizing of the edges of the "urban" in urban political ecology.

This leads me to propose five possible starting places here for (re) reading urban environments. These are by no means the only ways of reading, but merely a sample of what might open up for broader interpretation through an interactionist approach. The first is the *reading that emerges from the experts* as the starting point for many people who seek to claim an objective scientific or scholarly understanding of urban environmental issues in Africa. From there, we must move backward, to build from *a critical reanalysis of history*, in particular, the reshaping of urban environments brought to Africa with European colonialism and the multifaceted recasting of these environments by Africans. A third reading is *of the cityscape itself* as a physical environment but also as a socially and culturally produced environment, by critically analyzing the symbolism and meaning with which it is imbued. Fourth, there are the multiple and complex *readings of urban environments in the works of African writers, musicians, and artists*. Finally, I argue that we can reread urban environments *from the perspective of African social movements and community organizations*, from the bottom up. I suggest in the following five subsections some of the shape that these approaches take in successive chapters of the book. One caveat is that the kind of comprehensive, geographically focused ethnographic approach taken by the political ecologists from whom I take inspiration is not an option for me given the continental scope and encompassing comparison at the heart of the project. Instead, I employ a mix of methods and sources, including the use of my own qualitative research findings from Nairobi, Lusaka, Zanzibar, Dakar, and Cape Town over the last 20 years, archival and historical records, literary and music criticism, and secondary sources, in a similar manner to Mawere in his references to varied case studies.

The experts

In urban-environmental perspectives found in planning and policy realms, the concerns tend toward solid waste management, flooding, sanitation, air and water pollution, land degradation, haphazard construction, and the impacts of climate change, to name a few of the main issues, as *problems*. The Economist Intelligence Unit's (2011) *African green cities index* focused on energy and carbon dioxide, water, sanitation, transport, waste, land use, air quality, and environmental governance, for example. In terms of scholarly and scientific experts in urban studies or environmental studies, Africa's urban environments are beginning to gain attention but the broad picture is still rather neglected. On one hand, while urban Africa has gained a small foothold of interest lately in urban studies as a whole, the continent's environmental dynamics are less frequently touched upon. This is unfortunate given the invigorated attention to environmental issues in urban studies (Benton-Short and Short, 2008; Douglas, 2013). The popular *Sustainable urban development reader* (Wheeler and Beatley, 2009), for a simple example, had virtually nothing about Africa in its second edition's 494 pages—no case studies or examples, no excerpted readings, and certainly no African authors; the third edition (Wheeler and Beatley, 2014) added one small excerpt. On the other hand, even in the outpouring of scholarship on urban Africa over the last decade, environmental issues are generally sidelined. The general exceptions to these trends come in two flavors: scholarly-scientific studies of one issue in one city; and fairly dry policy documents (such as UN Habitat's [2014] *State of African cities*). I highlight both in Chapter One.

Africa's urban environments are more complex than either of these sorts of approaches can accommodate. Cities on the continent, like cities virtually everywhere on earth, cope with ever-greater potential for air pollution, water pollution, or land degradation. Rapid growth of the urban population leads to a rapid growth of needs for solid waste, sanitation, and water resources management. Urban population expansion in the absence of effective management or equally rapid economic growth can certainly expand environmental stresses. The potentially negative impacts of global climate change are not something to easily dismiss as brickbats of a Western environmentalist agenda. Not everything is glorious and wonderful about Africa's urban environments, from anyone's perspective. All this being accepted, we *still* need a broader way of reading—indeed, we need multiple ways of reading—African urban environments, and the modified urban political-ecology approach I take in the book can suggest that multiplicity. In Chapter One, I concentrate on the case of Nairobi, and plans and policies developed by experts for addressing the city's environmental dynamics, arguing for the necessity of seeing this urban planning and policy landscape from an interactionist UPE angle.

The past

Throughout the continent, clashes of visions over what the produced ecosystems of urban areas mean are common, and yet rarely examined. From the new planned gated communities and model neighborhoods of the 21st century to the informal squatter settlements alongside them, we can see a politicized and polarized environment in many cities. From its inception, the Garden City of Lusaka, for example, has had at least two very different visions of "gardens" and arboriculture, fractured by a highly uneven political economy (Pullan, 1986). While the colonial separation between ostentatious, ornamental, exotic white elite landscapes and the hard-scrabble urban agriculture of the poor African majority has lost much of its racial dimensions, class and cultural inequalities and fractures are easily read in the city's landscape architecture.

Historical-geographical research has documented myriad connections between imperialism and environmental discourse on the continent, and with urban planning legacies of the Garden City movement (Grove, 1995; Home, 1997; Njoh, 2003, 2012; Simone, 2004; Hodge, 2007; Bigon and Katz, 2014), but it has yet to wrestle much with the tangible environmental manifestations of these connections and legacies in today's cities in Africa. Moreover, very little has been written of pre-colonial urban settlements on the continent as planned or constructed *environments*. It is my contention in the book that we can deploy political ecology's critical analysis of colonial environmental discourse and of indigenous historical voices to recover the historical legacies and refractions of colonialism and, where applicable, of pre-colonial urban environmental consciousness in contemporary settings. In Chapter Two, after discussing a range of settings, I concentrate on the case of Lusaka and articulate the meaning of the past's produced environment for the contemporary city, arguing for the value of an interactionist UPE that is alive to and aware of the historical-geographical processes in urban settings.

The cityscape

The physical-environmental contexts of cities are often shortchanged in UPE. In Africa, this shortcoming is compounded by analyses of environmental change that do not account for the social and cultural production of that environment. I argue that we need to extend the analysis of intersections between cultures and environments in urban cultural practices-in-place if we are to fully read urban environments on the continent. Sacred groves, for example, are as much a part of urban imaginaries as rural in many parts of Africa. Spiritual and supernatural conceptions of urban environments are crucial, often hidden, dimensions of the produced ecosystems in Africa. The rise of Christian and Islamic centers within cities sometimes seeks to actively displace indigenous spiritual environments, but, in other ways, they blend with these, syncretically. There has been very little work that seeks to examine the physical environments together with the metaphysical (spiritual and symbolic) cultural-geographical environments of cities in Africa, as I work to do in Chapter Three.

My main focus in Chapter Three is on Zanzibar. I develop an argument for seeing the physical and symbolic landscapes of Unguja island (on which Zanzibar city is located) as a whole—rural, urban, and peri-urban areas. Building from the ideas of Raymond Williams, Denis Cosgrove, James Duncan, and Munyaradzi Mawere, I examine Zanzibari socio-natural structures of feeling embedded in dominant, residual, emergent, and hidden cityscapes. I concentrate on place names and everyday environmental consciousness, particularly in Zanzibar's rapidly urbanizing (but still peri-urban/suburban) West District.

The artists

In Chapter Four, I compare some key urban environmental moments in four novels, Ayi Kwei Armah's (1977 [1968]) *The beautyful ones are not yet born*, Nuruddin Farah's (2011) *Crossbones*, Chris Abani's (2004) *GraceLand*, and Ousmane Sembene's (1970 *God's bits of wood*. These four very different novels took on political-environmental stories in different cities at different times. I examine, in particular, their deployment of urban waste imagery in distinct ways in order to build toward a more comprehensive and honest understanding of the multiple dimensions of writers' readings and constructions of urban environments in Africa. I discuss Sembene in more detail than the others given the chapter's overall emphasis on Dakar. I then move outward from the literary analysis to examine waste and water issues (especially urban flooding) in both Dakar and its major edge city of Pikine. With the example of arts activists and hip-hop artists in Dakar/Pikine, I highlight the diverse and complex readings of urban environments found in the music and community arts institutions, in common with what we see in many cities in contemporary Africa.

Theoretically, in Chapter Four, I engage the literary criticism of environmental writing, often called ecocriticism, and seek to make a contribution to fostering further ecocritical understandings of African literature. I find that many of the challenges for ecocriticism in Africa connect well with what I have discussed earlier for UPE. Although ecocriticism and UPE differ in their direct subject of analysis and often in their epistemologies, they have much to learn from each other. Overall, artists offer a diverse range of fundamentally important cultural voices on urban environments on the continent. However, they are hardly the only cultural voices valuable to an African UPE, nor are artistic expressions the only means of seeing cultural visions of urban environments, as the overlap between Chapter Four and Chapter Five's grassroots activists reveals.

The grassroots

In Chapter Five, I am thinking first of ways that involve Olukoshi and Nyamnjoh's (2011) "local experts and communities" in the production and dissemination of understanding of urban environments. Any effort to build UPE from the grassroots in cities of Africa would probably begin not with novelists, historians, intellectuals, or policymakers, but from those who give "voice to the lack of representation" of informal settlements (Diouck, 2013). Some of that would entail the types of readings of the cityscape that I have discussed earlier, but my claim here is that this means much more forthrightly articulating the voices of ordinary people in marginalized majority communities in African cities.

UPE and political ecology more broadly are schools of thought where the agency of the marginalized poor is often a point of emphasis. If we are going to have a UPE that arises from African voices, it has to be built from outside the loop of the usual suspects, and it has to take seriously the multiple, sometimes contradictory, perspectives of environmentalisms of the poor, on a par with the intellectuals from the beginning. The radical potential, the level of both political and environmental consciousness, and the techno-scientific savvy of the grassroots are actually quite hard to read, or can, in fact, be read mostly as a source of conflict that runs counter to socio-economic justice, deeper democracy, or equity. Voices do not sing in unison from the grassroots about the urban environments of the continent. Chapter Five argues for the importance of—but also the multi-vocality of—everyday populist understandings of African urban environments and visions of socio-environmental justice and urban rights (Harvey, 2012; Parnell and Pieterse, 2014; Pieterse and Parnell, 2014). In Chapter Five, I examine the theoretical positionality of the grassroots in UPE and political ecology, making reference to grassroots issues in Dakar, Nairobi, Lusaka, Zanzibar, and other cities on the continent. My primary focus is on Cape Town, a city with a strong global reputation on environmental issues and yet one of the world's most unequal cities, and a city with a whole host of contradictions beyond that which make it a useful setting for the analysis of grassroots voices.

The book's Conclusion is not simply a summary of my arguments. I am also interested in what an interactionist UPE approach such as mine can offer in terms of activism, policymaking, and everyday environmental politics. I examine some examples or forms of interactionist UPE in action, in Nairobi and Cape Town in particular, as samples of what Pieterse (2008) terms "radical incrementalism'— small, progressive, and interactionist steps toward producing urban environments that are more just, equitable, and sustainable, while in tune with African ideas of the urban. Given the emphasis in that last sentence on "African ideas," in the Conclusion, I return to the works of a set of African philosophers who seek to find workable concepts for African re-imaginations of the environment, including the urban environment. I end with my goals for what a critical analysis of environmental politics for Africa's cities can offer to global UPE and for African activists and policymakers alike.

Conclusion

The recent outpouring of urban studies in Africa has only devoted moderate attention to environmental themes. The literature of environmental studies in Africa has had a fairly limited urban dimension. My aim is to bring African urban and environmental studies together. This Introduction has suggested some of the complexities on the conceptual terrain of that intersection.

One path for approaching this intersection leads to the conclusion that African urban environments are a mess. The voices of the experts taking this path actually comprise a diverse lot who trace causation for that mess to different sources, from neoliberalism and the global political economy to poor management and inefficiencies at the local urban scale in Africa. A second path, in effect, celebrates African urban environments as the outcome of alternative rationalities. It is common to see a collision ahead at the intersection, if you will, between these visions. My argument here is, first and foremost, that there are myriad other ways of reading urban environments in Africa.

I have suggested five different readings here: those that emerge from scientific and scholarly expertise; a critical rereading of the urban past; the physical, symbolic, and spiritual cityscape itself; literature and the arts; and the voices of the grassroots. These are not meant to be comprehensive, but they are illustrative of the potential for an interactionist UPE. UPE can benefit from the broadening of approach that an interactionist framework allows. The implications of fostering such a framework for reading urban environments are significant not merely for theory. Planners, policymakers, activists, and stakeholders well beyond academia gain from the breadth that this framework enables. At the very least, it creates a sense of humility about any uniformity of policy approaches to Africa's urban environments.

ONE

The experts

Introduction

African cities are a mess. Environmental calamities abound. Environmental settings and governance structures leave cities highly vulnerable to the negative effects of climate change. The soils are septic from so much overflowing human waste. The surface waters are putrid, left standing because what few drains there are get clogged with solid waste that does not get collected. What little water infrastructure that functions brings polluted water to the small percentage of residents with access. Road infrastructures are so poor and traffic so bad that air pollution chokes the multitudinous pedestrian passersby. Indoor air pollution from charcoal cooking in poorly ventilated small domestic spaces leads to as much toxicity inside as out. Earth, air, water, fire, solid, liquid, gaseous—no matter the element or state, it is in bad shape. Or so it would seem.

This chapter examines the scientific, scholarly, and policy analyses of the environmental crisis perceived to exist for cities in Africa—what I am calling the perspectives of "experts" on such factors as urban water supply, solid waste management, air pollution, forestry, transportation infrastructure, and climate change. After discussing this expertise, I narrow to a case study of its implications for the applied sphere of urban environmental planning, with special reference to Nairobi. It is initially crucial, though, that I talk more about who these experts are, at least for the purposes of placing some limits around what might otherwise be an unwieldy chapter.

Over the past 15 years, there has been a considerable expansion of interest in urban environments in urban geography, and in urban studies more broadly. Urban environmental studies now involve significant strands of the biophysical and atmospheric sciences, the social sciences, and the humanities. The literature of urban environmental history is, for example, increasingly sophisticated scientifically and international in scope (Douglas, 2013). Given this incredible range and depth, it is not possible to do justice to even a small segment of this urban environmental work—I cannot even pretend that the next segment of this chapter is a comprehensive literature review. The goal is to appreciate what is distinctive about prevailing experts' discussions of specific aspects of urban environments and environmental problems in Africa, and of how their expertise might impact planning and policies across the continent. I concentrate a bit more on works in the social sciences, especially geography and urban studies (as my own intellectual base), with some findings from biophysical sciences and the humanities included, and then focus on two key policy-oriented texts that have attempted more continent-wide urban analysis: the Economist Intelligence Unit's (EIU, 2011) *African green city index* and the UN Habitat's (2014) *State of African cities 2014.* My argument is that an interactionist urban political-ecology framework enables us to extend what is useful in this literature for understanding Africa's urban environments, even if that framework critiques the experts.

Scientists, scholars, policymakers, and planners on African urban environments

As urban environmental studies grows worldwide, the significance of African contexts has expanded. We can see this in the increasing discussion of Africa in major books from outside of African urban environmental studies. In Lisa Benton-Short and John Rennie Short's (2008) excellent textbook *Cities and nature*, for instance, we can see many of the strengths of the new urban environmental literature but also some potential shortcomings in relation to cities of Africa. Other ambitious works display a similar set of strengths and shortcomings, suggesting that *Cities and nature* can be a productive example (Boone and Modarres, 2006; Francis and Chadwick, 2013; Meyer, 2013; Douglas and James, 2015). The authors pay substantive attention to scholarship on environmental justice, and to the work of urban political ecologists. They also work to integrate material from urban Africa into broader discussion. There is some separation of the discussion along the conventional lines of "developing world" and "developed world" cities, but their use of this convention generally pertains to the relevant policy differences that do exist for well-resourced and less well-resourced cities.

What is more, Benton-Short and Short are careful to make distinctions within the developed and developing cities contexts. While they make mention of a wide range of environmental impacts of urbanization (including land use cover change, ecosystem change and fragmentation, increased resource use, and public health) they take the manageable step of focusing on water, air, climate change, and garbage as their central issues. Finally, their ecumenical approach allows for recognition that "the connection between urbanization and environmental deterioration is not a given," since sustainably planned and managed urban growth—including the growth of parks, for instance—can be more beneficial to the environment than some "disastrous effects of agriculture" in rural areas (Benton-Short and Short, 2013: 101).

The results of their inclusion of material from African cities are mixed. On one hand, their overview of global urban trends and urban environmental problems subtly weaves in examples from the continent. Nairobi is included alongside Shanghai, Rio de Janeiro, and Kabul in a chart on the "rise of big cities," Kabwe (in Zambia) is highlighted for its presence among the world's 10 most polluted cities, and Dar es Salaam and Accra are noted for the productivity of their urban agriculture. Perhaps the most interesting appearance of Africa material is in a discussion of Lagos, in which they draw the connection between the 2010 BBC documentary *Welcome to Lagos*, which "highlighted the incredible dynamism and energetic entrepreneurship of the slum dwellers," and the Nigerian government's 2012 effort to evict the residents of the slum on which the documentary focused, apparently because they saw the documentary as putting Nigeria in a negative light (Benton-Short and Short, 2013: 164).

Their arguments there and elsewhere are at least built from a reading of scholarship on Africa by African and Africa-focused researchers. There is very little Africa content, though, in the detailed discussions on water, air, climate change, garbage, environmental justice, or sustainability, even within segments on "developing" cities. Some of that absence is understandable given the comparative size of many megacities in Latin America or South and South-east Asia, as well as the comparative scope and scale of environmental issues there. Generally, Africa still has fewer large cities or megacities, and its environmental calamities—such as, say, industrial air pollution or severe flooding—may pale by comparison to those in cities of these other developing regions.

However, in other instances, the relative absence of Africa is a major missed opportunity, such as in their discussion of environmental justice, which bypasses the globally significant South African case. There is a brief mention of the 2002 World Summit on Sustainable Development in Johannesburg in a chart of the "international environmental timeline," but then virtually nothing at all about either Johannesburg or any other sub-Saharan city in the chapter on urban sustainability—when, for example, the United Nations Sustainable Cities Program of the 1990s and 2000s was largely an Africa-based program. More worrying is their tendency to still include hints of alarmist environmental stereotypes about Africa's massive slums and informal settlements, as in another discussion of the Lagos slums and their "myriad environmental problems, including inadequate fresh water supply, flooding, sewerage management and environmental contamination of air, water and soil. The mounting refuse poses major problems for public health, with increases in diseases such as typhoid" (Benton-Short and Short, 2013: 144). They argue that:

> the dysfunctional nature of Nigerian governance is partly responsible for the chaos that is Lagos, where it is not only the huge population upsurge that causes the environmental problems, but also the poor physical planning, inadequate enforcement of existing laws, inadequate funding and lack of proper coordination among agencies. (Benton-Short and Short, 2013: 145)

This textbook is certainly a marked improvement on past such books, for a variety of reasons. However, the problem that remains is that urban Africa too often appears as the dystopian victim of a crime that is its own doing. Benton-Short and Short (2013: 240) are correct that "much of the urban political ecology literature looks at how power is imposed more than how it is resisted." They then go on to claim, rather profoundly, that "reimagining urban political ecologies can be progressive and redistributional, not only changing the ecology and creating new socio-natures, but also tweaking relations of power and *transforming the very meaning of nature in the city and the nature of cities*" (Benton-Short and Short, 2013: 240, emphasis added). This argument resonates quite powerfully with Africa's cities, and yet there is little in the book to suggest that urban political ecologies from Africa exist or that they showcase—indeed, they may lead the way toward—the sort of transformational, redistributional understandings of power (as a contest) that Benton-Short and Short suggest urban political ecology (UPE) is capable of uncovering.

It is perhaps unfair to focus so much on a broad, general textbook by scholars whose main focus is not on Africa. My purpose in doing so is mainly to highlight that there is more to be done to take account of Africa's cities in global urban environmental studies, as in global UPE, and that Africa's cities can, indeed, be central to the development of ideas in both scholarly realms. In the remainder of the chapter, my goal is to suggest how this centrality to an interactionist UPE may be manifested through a review of Africa-focused urban environmental analysis of issues such as water supply, solid waste management, air pollution, transport infrastructure, urban forestry, or climate change analysis. When we turn to the work of scientists, scholars and planners, or policymakers who do focus on and in Africa, what are the issues that they emphasize? I see the works in three broad categories—the physical science approaches, the urban social scientists, and the policymakers or planners—followed by the Nairobi case.

A rapidly growing literature across many disciplines addresses African urban environmental issues—urban climatology, water resources, sanitation, solid waste management, soil sciences, energy, and the like—but typically by a case-study method based usually around one city. There have been few works, if any, among physical scientists that address urban Africa as a whole. The textbook *The physical geography of Africa* (Adams et al, 1999) has some excellent environmental analysis but little urban content. Most other environmental-science studies have focused on a particular environmental problem, and often in a particular city. These can be quite rich with data. For example, Balogun and Balogun (2014) produced an excellent study of the urban heat island effect and changing bioclimatological conditions for the city of Akure, Nigeria. Stoffberg et al (2010) were well ahead of many scientists in analyzing the carbon sequestration potential of indigenous street trees in their case study from Tshwane (Pretoria). An incredibly productive Czech–Zambian geochemistry research team has produced a bevy of studies assessing environmental impacts from copper smelting on the Copperbelt (eg Ettler et al, 2011, 2012, 2014; Mihaljevic et al, 2011). There are dozens more such valuable recent publications, which join similarly detailed case studies of specific issues in particular cities from a social-scientific angle, such as Van Dijk et al's (2014) analysis of financing strategies for sanitation in Kampala and Dar es Salaam or Khale and Worku's (2013) rigorous statistical assessment of the socio-economic factors impacting the delivery of municipal services across Gauteng Province (home to both Tshwane and Johannesburg). Among municipal services delivered, solid waste management is, arguably, the one realm where we more often see studies that bridge across between the physical and social sciences, such as Parrot et al's (2009) analysis of solid waste management in Yaoundé.

Building an interactionist UPE requires the voice of such scholarship to be analyzed and incorporated into the broader framework. The potential is vast for this to happen in the physical and social science literatures on urban environments, and in the planning and policy literatures. Unfortunately, these sets of experts seem to fall short of this potential for sharing across fields. There is a long history of criticism from ecological scientists about political ecology for its limited engagements with what they deem hard science, and, to some extent, this critique continues to ring true for the literature of UPE. The reverse, however, also remains a problem: the political critiques from political ecologists seldom inform the works of ecological scientists. Couth and Trois's (2010) survey and review of effective policies for African waste management to reduce its carbon emissions is a case in point. It is an impressive survey of waste issues as they relate to carbon emissions from an ecological or policy view, sensitive to the "positive social benefit" that might accrue from programs for the "organized scavenging and composting of waste" in terms of "job creation, education and environmental improvement" (Couth and Trois, 2010: 2344). However, it steadfastly avoids the murky political waters in which any landfill on the continent figuratively (and often literally) resides (Myers, 2005a).

Some of the best examples of work integrating the physical and social sciences with policy analysis in a political-ecological vein in Africa have long come from rural settings (eg Hiemstra-van der Horst and Hovorka, 2008, 2009). For example, JoAnn McGregor's (2005) analysis of the politics of conserving the Nile crocodile in Zimbabwe contains both a scientific assessment of the ecological niche of crocodiles, social science research on harsh local reactions to efforts to preserve it, and a powerful, meaningful critique of these conservation policies. She asks the provocative question of why the "significant losses of human life, impoverishment and harassment from wild animals" are apparently "acceptable" and fail "to provoke media attention, public outrage and fierce debate" among conservationists and preservationists for Africa when similar circumstances in Western countries (eg mountain lions in Colorado towns) do so (McGregor, 2005: 354). Her work not only threads the three angles together; it does so while opening the Western-dominated literatures on animal geographies or non-human agency in and around political ecology to appreciate the profound and tangible differences that such theoretical literatures face in African contexts.

It seems to me that similar work is not only possible, but also necessary, in urban realms in Africa, where "significant losses of human life, impoverishment and harassment"—not often from wild animals (albeit occasionally)—are likewise consequences of environmental policies and politics. Admittedly hard (for so many reasons) as this sort of combination is to pull off in Africa-based research, it would make richer comparisons possible across the continent regarding the processes and contestations in the interwoven physical science, social science, and planning/policy dynamics of Africa's urban environments. At present, we really have only two main attempts toward gaining that broader comparative lens: the EIU's (2011) *African green city index* and UN Habitat's (2014) *State of African cities 2014*.

The African green city index

The EIU's (2011) *African green city index* studied the environments of 15 cities on the continent in eight categories: energy/carbon dioxide, water, sanitation, transport, waste, land use, air quality, and environmental governance. Their index "measures and assesses the environmental performance of ... [these] cities across a range of criteria, and highlights green policies and projects that other cities can learn from" (EIU, 2011: 6). The EIU researchers talked with a wide range of (often local) experts who work in and on the urban environments of the surveyed cities, and they effectively summarize this expertise, with some hard-hitting critiques.

The report suffers from a number of flaws, though. The first resides in the choice of cities. Apparently for reasons of data availability and reliability, a great number of important major cities were left out of the study—Kinshasa, Dakar, Khartoum, Abidjan, Abuja, Ouagadougou, Ibadan, Kano, Yaoundé, Douala, Bamako, Antananarivo, and Ekurhuleni, for example, are all cities estimated to cross the 3 million mark in population by 2020, and yet they are absent here. Of course, as I have argued in the Introduction, it is impossible to expect a study to even begin to be comprehensive, to account for all of urban Africa. However, the *African green city index* suffers most glaringly from its lack of attention to Sahelian cities given the study's focus on the impacts of climate change on cities and the frequent prediction of dire climate change impacts on the line of cities from Dakar across to Khartoum. Five cities of at least 3 million people by 2020 are located in the Sahelian zone, but the *African green city index* can report nothing on them. Adding in the other eight major cities missing, to say nothing of other large cities not studied in the *African green city index*, we can say that it is a report with huge gaps in Central Africa (no city studied, if we place Luanda and Lusaka in Southern Africa, as they typically are placed) and francophone Africa (amazingly, only Casablanca is included), as well as the Sahel. By contrast, both the cities of the Republic of South Africa (Cape Town, Johannesburg, Durban, and Pretoria) and those of North Africa (Cairo, Alexandria, Tunis, and Casablanca) are well represented. Furthermore, these eight largely outperform the other seven cities on nearly every measure of a "green city" given the huge wealth and resource differences between South African or Northern African cities and those of the sub-Saharan zone. Ultimately, no cities studied were judged to be well above average, but those listed as "above average" are Cape Town, Casablanca, Johannesburg, Tunis, Durban, and Accra—and only Accra is located in the sub-Saharan tropics. Addis Ababa and Lagos come in as "average" performers overall, alongside the other Northern or South African cities (Cairo, Alexandria, and Pretoria). Luanda and Nairobi were classified as below average and Dar es Salaam and Maputo as well below average. Indeed, based on their survey, the EIU concluded that tropical sub-Saharan African cities "are in a different league" from those of the far north and far south on the continent.

In reality, the whole assessment mechanism in the *African green city index* is problematic. This seems to be yet another means of measuring the cities of Africa by the standards of Western cities, positioning them in the relegation zone of the league table (eg last place, sent down to the minor leagues) for "Green Cities," just as UN Habitat (2013a) does for Africa's cities in its City Prosperity Index in the latest edition of its *State of the world's cities*. At the same time, in EIU's analysis sections based on local experts—in fact, in the quotations from these experts—there are kernels of what could have been a UPE argument.

The UN Habitat State of African cities *report*

Reading documents like the *African green cities index* or UN Habitat's (2010) *State of African cities 2010*, it is easy to become deeply depressed about the state of the environment in Africa's cities (see also: UN Habitat, 2013b). For Habitat in 2010, Africa's cities were bedeviled by crises that result from poor planning and bad or non-existent urban environmental management. The list of crisis points ran the gamut from waste management to climate change, with the UN touting, as a counterweight, the benefits of its form of sustainability and a "green" urban economy. The UN Habitat's 2010 vision of Africa's urban *environments* was dominated by the need for climate change mitigation and advocacy for technocratic sustainable management. The general tone, particularly after the more stimulating first chapter, was techno-managerial, where urban environmental woes could be effectively addressed with better policies, more efficient markets, and spatial planning.

Both UN Habitat and the master planners of the continent have often seemed untroubled by the apparent incompatibility of their generally outsider-driven agendas for climate change mitigation and "sustainability" with African demands for socio-environmental justice, or with the diverse perspectives of urban Africans on the urban environment. It thus comes as something of a pleasant surprise to say that the *State of African cities 2014* from UN Habitat (2014) is the closest to a UPE approach that is continent-wide among any works that have yet appeared in print. The author list for this report is comprised almost entirely of African or Africa-based scholars, scientists, and planners—an important segment among experts on the continent's urban environments. In many respects, this network of experts replicates the network of the late colonial era in Africa, where "specialist advisers, scientific researchers, and technical experts involved in colonial policy debates and project planning" showed "increasing sensitivity and awareness of the complexities of local conditions articulated by technical officers and researchers working on the ground" (Hodge, 2007: 4). The differences in tone and argument between the 2010 and 2014 editions seem to reflect that "increasing sensitivity and awareness."

This 2014 edition of the *State of African cities* report comes with the subtitle *Re-imagining sustainable urban transitions*. There is much to appreciate and build upon in this volume. Unlike the 2010 edition, even though climate change is the primary theme for urban environmental discussions, this time, UN Habitat's authors have targeted directly tangible climate-change-related issues facing the region's cities, and they have linked these coherently with both policy and politics. They cast a wide net, in making use of research across the physical and social sciences, as well as policy realms, while not entirely shying away from political ecology. What is more, they do not sever the urban analysis from rural, national, and global dynamics. It can thus serve as the fullest statement yet of the voices of "experts" on Africa's urban environments.

As with the previous *State of African cities* reports, the main document consists of chapters on each of five subregions of the continent (Northern, Western, Central, Eastern, and Southern Africa). Each of these chapters has six subsections, regarding: population and urbanization; global change and implications for urban development; social and environmental vulnerabilities; urban planning and resource management; urban culture and change agents; and emerging issues. I utilize the report's data and some analysis of Nairobi in the subsequent case-study section, but let me further explicate several strengths and shortcomings of the UN Habitat approach here.

The report's vision of what the urban environmental problems are on the continent is familiar: water scarcity, flooding (and sometimes, paradoxically, urban Africa experiences both of these first two at once), water pollution, poor waste management, health and sanitation, and recurring environmental disasters. The main culprits are also fairly familiar: environmental change and climate change, weak governance, and poor management. However, from these familiar tropes, the report's authors take off in fairly new and intriguing directions. First, the effort to tie urban and rural dynamics together brings the authors to effectively attend to issues of (urban and rural) food security (eg in the West Africa chapter's discussion of the geographic networks across the region that impact urban food security), energy security (eg in cogent analysis of links between lower rainfall totals and reduced electricity supply in many countries highly dependent on hydroelectricity, such as Tanzania), and droughts (increasing with climate change in certain areas, further impacting urban food and energy security).

Second, the report is highly critical of the way in which urban planning has performed across the continent, not for stereotyped reasons ("corruption" in Africa, say), but, instead, due to the heavy influence of "the normative orientations of urban planning in the Global North" (UN Habitat, 2014: 11). These orientations lead planners to obsessions with master planning, building regulation, and control (of buildings and people); furthermore, when planners do turn to the environment, "expensive green technofixes" divert attention "from needful communities to provide elite green enclaves that entrench inequalities" (UN Habitat, 2014: 37).

Third, this leads the authors to boldly declare that "Africa and the world community need to rethink what constitutes a city since the Western concept is no longer the sole legitimate template for its application in Africa" (UN Habitat, 2014: 37). They thus call for "a radical re-imagination of African approaches to urbanism" (UN Habitat, 2014: 7). This call is, at times, rather vague: "African cities should actively explore and embrace diverse growth opportunities, decoupled where possible from unnecessary resource exploitation and ecological degradation. This would enable them to implement a sustainable development direction" (UN Habitat, 2014: 25). Yet, at other times, there are detailed or specific recommendations that might be workable, like the call for a "radical decentralization of powers" to foster "community self-organization" that could happen with a "devolution of controls over revenue collection" in a "bottom-up system of government" (UN Habitat, 2014: 11). They are realistic in acknowledging that such radical changes would have to be introduced incrementally, but sharp-elbowed enough to argue that without that radical decentralization, many urban informal areas "will detach themselves even further from effective government control" (UN Habitat, 2014: 11).

Given that the report shows that "the road to truly democratic governance systems often provides for a rough ride" (UN Habitat, 2014: 16), it is inspiring that UN Habitat remains committed to the promotion of "inclusive, progressive and productive dialogue among urban stakeholders" (UN Habitat, 2014: 30). Without such dialogue (particularly including African urban youth), "growing environmental and social strains may exacerbate urban poverty and conflict in the region. The spectre of violence looms large" (UN Habitat, 2014: 30). The authors see that evident links across scales—global and regional-scale geopolitics and climate change, as well as relations between national and municipal governments and governance networks—all play roles in urban environmental dynamics.

This all sounds like political ecology. Oddly, the one time when the authors do use the term—"analysis of the political ecology of urban poverty in Africa may lead to a polarized and luxurious debate of whether, for example, solid waste is a health hazard or a livelihood resource" (UN Habitat, 2014: 33)—it is in a backhanded, almost dismissive, way (and with a citation only to Mark Pelling's [2003] work in Guyana, not to any political ecology from Africa), as though all political ecology can do is engage in luxurious debate. If we re-engage with what drew African and Africanist scholars to political ecology in the first place, it is surely not to luxuriate. (For all my concerns noted in the last chapter, Loftus's [2012: ix] *Everyday environmentalism*, after all, begins with this line: "this book is about remaking our world'—hardly luxurious stuff!) In fact, the clearest way to strengthen this report would be to put its findings into dialogue with an interactionist UPE, as I seek to do throughout the remainder of this chapter.

To begin that process, let me turn to other shortcomings of the report. To be fair, the report's primary focus is not on urban *environments*. Inevitably, there are aspects of the environmental analysis that are therefore limited, such as the assessment of air pollution, but I do not critique them for this, remembering that the report is not attempting to be comprehensive environmentally. Several other problems with the report take precedence: the degree to which it shies away at key moments from the political, the cultural, the historical, and the spiritual.

While there are aspects of the political analysis that are hard-hitting and cogent, UN Habitat pulls back, probably strategically, in a number of controversial areas. For one example, while noting that Ethiopia's regime "is valued by Western governments for its assistance in curtailing Islamist extremism" (UN Habitat, 2014: 153), they largely avoid any critique of that authoritarian regime, probably for related reasons, even though its recent master plan for Addis Ababa that calls for the city's expansion led to violent, deadly protests by residents of surrounding communities (Ademo, 2014). A more worrisome dance around politics occurs in relation to Rwanda. The report acknowledges the "somewhat authoritarian nature of governance in Kigali" as a subject that has "generated some controversy—and may ultimately prove unsustainable" (UN Habitat, 2014: 29). Yet, in the next breath, the regime of strong-arm President Paul Kagame is praised: "the pace of urban development has been impressive, earning the city a UN Habitat Scroll of Honour" (UN Habitat, 2014: 29). They contrast Kigali with Kampala, Uganda, whose government is disparaged for "catering to the interests of voting blocs" (UN Habitat, 2014: 29). It is apparently the fact that in Kigali, "memory of Rwanda's past violence and instability remains strong, and the government prioritizes the provision of stability and order" as a "natural outgrowth" (UN Habitat, 2014: 29). Kagame's regime may use the "security threat to maintain a firm grip on political life, and the economy is centrally managed," but this is forgiven because it is all done "efficiently," and the regime has created a plan for sustainable resource management (UN Habitat, 2014: 154).

This Rwanda material is deeply problematic. It is exceedingly difficult to conduct research that even remotely touches on anything political in Kagame's Kigali given the "rather restrictive political environment" (Miller, 2012; Goodfellow and Smith, 2013: 3186). Yet, even non-political research has shown that Kigali has not been effective in maintaining tree cover, indigenous forest, or green space in this era of the rapid expansion of the city (Seburanga et al, 2014). More than 60% of Kigali residents live in informal settlements—officially a higher percentage than infamous Nairobi—and the regime has been ineffective in providing any sanitation services for these mushrooming areas of the city (Tsinda et al, 2013; Okurut and Charles, 2014). Industrial pollution in this era of intensified industrial development has led to metals contamination in the food supply produced in one wetland farming area of Kigali at four to seven times the World Health Organization's safety standards (Etale and Drake, 2013).

Perhaps most significantly, the menacing state's "control in most spheres of life and the constriction of political space" certainly seems to "have less positive implications for urban stability over the long term" (Goodfellow and Smith, 2013: 3186). Securing more than a billion US dollars in aid annually as of 2010, much of it flowing due to "donor guilt" for failing to prevent the 1994 Rwanda genocide, the Kagame regime showed its savvy in playing up its "genocide credit" (Reyntjens, 2004, as cited in Goodfellow and Smith, 2013:

3190–3191). I witnessed this in Kagame's 2012 lecture to the University of Hartford's Holocaust and Genocide Education Initiative at the Maurice Greenberg Center for Judaic Studies, as he cleverly played this genocide card for a receptive, wealthy, donor audience. Yet, at home in Kigali, the government has ruthlessly eliminated dissent, severely restricted even modest criticism, and deeply penetrated most aspects of social life—notably, through its program of "decentralization" that UN Habitat praises (Human Rights Watch, 2008). The 2007 Master Plan for Kigali, which talks a good game around environmental sustainability, has been far more effectively used as a tool for securing the power bases and elite spaces for Kagame's Rwandan Patriotic Front and its allies (Goodfellow and Smith, 2013).

Admittedly, there are political problems in Kampala, too—but is "catering to the interests of voting blocs" precisely not what vibrant, participatory democratic politics brings about? So, the (eventual) trains (will) run on time in Kigali, the buildings in the elite and expatriate areas will gleam, the streets will have no plastic bags. On the surface, there is nothing wrong with working toward a "corruption-free environment and a well-managed and governed, clean capital city" (UN Habitat, 2014: 183). No one would ever wish for a return to the genocidal politics of the early 1990s. However, UN Habitat wants to go along with the charade that Kigali is suddenly now the "Singapore of Africa" (UN Habitat, 2014: 183) without returning to, and applying, its own critique of non-inclusive governance in Africa's cities *to what is happening in Kigali*, let alone discussing what might be problematic about Singapore itself politically. Where is the "inclusive, progressive and productive dialogue among urban stakeholders" in Kigali, or in any city of the eastern Democratic Republic of Congo (DRC) destabilized by Rwanda's regime?

Other problems with the *State of African cities report 2014* run together: while it is encouraging that the report pays some attention to cultural change agents (youth, hip-hop artists, women, and gender activists), there is little in the way of systematic analysis or deployment of their inputs or views on environment or development. The report's users are urged to include the work of groups like Cities Alliance, Slum/Shack Dwellers International, and the Urban Poor Fund International, without recognition of the short grassroots these groups have in many parts of the continent, or of critiques of their non-democratic, non-progressive actions in several African contexts, including Cape Town (Robins, 2006). If, as UN Habitat (2014: 42) claims, "African urbanism needs to be rethought 'from the slums,'" then we need to hear much more from the voices of artists and the grassroots—youth movement leaders, hip-hop performers, women's activists, and more—from those slums.

Further, historical forces and factors shaping urban environments rarely make appearances. The "robust" recent economic performances of Angola, Ethiopia, and Nigeria and the "sustained growth" of Cote d'Ivoire, Ghana, Kenya, South Africa, Tanzania, and Uganda are highlighted with only signposted notions of the troubled histories of these contexts for growth (most of which are hydrocarbon- or natural resource-fueled). African regimes are criticized for "the choice against developing denser railways networks," considering that the "longer-term benefits" may balance out the high "upfront expenditures" (UN Habitat, 2014: 20); yet, the spatial outlays of infrastructure under European colonialism historically skewed development, weighted heavily toward extractive industries and white enclaves, in ways UN Habitat leaves unreported here. The report does note that "the segregation that characterizes many Eastern African cities involved the deployment of European urban planning processes of instruments of division and control over colonial cities and their populations, segregating them along racial, ethnic or political lines," and they show how little post-colonial regimes have done to move past that legacy (UN Habitat, 2014: 163). However, there is less consideration of the unequal colonial histories of infrastructure and service provisions that gave rise to the "dualistic nature of urban development" (UN Habitat, 2014: 163), and produced two distinct, yet interlocking, urban environments in many cities, beyond just Eastern and Southern Africa.

Lastly, the spiritual and symbolic realms of those urban environments are likewise shortchanged. There is an occasional reference to "faith-based organizations" (UN Habitat, 2014: 173) or "religious radicalization" (UN Habitat, 2014: 37), but there is little sense in the report of the depth of meaning and feeling produced in Africa's urban places or the symbolism embedded in the urban environments for which UN Habitat seeks a "radical re-thinking." There is much more depth and complexity to the spiritual dimensions of Africa's cityscapes than UN Habitat suggests.

Ultimately, then, while Habitat's *State of African cities 2014* is the best work yet published in terms of an attempt to address urban environmental issues in Africa comprehensively, I argue that its shortcomings might be addressed with an interactionist UPE that could account for the multi-vocality on urban environmental issues beyond the voices of experts. This is not about luxuriating in a debate. The type of "radical re-thinking" of urbanism around the world and of African cities in particular that UN Habitat calls for surely begins with interactions of perspectives, with the multi-vocality that the report only hints at. I seek to show this with the case study on urban environmental planning for Nairobi—and throughout the book.

As UN Habitat (2014: 150) put it in the *State of African cities*: "catering preferentially for the ... needs of rich urban populations may backfire" in planning since all cities require "cleaners, waste collectors, gardeners, *askaris* (watchmen) and other low-income service providers" whose needs are largely ignored in most of the new wave of grand master planning for cities across the continent, including Nairobi. It is easy to see why ordinary urban Africans would ask, with Nairobi-based urban planner James Wanyoike (2013), whether urban planning in Africa is "a tool for prosperity or paucity." One might just as well ask if environmentally sustainable planning is a tool for the elite's environments or those of the continent's poor urban majorities. With Wanyoike's question and my extension of it lingering, I now turn to an in-depth case study of Nairobi's environment and the experts' plans for it in the 21st century.

Planning and Nairobi's environment

UN Habitat's (2014) estimate for Nairobi's 2011 population was 3.363 million, with a rather high 2010–20 growth rate of 5.26%. They estimated that by 2025, Nairobi would be a city of 6.1 million (see Figure 1.1). In 2014, the newly established Nairobi City County's web portal (see: www.nairobi.go.ke) had a home page image that directly played off the city's claim to being the "Green City in the Sun": it is the rich green grass of the city's Uhuru Park, lightened by the bright blaze of the sun that is just peeking out from behind a tree in the park. Nearly every introduction to the city notes this nickname, as well as the city name's origins in the Maasai phrase, "place of cool waters." In reality, Nairobi's environmental setting is much more complicated than such enticing phraseology or simple rendition of rapid growth would suggest. To begin, Nairobi's greenness, literally, varies both seasonally and spatially across the city given the location on the edge of climate zones and biomes. The western areas of the city are more wooded, hillier, at generally higher elevations (up to 1,850 meters above sea level), and receive more rain, while the topography flattens toward the eastern segments, which are not only at lower elevations (1,600 meters), but also on a plain crisscrossed by stream channels and interrupted by wetlands and swamps.

Experts have, helpfully, devoted a substantial amount of time and energy to the analysis of Nairobi's environment, making it an ideal case study for the book in this regard. As we have seen earlier, the *African green city index* rated it as "below average," one of the four tropical sub-Saharan African cities at the bottom of that ranking. Within its eight categories, the EIU rated Nairobi "average" in land use, waste, water, and sanitation, and "below average" in energy, transport, air quality, and environmental governance.

What the EIU saw as a good policy base for green-space preservation and water management helped the city reach "average" in the former areas, while weak policies on air pollution and transport, as well as poor access to electricity across the city, brought Nairobi down in the EIU's other categories. They cite the Kenya Wildlife Services' Green Line Project, planting trees meant to separate Nairobi National Park from the new housing developments on its southern edge, as "part of a wider initiative led by Nobel Prize winner Wangari Mathai [sic] to plant new trees throughout Nairobi to improve water catchment and biodiversity" as a cause for pushing the city up to an "average" mark in land use (EIU, 2011). They also praise the city's efforts to build new road infrastructure, including the Southern Bypass Highway and Thika Superhighway. In highlighting these two "positive" factors, they somehow avoided the collision of them, to say nothing about the multitude of highly political controversies on Nairobi's green spaces over the last quarter-century (Manji, 2015).

The city government is seen as making some positive changes to waste management, despite only collecting a city-wide average of about 40% of residential waste, mostly from wealthier areas. Although many city residents (93%) were cited as having access to potable water, shortages were deemed likely to increase as the city grows and waste clogs most of the city's rivers and streams. The city's sanitation system is assessed as unable to service the population efficiently or effectively. Air quality suffers because of traffic congestion and "fecal dust" from the informal settlements. However, Nairobi's biggest problems, according to the EIU, are with environmental governance. This is not for want of an agency to manage Nairobi's environment because the local government has one. The EIU (2011: 83) says that in 2010, the city council's "annual environmental budget was about US$5.9 million, or roughly 5% of the total annual city authority budget of US$107 million." Yet, the city apparently does a poor job of monitoring its environment, and the National Environmental Management Agency is seen as doing little to assist the city in this.

The EIU ends its Nairobi chapter by praising the UN for its investments in green planning and green technology for its Nairobi campus in the leafy Gigiri neighborhood. As the home base of both

Figure 1.1: Map of Nairobi

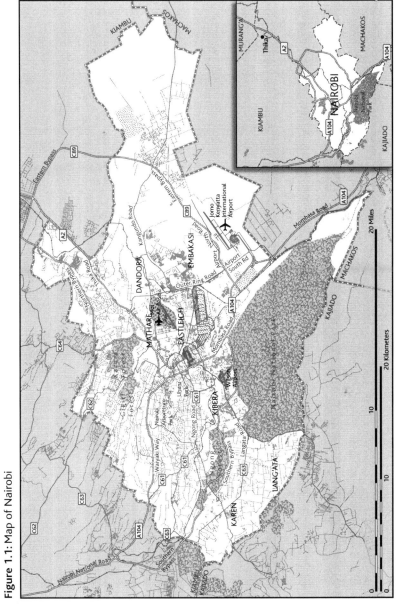

UN Habitat and the UN Environment Program (UNEP), Nairobi is a common focus of the research and analysis of these two offices. UNEP (2009) produced an Atlas entitled *Kenya: Atlas of our changing environment*, where one of the five chapters was devoted entirely to Nairobi's environment. Habitat's host city was portrayed in the 2014 *State of African cities report* as emblematic of cities facing what Habitat's executive director called "the overarching challenge for Africa"— "massive population growth in a context of widespread poverty" that together "generate complex and interrelated threats to the human habitat" (Clos, 2014: 3). Poverty, informality, water shortages, sprawl, slum development, weak and unequal environmental service delivery (such as for solid waste), food insecurity, poor wastewater treatment, and other environmental vulnerabilities all intersect in Habitat's portrait of Nairobi's highly fragmented social and physical environment. At the same time, UN Habitat (2014: 154) noted that the city had a growing economy, fueled in part by tourism (which is said to have "held up remarkably well" in spite of terrorism), construction and real estate development, and, indeed, by its "status as a diplomatic hub." UN Habitat saw Kenya's new 2010 constitution ambivalently: on paper, it would seem a step toward the kind of devolution to local authorities that Habitat was advocating; in practice, they seemed to join many Kenyan officials in fearing that the new system would prove "financially and politically unworkable" (UN Habitat, 2014: 163).

Indeed, urban environmental planning in Nairobi has often been ambitious, but financially and politically unworkable. Planning in Nairobi has been defined by a glaring contradiction for more than a century. On one hand, city leaders seek to make Nairobi fulfill a modernist vision of world importance. Nairobi's planners and elites have long seen the city as a model—for a European settler colonial city (White, et al, 1948), for a garden city, for a green city in the sun, for a city of multiracial harmony, and, lately, for a "world-class city-region" in the age of economic globalization (see Figure 1.2). On the other hand, all along, Nairobi has looked very differently to its majority of citizens. The inequalities and injustices of Nairobi's environment are as dramatic as its spectacular skyline or its leaders' grand ambitions, and many of its settlement areas and lower-class estates simmer with small-scale violence and socio-political unease, occasionally erupting to gain the world's attention (Obudho 1997; GoDown Arts Centre and Kwani Trust, 2009; Githongo, 2010; Kanyinga and Long, 2012).

Figure 1.2: Weekend roller-skate park, downtown Nairobi

As a consequence of the rapid rate of growth, ineffective urban planning, and the global/local political economy of the city, post-independence Nairobi became an even more deeply divided urban area than it had been under colonial rule (Kingoriah, 1983; Njeru, 2006; Charton-Bigot, 2010). The most visible, visceral manifestation of this appears in the rapid expansion of dramatically underserviced informal settlements, not only on the colonial map's "African" eastern side of Nairobi, but in deep pockets amid the wealthiest city areas in the west (Médard, 2010). Most of these informal areas have, in essence, their own rules of operation, which more hopeful analysts point to as a continuation of the "self-help city" that Nairobi had been (Hake, 1977; Gatabaki-Kamau and Karirah-Gitau, 2004), but which less sanguine observers see as a further manifestation of longer-term processes of the production and reproduction of poverty and inequality (Amis, 2006; Bryceson, 2006; Médard, 2010; Deacon, 2012). While the early independence period witnessed the creation of a number of government housing estates, housing supply never came close to demand; even recent informal private-sector tenement construction in slum areas not only fails to meet demand, but also falls far short of acceptable standards (Huchzermeyer, 2011; Owuor and Mbatia, 2012). Government response to the growth of informal housing veered from profound indifference to ruthless demolition, depending on the political moment (Otiso, 2002; Kinuthia, 1992; Médard, 2010). Violence—both organized and petty, both politically inspired and merely criminal—became a banal feature of everyday life in informal areas like Kibera and Mathare, and long-time President Daniel T. Moi's long departure in 2002 did little to reduce it (Murunga, 1999; Murunga and Nasong'o, 2006; LeBas, 2013).

In 2008, the national government established the Ministry of Nairobi Metropolitan Development (MoNMeD) as a moment of seemingly tangible evidence of the intensification of efforts at urban governance and urban planning reform in the post-authoritarian era. MoNMed was able to produce a bevy of new planning documents, including a new spatial planning framework (Government of Kenya, 2011), an updated framework for improving urban services (Kithakye, 2011), a new metropolitan transportation plan with a limited commuter rail network (Oirere, 2012), and new forms of communication with the general public (Limo, 2011), alongside a general rethinking of the relationship of planning to the city (Gathanju, 2009; Owuor and Mbatia, 2012). The biggest example of MoNMeD's impacts came in the form of the master plan *Metro 2030* (Government of Kenya, 2008a), but even for a city with a substantial planning history, Nairobi in 2008–12 had a remarkable flurry of formal urban planning activity (Ngau, 2013). Clearly, some environmental planning innovations, even in slum areas, were set in motion by the apparent retreat of authoritarianism after 2002 (Gendall, 2008; Njoroge, 2009; Ngau, 2012, 2013; University of Nairobi, 2012). Numerous examples have been documented around the city, however, of local-level disenfranchisement, resistance to supposed reforms, and expansion of socio-environmental injustice (Bousquet, 2010; Njeru, 2010, 2013; Thieme, 2010; Kameri-Mbote, 2012).

Kenya's citizens did endorse the potentially transformative and progressive new constitution in 2010 (Whitaker and Giersch, 2009; Burugu, 2010). The urban-environmental planning implications of this constitutional change for Nairobi, particularly given all of the new activity, are substantial. In July 2012 fieldwork, city planning officials expressed uncertainty, particularly amid the process that they were then experiencing of the city council being merged with the new county government (Muema, 2012; Odongo, P.T., 2012). Since the new constitution also limited the number of government ministries to 22 (there were formerly more than twice that many ministries), these planners saw the Ministry of Nairobi Metropolitan Development, created just before the new constitution's passage, as among the easiest of cabinet posts to be scrapped (Odongo, P.T., 2012), and it was, indeed, abolished by Kenya's new president, Uhuru Kenyatta, soon after his 2013 election.

The new county structure provided for no mechanisms for planning for the whole of the Nairobi metropolitan area—for which the *Metro 2030* master plan had at least provided a map. However, there were even more grand questions afoot after 2010. As planner Peter Ngau (2013: 17) put it:

> planning is centre-stage in this new era [after the 2010 constitution]. Given the history of planning in Kenya, it is important that planners now act with integrity. We must ask ourselves fundamental questions. Are we, as planners, going to champion the changes brought about by the new constitution or are we again going to serve the interests of the rich minority?

There are certainly dynamic, innovative and progressive local plans set in motion in Nairobi outside of the new city county planning structure, some of which have environmental issues in focus. The formal government planning for the city, though, has a more doubtful prospective answer to his question, particularly in attempting to follow the *Metro 2030* map, literally and figuratively.

Post-election violence

Before analyzing that map and the master plan to which it belonged, it is essential to detail the political context that both made them possible and foretold their undoing. Above and beyond the planning context for making Nairobi a "world class city-region," this political context looms large. The greatest aspect of that is the hangover from what is universally spoken of as the "post-election violence" in Kenya after the 2007 national elections (Juma, 2009).

The late December polling produced a "poison" with devastating consequences (Wolf, 2009). Incumbent President Mwai Kibaki was returned to the presidency and quickly inaugurated despite massive irregularities and evidence of rigging. Supporters of his main opponent (and the apparent victor), Raila Odinga, were outraged, and both sides mobilized militant (mostly youth) supporters and criminal gangs to commit acts of heinous violence on supporters of the other candidate. This mobilization came at the end of a long arc of the politicization of ethnic identity. Although rural areas within districts also had violence, it was in cities and towns where all sorts of ethnic identities mixed and matched—and especially those at the boundaries of ethnic regions—where the post-election violence hit the hardest (Waki Commission, 2008; Tarimo, 2010). More than 1,100 Kenyans lost their lives, and more than 250,000 became Internally Displaced Persons (IDPs), particularly around the edges of Nairobi and major towns of the Rift

Valley, notably, Nakuru and Eldoret—more than 500 fatalities came in these three cities alone (Waki Commission, 2008).

While many conflicts in the Rift Valley areas had origins in "land clashes" dating at least to the early 1990s (Waki Commission, 2008; Harbeson, 2012), Nairobi's informal settlements were among the hotspots of the post-election violence in part because the rival parties' followers resided in close proximity or even among one another, but, more importantly, because the rivals' campaigns "exploited long ethnicized landlord–tenant tensions in Nairobi's 'slums'" (De Smedt, 2009; Huchzermeyer, 2011: 150). In Nairobi, as in the Rift Valley towns, the Kikuyu-origin Mungiki gang syndicate was deeply implicated in planning and orchestrating the violence, alongside other criminal gangs (Waki Commission, 2008; Katumanga, 2010; LeBas, 2013). LeBas (2013: 251) and the Waki Commission both report that "Mungiki used the post-election violence period to opportunistically evict squatters from rental properties and also took pay from local politicians for intimidation and other political tasks." The result was an almost surreal bifurcation of the city: the gated communities and middle-class housing estates had one narrative of peaceable democratic transition; and the streets and alleys of the informal settlements and lower-class estates, particularly places like Kibera, Dandora, or Mathare, were wracked by calculated violence. The roots of the violence were much more complicated than some illusory, primordial "tribalism," with carefully deployed political constructions of ethnic politics in the interests of furthering the calculated agendas of rival elites combining with criminal militia interests to produce harrowing results from which the city is still recovering.

For urban environmental planning purposes, one impact of the post-election violence was the staggering problem of the internally displaced, as yet still unresolved in many Kenyan cities, including Nairobi. Some city parks and open spaces had IDP encampments long after the violence subsided, and some businesses and market areas burned in the violence disappeared forever (Owuor and Mbatia, 2012). Many other legacies detrimental to planning possibilities linger in gang violence, disrupted services, and still-simmering and heavily politicized ethnic tensions. However, another impact seems to have been the master plan, *Nairobi metro 2030: a world class African metropolis* (Government of Kenya, 2008a), created in 2008 by the now-defunct Ministry for Nairobi out of the wreckage of the violence. The power-sharing agreement reached in early 2008 between Kibaki and Odinga (which created a previously non-existent post of prime minister for Odinga) led to far too few reforms in the behavior of political leaders

(Gîthînji and Holmquist, 2012). Furthermore, the national *Vision 2030* development plan (under the guidance of which *Nairobi metro 2030* can be said to fall) had technically been developed in 2006, before the disastrous 2007 elections (Government of Kenya, 2008b). However, the state of shock that characterized the aftermath of the violence did somehow lead to a rethinking—at least on paper—of planning in Nairobi.

Analyzing Nairobi metro 2030

The master plan has been critiqued as superficial, highly business-oriented, unrealistic, embedded with "destructive modernist ideas" (Huchzermeyer, 2011: 236), and wedded to "the colonial motto of the 1950s, 'Nairobi, the green city in the sun,' with today's global stakes" (Steck et al, 2013: 154). This may indeed be a valid, and damning, critique, but I want to take the examination of it a step further with a full deconstruction of its content as a major applied statement of the "experts" on what to do with Nairobi's urban environment. As a document, the plan also bears at least the superficial marks of scholarly integrity and seeks to connect Nairobi's trajectory to, for instance, Cape Town as a regional hub for business, industry, and tourism. It took a very ambitious broad perspective, looking not simply at Nairobi, but also at 14 other municipalities around it, stretching south to the Tanzania border, west into the Rift Valley, north into Kikuyuland, and east into Ukambani (Owuor and Mbatia, 2012). This was the first plan in Nairobi's planning history to think about the city regionally or globally, and its reach and ambitions were particularly remarkable given its creation immediately following the worst political violence Kenya had seen. Although they would later seem to have been operating two different governments, President Kibaki and Prime Minister Odinga both endorsed the plan, wrote introductions, and invested in it—from these rivals to the UN, to outside investors, and back again to a broad cross-section of Kenya's viciously fractured elite, the plan won a substantial amount of powerful support at the outset.

The map of what the plan sees as constituting Nairobi as a city-region is intriguing for several reasons. First, since the planners could not have known that the governance system would begin to shift, scarcely two years later, toward the county-based devolution of the 2010 constitution, it is not an exact fit to map the 2008 proposal onto the current counties through which the region is governed. That being accepted—and most county boundaries do dovetail with the former districts, even if the names were sometimes changed—it is mostly for *how* the 2030 vision plan expanded "Nairobi" geographically that the map warrants discussion.

Most dramatically, one sees the expansion southward, all the way to the Tanzanian border, including the former Kajiado District (now Kajiado County). The three other former districts that the plan envisioned absorbing into the metropolitan region, Machakos, Kiambu, and Thika, have intrinsic economic links with the city. However, Kajiado is rural, arid to semi-arid, and mostly a part of Maasailand ethnically. It has connections to the Nairobi economy, to be sure, from the industrial trona mine at Magadi to the long-time supply of some meat and hides, and it has value to the national tourist economy through Amboseli National Park (Myers, 1986). However, beyond the southern Nairobi suburbs on Kajiado's northern edge, it is hardly a part of anyone's "world-class" metropolitan region. Possibly, this is an example of planning expertise seeing the sort of integration of urban and rural dynamics that I have suggested as a crucial part of UPE in Africa. However, by contrast, *Metro 2030* did not propose extending Nairobi's metropolitan reach much to the north or west, even though there are densely populated but largely rural counties there (the former districts of Murang'a, Maragua, or even Nakuru) with much stronger ties to its economy. Although the plan's authors detail their technocratic criteria for the geographic choices, inevitably, in practice, such a metropolitan region would prove grossly unequal in needs, resources, demands, or political influence, and not the interactionist rural–urban "rethinking" that the map might imply.

Content analysis of the plan reveals some illuminating patterns. The seven most frequent themes of the text make the plan's emphases quite plain: development, economy, investment, infrastructure, global, world-class, and business are key words that appear at least 90 times each in the document. Other very common words or themes in the plan belong to a similar vocabulary of neoliberal globalization: city/place-branding, competitiveness, tourism, business environment, and market. Finance, trade, economic growth, and innovation occur in the text a bit less frequently, but they add to the obvious overall thrust. In line with entrepreneurial urbanism elsewhere (Hall and Hubbard, 1996), the message is very clear: Nairobi is open for business. Nearly every one of the 14 strategies that Sager (2011: 152) identified as common to neoliberal urban planning around the globe (such as city marketing, economic development incentives, public–private partnerships, the state as facilitator of infrastructure for developers, or the liberalization of housing markets) are front and center in *Metro 2030* (Government of Kenya, 2008a: vii), which aimed to make Nairobi a "regional and global services centre." The plan's seven key "result areas" follow this discursive playbook, focused on place-branding, prosperity, infrastructure, transportation, the quality of life, "world-class governance," and security.

Given the important role and influence of UN Habitat's Nairobi headquarters, it is not shocking to see the fairly common recurrence of Habitat's sort of vocabulary for environmentally oriented sustainable urban planning subsumed beneath the aforementioned standard neoliberal lingo. Environment (when used other than in the phrase "business environment") and waste are the only words in the top 10 most frequent keywords that are not immediately identifiable as belonging to neoliberal globalization. Sustainability, inclusion, and public transport warrant more than 25 mentions in the text. This appears to be a form of greenwashing the document, though, since little content is devoted to actually planning for waste management, water resources, or genuine means for inclusivity.

Indeed, the absence of or at least infrequent reference to other potential themes can be as revealing as any frequent themes, content-wise. Violence, inequality, social exclusion, unemployment, underemployment, women, youth, or the elderly are terms or themes that appear very rarely in the plan. Despite the document's emphasis on transport infrastructure, the word "traffic," a problem that Nairobi residents from every *walk* of life would identify as critical to improving the city's environment (Kiberenge, 2014), appears exactly once in the master plan. As Huchzermeyer (2011) points out, despite the huge emphasis on transportation planning that it set in motion, *Nairobi metro 2030* makes no mention of the massive, thriving *matatu* (mini-bus) transport sector that serves most of the city and particularly its informal areas—when its 2014 *matatu* strike that brought the city to its knees amply demonstrated the centrality of the *matatu* to Nairobi (Kiberenge, 2014).

Perhaps the most intriguing lacuna has to do with informality. The word "slum" appears some 16 times, but mostly in a few charts; the phrase "informal settlement" occurs once, for a city with dozens of profoundly poor slums (Gulyani et al, 2012), the eradication of which (as a part of poverty eradication) this document claims to seek. The most famous of these slums, Kibera, warrants one mention. The next-largest, Embakasi and Mathare, go unmentioned. Despite its supposed role in creating "a framework for comprehensively addressing a broad range of policy areas," among which "slums and housing" are included (Owuor and Mbatia, 2012: 125), the plan actually offers these areas next to nothing, with the possible exception of eviction to implement transportation plans:

> residents of Nairobi informal settlements ... have experienced forceful evictions that have left most of them homeless and poorer through loss and damage of property. These evictions have usually involved land allocated for government projects or private developers claiming ownership of land on which the informal settlements stand. (Mwelu, 2012: 1)

Yet, nothing in the plan addresses this concern whatsoever. As Huchzermeyer (2011: 236) puts it, in *Nairobi metro 2030*, "a land-hungry and unsustainable modern spatial order continues to be rolled out. Those evicted to make way for this spatial order can stage only a weak challenge."

Implementing *Nairobi metro 2030*

There have been efforts to implement some elements of the plan, and particularly during the first four years of its existence, coinciding with the lifetime of the Ministry for Nairobi Metropolitan Development. Despite its ideological bias toward modernist and neoliberal ideas of what cities are, many potentially good outcomes for the city's majority and its environment can be gleaned from the plan for the Nairobi of 2030 were it to be implemented. "World-class infrastructure and utilities" are a priority of the plan, and tangible investments have been going into this aspect of it. For example, the new plan for commuter rail development that is slowly coming into being, along with bus rapid transit and new roads, might reduce the stultifying traffic of Nairobi, and thereby reduce air pollution. However, as one Nairobi planner told me anonymously in 2012:

> "we can all see the problems with traffic, and the Chinese have come in and built this Thika Road we call a superhighway. But they just build. There is no opposition there in China to anything the planners do. They come here and they just build."

This sort of approach to implementation is far from the UN Habitat ideal of an inclusive city, let alone any more radical vision of democratized, participatory, and relational planning or "radical rethinking" of urbanism (Pieterse, 2008, 2010; UN Habitat, 2014).

It is ironic that the most notable and tangible environment-related achievements of the Nairobi 2030 plan are the road and rail projects because they have been achieved through non-democratic, and sometimes draconian, means (Klopp, 2012; Manji, 2015), when the plan aimed for "world-class governance systems" that would foster a more transparent and accountable type of planning along the lines of Habitat's ideals. In President Kibaki's preface, he pledged to "work with local communities in nurturing effective civic engagement" (Government of Kenya, 2008a: xviii). Prime Minister Odinga spoke of the need for "a shared vision for local communities" to create "a better quality of life for all" (Government of Kenya, 2008a: xx). Implementing the plan in the context of not just the divisions of the "Grand Coalition" regime of these two leaders, but also the expansion of the broader inequalities and injustices that have defined Nairobi from its foundation onward, would inevitably be a daunting task. As another planner put it (anonymously):

> "planners are always caught in a bind, with politicians and elites wanting to talk about the problems of plots in Kiambu [the rich county just to Nairobi's north] when not one of them is talking about Kibera or the planning needs in slums."

Some 20 years on from a city summit that had set out to envision "the Nairobi We Want," it is even harder to imagine how the "we" of this phrase could ever form a consensus behind a master plan that has the shape that this one has (Myers, 2011, 2015b).

The Southern Bypass Highway is the perfect example for highlighting these issues (Manji, 2015). The bypass plan sliced directly through the middle of the Ngong Forest Reserve, skirted the southern edge of the Kibera slum, called for demolitions of many homes in Lang'ata estates, and cut through the northern boundary of Nairobi National Park, all to make the route to the international airport more convenient for some of Nairobi's richest (and historically whitest) neighborhoods (like Karen, named for Karen Blixen, the colonial-era white settler author of *Out of Africa*). Ngong Forest was one of the last major urban forests in the city (Gigiri, where the UN is based, and Karura, adjoining the smaller Gigiri, are the others), and its ecological integrity was irreparably damaged by the highway. What an irony that it went under the knife with barely a whimper, and with even the praise of the EIU and UN Habitat for efficient road-building, when the other major urban forest,

Karura, had been the site of Wangari Maathai's famous stand against its de-gazetting and private sale to local elites (Njeru, 2010)! The Lang'ata demolitions caused more opposition than the forest bisection did, and the project has still been prevented from carving a route through the National Park at the time of writing, with an alternate route just grazing the northern gate under way.

Rumors of lion sightings and even lion maulings were rampant in the communities nearby to Ngong Forest and the National Park from my first stay in the area in 1982 through my 2012 fieldwork. Then, in June 2012, just south of the park in Kajiado County, residents ambushed and killed six lions who had escaped from the park and who had been claimed to be responsible for killing local livestock (Kameri-Mbote, 2012; Odongo, P., 2012). Even seasoned environmentalists began to recognize that for many real estate developers and business elites—as well as many of the poor residing adjacent to the park in Kibera or in rural Kajiado—"the park will have to go" (anonymous interview in 2012), like the now-bisected forest. The Southern Bypass subsequently became an engine for urban redevelopment through the sorts of shady land deals for which Nairobi has become infamous in the neoliberal era: in 2015, Kenya police fired tear gas on schoolchildren protesting at the illicit sale of their school's sports ground to private developers in Lang'ata, directly adjacent to the new highway. In this case, President Kenyatta did eventually intervene on behalf of the children, but many other, small injustices leap forward with each of the new road projects and real estate schemes around the city (BBC, 2015; Kaberia, 2015).

The already bitterly politicized context for urban environmental planning was also further enhanced by the tensions surrounding the March 2013 elections. These were the first national elections after the public approval by referendum of the new 2010 constitution. The election process was more peaceful than the December 2007 disaster, but the city and the country were still highly fractured, and facing the possibility of a president (Kenyatta) and vice-president (William Ruto) governing from a cell in the International Criminal Court, each having been charged with crimes against humanity for their role in orchestrating the 2007–08 post-election massacres. Eventually, the Kenyatta case was dismissed in The Hague, but the abolition of the Ministry for Nairobi Metropolitan Development did not bode well for any movement toward implementing the master plan that that ministry created, or any more progressive environmental plan for the city. Samuel Owuor and Teresa Mbatia (2012: 138) argued that "to make Nairobi inclusive and sustainable, there is a need for a radical change of mindset, new strategies and, finally—but crucially—new governance structures to support development and foster a new generation of urban leadership." The Kenyatta regime's first steps did not at all suggest any "radical change of mindset," and its failure to work with and select for meaningful posts any of the "new generation of urban" leaders who had played such a critical role in securing a relatively peaceful election suggests little in the way of the tangible structural governance changes that Owuor and Mbatia advocated as a route toward planning a more sustainable and equitable urban environment.

Then, very early in its first term, the Kenyatta regime faced the shocking armed attack by apparent al-Shabaab Islamic militants on Nairobi's Westgate mall on 21 September 2013. For the purposes of this chapter, what is most significant is that the attack, in which at least 67 people were killed and the mall utterly destroyed, highlighted the "incompetence and infighting among the authorities" (Howden, 2013: 1) that have been, thus far, the hallmark of the Kenyatta administration across nearly all spheres of urban management. The net result is that "insecurity in the city has become the order of the day and no one is safe anymore" (Kiberenge, 2014: 6). In this context, it is a challenge to return to any grand environmental planning agenda for the city.

The new Nairobi City County Council attempted to do so through a grand-vision blueprint master-planning process as a direct follow-on from the Nairobi Vision 2030 plan. It is notable to compare the results thus far from their supposedly participatory planning process and the GoDown Arts Centre's community-created multi-site festival, entitled "*Nai Ni* Who?" ("Who is Nairobi?"), in 2013. According to Joy Mboya (2014: 69), "the festival was all about allowing people into processes and making space to provide input." She contrasts its popular energy and engagement with the county's master plan, which largely failed to generate popular participation, public comment, or attendance at open events.

What could Nairobi be if its elites were not so caught up in achieving global status, and were instead more engaged in the dynamic participatory planning agenda of youth organizations, women's organizations, the GoDown Arts Centre, the Center for Urban Research and Innovations, and other development non-governmental organizations (NGOs) in the city? There is a considerable degree of readiness, primed by political activism, for poor, informal settlement residents to engage in transformative, democratized planning at the grassroots, but these grassroots are disconnected and estranged from much of the formal state-led planning, left out of the vision for Nairobi in 2030 that appeared in the 2008 master plan.

This lack of inclusivity has rather deep roots in Nairobi; to fully understand its contemporary vestiges would require a rereading of the history of non-inclusive urban environmental management for the city, from the colonial era on. Further, how do we read Nairobi's cityscape and its spiritual and symbolic meanings? Clearly, overcoming the clash of rationalities between al-Shabaab and its followers, or criminal gangs like Mungiki, on one hand, and Nairobi's substantial bible-believing, Pentecostal, evangelical Christian population or its sizeable moderate Muslim minority on the other, is central to any possibilities for dialogic or argumentative, stakeholder-driven urban environmental planning. What do Nairobi's writers, musicians, hip-hop artists, visual artists, environmental activists, grassroots organizers, youth leaders, and voices out of the "slums" (or even ordinary middle-class or working-class estates) have to say? What is their vision of the urban environment and how to plan it? We see almost none of this from expert documents like *Metro 2030* or from the efforts to implement it. Seeing Nairobi in its historical, cultural, economic, ecological, and, crucially, political contexts and from multiple perspectives is essential to rigorous analysis or a "radical rethinking" of environmental planning for it.

The same questions that I have asked about Nairobi here can be asked of many cities across sub-Saharan Africa, and the answers will likely point toward the same sorts of disconnections between planners and many experts as opposed to ordinary people, the poor, artists, activists, and others. The UN Habitat (2013c: 1) claimed "a new mood of optimism about the prospects for Africa." However, the optimism one senses in the ambitious new round of urban planning across the region is actually more than jaundiced by the glance backward or around at the environmental, political, economic, or cultural realities confronting cities. A great many of the grand-planning schemes merely represent a return to faith in elitist, modernist visions for metropolitan development wildly at odds with what grassroots organizations say, think, or plan for in these cities' majority areas, without genuine efforts toward progressive environmental policymaking. To be sure, there are still notable achievements in grassroots participatory planning in Nairobi, as in cities around the continent, which can improve and have improved environments. However, until the yawning gap is narrowed between the elites' visions and the experiences of ordinary city residents, all the master plans in the world will not lead to the growth of inclusive, relational cities with an improving quality of life, declining rates of inequality, and radically improved environments.

Conclusion

Scholarship and policy expertise on African urban environments generally places cities in crisis mode. African cities do face myriad environmental issues, and many cities, perhaps most, offer a weak hand for the governance and management of these issues. On one hand, we are learning more and more, in many sophisticated studies in an increasing array of cities, about urban environmental problems on the continent. This expertise is beginning to filter into work on urban environments around the world. Furthermore, the generally grim expert picture is not without cause. However, when we apply an interactionist UPE lens, we see this expert map of urban environmental problems more complexly. We need to see the issues in their historical, cultural, political, economic, spiritual, and ecological dimensions, and to hear the great variety of local perspectives on them.

Benton-Short and Short (2013) have argued that a re-imagined UPE can be progressive and redistributional, offering the possibility for changing unequal power relations and transforming the "very meaning of nature in the city and the nature of cities." Although this is a daunting, ambitious claim, I believe that African cases can contribute to this quite directly. UN Habitat's (2014) *State of African cities* takes us part of the way there—and certainly further than the *African green cities index*—but it is not enough. The most crucial absence in that report is the rigorous, *critical analysis of environmental politics*; this is my book's subtitle because I seek to offer a fuller suggestion of what that entails. Habitat also falls short in analysis of the historical, symbolic, cultural, and grassroots-activist angles on urban environmental issues on the continent. I have tried to use the Nairobi case to argue that we need the multi-vocality of an interactionist UPE to see the issues or problems clearly, to challenge the meaning of nature in cities, and to offer ways to do more than "tweak" the power relations in the city. Urbanization can be a progressive, transformative process for the socio-natures it impacts and that impact it. African cases can help re-imagine urbanism, urbanization, and urban environments across the world. Expert voices only take us so far toward a complex, situated understanding of the environmental dynamics of the continent's urban areas. Re-imagining these environments "from the slums" means, really, practically providing for "inclusive, progressive, and productive dialogue among urban stakeholders," and truly re-imagining who *holds* a *stake*.

Figure 2.1: Map of Lusaka

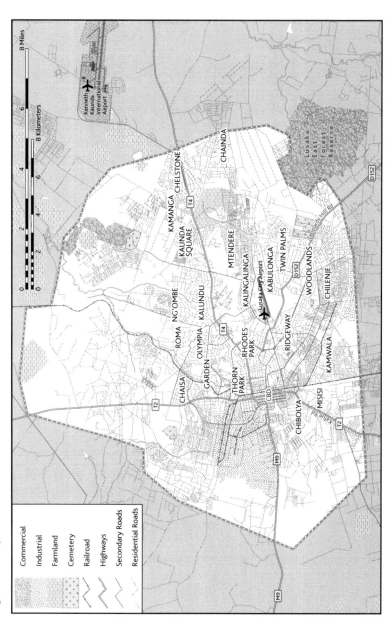

TWO

The past

Introduction

The British colonial official and town-planning expert Eric Dutton (1937: 43) once wrote that "it can be truly said of Africa, trees hide a multitude of sins." Dutton wrote this in *The planting of trees and shrubs*, a manual for the work he had undertaken from 1932 to 1936 to implement the plan creating Lusaka, Northern Rhodesia's new capital, as a garden city for Africa. After Dutton's work on the tree and shrub planting for Lusaka as part of his shaping that garden city (which the colonialist writer Elspeth Huxley [1983] called his "brain-child"), Dutton (1983: 133) spoke of the pride he felt in seeing the trees he had planted upon returning to Lusaka in later years: "There was something spellbinding" about visiting "those youngsters from various parts of the world struggling to accustom themselves to the rigours of the high veld." This sentiment fits very well with cultural analysis of animated elite English relationships with trees, wherein even scholars are apparently "drawn to their aesthetic beauty and their shadowy meaningfulness" (Jones and Cloke, 2002: 2). However, what does this archaic, exotic arboriculture mean to Zambians now—does it have anything like that "shadowy meaningfulness" for Lusakans? What are Zambian residents' views of the trees in the original garden city's main segment? What trees do Zambians over a broad cross-section of the city plant, and why? What does the whole colonial idea of a garden city mean for contemporary Lusaka's environment?

These specific questions about Lusaka are linked to similar questions in many cities of the continent about their comparative indigenous and exotic biogeographies and environments, about the meanings of the past environments for the present-day cities. Scholars are only really beginning to ask these questions about the contemporary social meanings of urban environmental histories and produced natures across the continent (Shackleton et al, 2015). Although there are some exceptions (Sheldon, 1996; Coquery-Vidrovitch, 2005; Freund, 2007), most African urban historical studies have paid fairly limited attention to environmental dynamics. Most of the recent spate of environmental science research in the continent's urban areas has lacked sufficient historical analysis. I argue that in order to develop a full and critical reading of today's urban environments in Africa, it is essential to reread their pasts through an interactionist urban political ecology (UPE). This may be a particularly pronounced need for Lusaka given its significance as a created environment meant to manifest the British colonial order.

However, before we get to Lusaka's historical geography, or that of any of the continent's cities, we need to look around at the present: one of the reasons for thoroughly interrogating the past lies with the broader context of *contemporary* African development. Across the continent, the 2010s have been a time of rising optimism in many countries in terms of economic development. This discourse of a rising Africa often includes an erasure of the past. There are understandable reasons why that erasure takes place, or reasons why people would want it to—for example, since European colonialism ended a long time ago, and many indigenous cities were in ruins even before the Europeans came, some might wonder what relevance these supposedly dead stories could have for the booming metropolitan realms around them in Africa. However, ahistorical ideas of a rising Africa risk fostering some ugly silences. These growing cities, no matter the overall economic numbers (even if these are accurate), still have incredible poverty, inequality, and injustice—these factors have often increased in this supposed era of a rising Africa.

Other ugly silences concern the environment. I argued in Chapter One how some expert opinions on the environmental crises in urban Africa often lack a grounded historical outlook. When one asks why Cape Town has such poor air quality, why Pikine in Dakar has persistent flooding problems, or why Kibera in Nairobi has severe sanitation problems, surely the answer is not that colonialism is the cause of every calamity. At the same time, colonialism's environments are still very much a part of why things are as they are in many cities of Africa. If Africa's urban environments are the "mess" that so many experts claim, this mess did not appear *sui generis*.

The past of African urban environments also does not begin with European colonialism. From Swahili cities, to Tswana agro-towns, to Yoruba and Hausa cities, African urban environments had varied patterns from the beginning of urbanism on the continent through the rise of European influence. There was no one single way of relating the city and the environment as Africa's pre-colonial urbanisms came in many varieties. As Catherine Coquery-Vidrovitch (2005: 3) put it:

> from the confines of the desert to the rain forest, from
> the high plateaus of the eastern and central savanna to

the Mediterranean climatic areas, either in Maghreb or on the shores of South Africa, the ecological contrasts are enormous.

Some cities exhibited profound connections with the natural world, while others had less intimate links. This chapter works toward a case study of the present significance of the past of Lusaka's environment by situating that city in the broader geographical and deeper historical contexts of pre-colonial and colonial urbanisms across the continent, as an example, but by no means as a single case meant to stand for all of Africa. I emphasize variations across pre-colonial Africa, and diverse combinations of exploitation and neglect that characterized colonial efforts to shape urban environments. I begin with a discussion of pre-colonial urbanization, highlighting the variations, but also some commonalty, across the continent in terms of urban environments, via several notable example regions.

Pre-colonial urban environments in Africa

As Liora Bigon (2015: 77) argues, "the physical landscape" of cities in Africa has been "to a great extent an outcome of representational and ideological realms of the involved interest groups, and a contested sphere of the memories and invented traditions of these groups." Furthermore, these outcomes, inevitably, vary substantively across the vast continent. As Bigon (2015: 55) has shown, "large trees served as symbolic socio-political institutions … in the configuration of the historic royal capitals" of the Senegambian region. Bigon (2015: 55) notes that the rise of Islam in Sahelian West Africa led to the placement of mosques at the center of towns, but mosques were typically "situated in the central square next to a large tree or several large baobab or kapok trees." Even with the new centrality of Islam in these medieval urban contexts, it was trees that typically "symbolize[d] the center of the universe" (Bigon, 2015: 55).

Since "cities existed in a wide range of African environments in the precolonial era" (Grant, 2015: 88), it is impossible to justify sweeping continent-wide claims for their socio-environmental character. Along the East African coast, medieval Swahili city-states did not necessarily have the same deep central symbolism for trees since their urban form lacked the sort of tree-and-mosque open central square that Bigon identifies in the West African region. Yet, the "sacred and spiritual roles" of cities in the Swahili region were often inextricable from the natural world as "urban and rural mesh[ed] in original ways" (Grant,

2015: 90). Indeed, across a broad swath of the continent in pre-colonial times, one can make the case that with urban agriculture, multi-use compound housing, buffer zones around the urban edges, and broad popular participation in urbanism, many "indigenous urban forms and architecture in early African cities were sustainable," or at least much more so than their colonial and post-colonial descendant cities (Grant, 2015: 326).

Many ancient and medieval towns in Africa, such as the Great Zimbabwe, the capital of the Kongo Kingdom at Mbanza-Kongo, or the medieval Saharan or Sahelian towns like Agades, Timbuktu, or Jenne, became elite settlements because of their control over agricultural areas, livestock, and/or (often long-distance) trade in natural resources (Coquery-Vidrovitch, 2005). Swahili city-states of the medieval era were as integrated into the "ecological and cultural milieu" of the coastal hinterland as they were into "wider Indian Ocean commercial and social networks" (Kusimba et al, 2013: 399). Let me use the Swahili coast settlements as an example of the hinge-type of pre-colonial urbanism common to many trading zones. Mark Horton's (1996) extensive work at Shanga on Pate Island showed how the indigenous settlement grew from a very modest village in the 700s to an important city-state by the 1400s (see also Kusimba, 1999: 60). Fishing, farming, and herding provided Pate with its base as it steadily expanded through trade both across the Indian Ocean and in its African hinterland. In fact, the interactions with the hinterland emerging in recent scholarship point toward a much more integrated understanding of the boundaries—or lack thereof—between city and countryside in the medieval Swahili realm. Shanga was subdivided into neighborhoods that seemed to vary in wealth somewhat, but this was not a segmented or segregated society like the later colonial cities, and its residents had deep links to the hinterland.

Chapurukha Kusimba has been a major contributor to the reorientation of the historiography of Swahili towns. In *The rise and fall of Swahili states* (Kusimba, 1999), he shows how the "coastal environment was a critical player" in the growth of these city-states, both in terms of farming, fishing, and herding conditions, and in terms of the wealth of natural resources that formed other commodities in long-distance trade patterns. Mangrove poles, tannin oil, forest timber, wildlife products, iron, coral, lime, and other goods were in plentiful supply. Swahili farmers practiced shifting cultivation using rotational bush fallowing and crop rotation, which made the best use possible of the precarious and unpredictable climatic and soil conditions in sustainable ways. Each settlement would have a committee making decisions on the rotation process, typically led by women elders. Swahili fishers used careful management of fishing grounds, with regularized ownership of coastal zones of the ocean and collective decision-making on fishing practices led by male elders. Although the more hierarchical institutions of a "guardian of the soil and a master of the sea" led to a growth of inequalities in the settlements, most analysts see interdependence within the town's society, and between it and its hinterland.

There was, though, also great variety along the Swahili coast, both in terms of the base environments and in terms of the size or reach of cities. Of the more than 400 Swahili settlements of the medieval golden age, Kusimba makes a distinction between those that had walls and those that were either closely built or dispersed, in a gradation toward small hamlets. His classification followed those of Stiles (1992) and Wilson (1982), who identified five size classes of Swahili settlements. The largest of these classes, One and Two (cities and towns), he reserved for sites of greater than 5 hectares (and with cities at greater than 15 hectares), with at least two or three mosques, from 50 to more than 100 coral stone houses, and evidence of wards. Richer hinterlands, river mouth settings, and islands with good harbor sites helped settlements like Mombasa, Lamu, Kilwa, Malindi, and Sofala to grow into the largest urban settlements.

Tumbatu Island off the north-west tip of Unguja (Zanzibar) Island was home to one of these major city-states of the Swahili coast's Golden Age. As many as 25,000 people resided in this city-state, adjacent to the contemporary town of Jongowe on the southern end of the island. From the Arab geographer Yaqut's prominent reference to "Tumbat" in the 13th century, through the 1989 recovery of a "Shirazi" ("Persian") inscription from an early 12th-century *qibla* (prayer niche), to the recognition that the occupying Portuguese established administrative centers in the 16th century at Limbani in the present environs of Jongowe and on Zanzibar (Unguja) Island at Fukucheni directly opposite the Tumbatu city site, there is ample evidence of that city's medieval significance (Pearce, 1920; Ingrams, 1931; Trimingham, 1975; Sutton, 1990; Horton, 1996; Horton and Middleton, 2000). Tumbatu was one of the main culture hearths of Swahili civilization from at least the early 12th through the early 16th centuries, when the island and its city dominated the northern half of Unguja. The island lent its name to the culture group that predominates in what is today's Unguja-Kaskazini Region of Tanzania. Tumbatu's Swahili culture has material evidence of the island's long arc of global connectivity: their dhows, fishing boats, and *ngalawa* (catamarans) evolved from different societal traditions beyond Africa, as Tumbatu peoples mingled with and borrowed from ancient and medieval Arab, Axumite, Indian, Persian, and Polynesian (Malagasy) traders or travelers (Gray, 1963).

Today, Jongowe manifests in its urban structure and its indigenous urban management structure a surprising number of medieval Swahili institutions of particular relevance to the understanding of those older Swahili city-states' environs. These legacies begin with the settlement structure itself. The town is built away from the beach, with a sacred grove of trees between its fishing harbor and the residences. The small forest is the town's burial ground and the home, literally and also metaphysically, to its ancestors. It also serves as a buffer for the village from onshore winds and storms moving onto Tumbatu from the open ocean—residents see the forest as a principal source of protection from the 2005 Indian Ocean tsunami, which disrupted local tides and sent fairly substantial waves inland. Jongowe's central ground consists of its Friday mosque and town hall; the edges of its residential quarters—and there are, indeed, four quarters—intersect at the town hall.

In the 21st century, Jongowe still practices a regular village cleansing ceremony, where trash is cleaned from all footpaths and yards, but this is inextricable from social, spiritual cleansing. Cleansing coincides with the celebrations of the Prophet Mohammed's birthday (Maulid) and of the Persian calendar's New Year. On the latter occasion, every resident of the settlement bathes in the ocean, by category (men, women, and children) and age-set. Jongowe's settlement structure includes both local farmland on Tumbatu and the waters of the Tumbatu channel. Every ecological segment of the channel between Tumbatu and Unguja is mentally mapped, named, and associated with a particular spirit; older residents give burnt incense offerings as appeasement to the ocean spirits prior to fishing these waters. Many younger Jongowe residents scoff at such un-Islamic practices, and they may be slowly diminishing. However, this example does give hints of the types of older socio-natural co-production found on Swahili coast city-states during the coast's Golden Age.

Some vestiges of the Swahili city-states' relations of city and nature endured into the late pre-colonial period, prior to the dramatic changes of the 19th century. However, this sort of urban socio-nature differed significantly from, for example, that of the Atlantic West African cities of the 1500s–1700s. Ports there grew dramatically with the Atlantic slave trade, which transformed and threw off-kilter prior relationships of the town and its environs. The "demographic disasters" that the slave trade inflicted upon West and Central Africa's interiors, combined with the demands for intensified agricultural production and natural resource exploitation near to coastal ports, produced imbalances regionally in urban relationships to the environment (Coquery-Vidrovitch, 2005: 153). Older cities slightly into the interior, like Oyo or Benin City in the Yoruba culture area or Kumasi in the Asante area, also saw their environments totally transformed by the intensification of trade with Europe and the New World in that era. The effects of the slave trade across the region socially, culturally, economically, politically, and ecologically were "fearsome" (Coquery-Vidrovitch, 2005: 169) on a scale that dwarfed that of European (or Arab) Indian Ocean slaving on the Swahili cities and environs.

The 19th century eventually brought an end to the Atlantic slave trade, and the parallel rise of the so-called legitimate trade. Some cities in West Africa were able to effectively transition from slave towns to legitimate towns, often based around commodity exports to Europe. However, by the close of the 19th century, virtually the entire continent came under the formal control of European powers. Formal colonial rule lasted for less than a century in most areas, but its impacts on cities, and on urban environments, have proven stubbornly haunting.

Africa's colonial urban environments

Indeed, colonialism irreparably disrupted the pre-existing relationships between cities and environments, overturning "indigenous spatial and physical arrangements" (Grant, 2015: 97). In some cases, this occurred through the creation of entirely new towns for the twin purposes of administration and exploitation. Zambia provides us with examples leaning toward each of these twins, from the new administrative capital that Dutton helped to shape in Lusaka in the 1930s to the Copperbelt towns further north that had begun a decade or so beforehand. Since I devote the latter half of the chapter to Lusaka, let me focus here on the Copperbelt.

There is little escaping the idea of the Copperbelt urban agglomeration today as a poisoned place. The Copperbelt's air quality places it among the world's worst, in large part due to copper mining, processing, and smelting (Vitkova et al, 2011). Its soils are toxic, particularly in unforested (cleared) areas accessible for farming (Ettler et al, 2011, 2012, 2014). Its surface waters and groundwater contain heavy metals and carcinogens well above standard levels for human consumption (Von der Heyden and New, 2004; Sracek et al, 2012). Its plant life is "rich" in arsenic, cobalt, and copper contamination (Kríbek et al, 2011; Mihaljevic et al, 2011). The animals, even worms, are not immune from this uptake (Nakayama et al, 2013). Farms in its Kafue

River valley utilizing leaking sewage pipes for irrigation show how this toxicity finds its way into the human food supply (Kapungwe, 2011). People's bodies ingest the arsenic, zinc, copper, cobalt, and manganese of the fire, air, earth, and water.

We could take the expertise of Chapter One or the impressive recent work of the Czech and Zambian scholars cited in the previous paragraph to depict the Copperbelt today as a set of carcinogenic cityscapes, and stop there. However, the historical geography and metabolic conceptualization of a UPE demand the tracing of this ecological poisoning backwards in time and outward in geographical space. Why does the Copperbelt exist? Certainly, there was some trade in its copper resources before the 20th century—indeed, from as early as the 7th century, there is evidence of copper mining there (Roberts, 1976)—but the large-scale exploitation of its resources is inseparable from the imperial project of the British South Africa Company (BSAC) and its founder, Cecil Rhodes.

Present-day Zambia drew the attention of Rhodes and the BSAC for its apparent mineral wealth, but major copper mining did not begin until the 1920s. While the Great Depression of the 1930s interrupted its development somewhat, the Copperbelt attracted a range of international mining investments and by the 1940s and 1950s, it had become a zone of rapid industrialization and urbanization (Fraser, 2010). It even became a globally significant region for science and especially social science research into the impacts of industrialization and urbanization on African society (Mitchell, 1956; Epstein, 1958; Powdermaker, 1962; Macmillan, 1993, 2012; Frederiksen, 2013). Although sociology and cultural anthropology were at the forefront of these colonial-era studies, environmental issues occasionally surfaced— notably, in Audrey Richards's research into the region's *citimene* agricultural system and impacts of labor migration to the Copperbelt on rural deforestation (Moore and Vaughan, 1994). Furthermore, the new Copperbelt towns (Ndola, Kitwe, Chingola, Luanshya, Mufulira, and Chililabombwe), each associated with different copper mines, smelters, or both, grew to have their own separate "garden cities" (really, leafy suburbs) for their white residents (Padfield, 2011).

Colonial Zambia (then known as Northern Rhodesia) was heavily reliant on copper mining for its economic survival, and independent Zambia continued this dependence. For most of the independence era, more than 90% of Zambia's foreign exchange has come from copper, a significant amount of which is exported as raw ore. Having gone through the post-independence nationalization of the mines and the steady decline of global copper prices, the Copperbelt is today experiencing an unsteady boom (Fraser and Larmer, 2010) and an expansion of copper mining further west into what is being called the "New Copperbelt" (Hampwaye and Rogerson, 2010; Van Alstine and Afionis, 2013; Negi, 2014). The region's boom-and-bust cycles, heavy external dependence, and serious environmental costs stretch back to the beginning of the colonial-era exploitation. It is impossible to see the current patterns—even if they involve Chinese, Indian, and South African capital—outside of the long sweep of that history (Negi, 2013). It is also hard to see the collective Copperbelt conurbation outside of its rural surroundings—especially with the "wavering urban character" and frequent recourse to "return" migration to those rural areas or cyclical migration between them and the Copperbelt towns (Potts, 2005; Mususa, 2012). It was, in the first place, an urban environment created by colonialism to be nakedly exploited; it remains one. Its colonial environment did much to shape its contemporary urban political ecologies.

Across Africa, substantial variation exists in this narrative, from cities or urban settings created entirely for colonialist exploitation like the Copperbelt or administrative control like Lusaka, to those transformed in other ways to serve colonial interests. Mombasa, Kenya, a substantial city from the 9th century onward, had its environmental dynamics forever altered by its selection as the terminal port of the Uganda Railway; Dakar, Conakry, Dar es Salaam, Abidjan, Lagos, Luanda, and other cities faced the same fate at the end of other colonial rail lines. Other cities were transformed by the absence of colonial infrastructure. Mombasa's rival city-states of the Golden Age of Swahili civilization, such as Lamu or Malindi, were bypassed by the railway and withered as important ports. For every other example railway terminus just mentioned, one could name rival cities and towns that foundered as a result of being left off the line.

The point is that all across the continent, the spatial impress of colonialism on urbanization had multiple and overlapping environmental consequences that still affect the cities (and the countrysides). Even where those impacts were far less pronounced or enduring than they have been for the Copperbelt, they cannot be ignored. It is crucial to understand the environmental dynamics of the continent's cities today against that deeper historical backdrop, as I seek to do below for Lusaka.

Lusaka past and present

Lusaka is a city of 1.7 million people as of the latest national census, with most scholars and planners who study it estimating that its actual population is well over 2 million. The contemporary settlement began as a railway watering-station settlement in 1905 on the site of a Lenje village whose local leader, Lusaaka, gave the town its name; it officially became a town in 1913, serving a very small community of white settler farmers in the area. In the 1930s, this small town was utterly transformed with the establishment of Lusaka as the capital of the colony of Northern Rhodesia. The capital was redesigned along the general ideas of a garden city for Africa, and it was opened as the new capital by King George V to much fanfare in 1935 (Bradley, 1935). Working from a template suggested by the architect and town planner S.D. Adshead, local colonial officials—mainly, engineer P.J. Bowling and Dutton, then serving as assistant chief secretary—fashioned and built a layout for a low-density, white-only town of large lots, wide, spacious parklands, tree-lined boulevards, and the prominent new central government area, the Ridgeway, on the town's highest rise (Myers, 2003: 55–6).

What was the environment or socio-nature into which this modern city was placed? There is evidence of human occupation in the vicinity of Lusaka as far back as the 6th century; by the 11th century, in the hilly eastern area of today's neighborhood of Olympia, there was a village of goat-herding, iron-smelting people living in round huts (Roberts, 1976: 33). The Lusaka area and its environs saw numerous peoples come and go after these early residents, though. In the 17th–18th centuries, both the Soli and the Lenje (who together comprised the majority of indigenous people around Lusaka just before colonialism began) came under the influence of chiefship systems that originated in the Luba empire of late-medieval southern Congo. In the 19th century, both groups were buffeted (and sometimes enslaved) by the incursions of militant outsiders from Eastern and Southern Africa (the Ngoni, Makololo, and the Yao/Swahili), as well as from Portuguese East Africa, well before the BSAC came through. Both were also active in long-distance trade for ivory and metals; their settlements in the area were small and likely fairly transient, especially given the extensive bush-fallowing agricultural system they used.

The bio-physical setting is generally less favorable for farming than much of southern Zambia, but a bit better than the Copperbelt. Dominant tree species of the pre-colonial era would have been the typical small trees of the *miombo* woodlands, *Brachystegia Isoberlinia* and *Julbernardia*. Certain stretches of the countryside would have been covered with *Acacia*, *Combretum*, and *Afrormosia* trees, referred to locally as the *munga* woodlands. In either the *miombo* or *munga* areas, tree cover was actually widely scattered, with significant grassland areas between,

Figure 2.2: Trees along the Ridgeway of the colonial capital area, Lusaka

and seasonally flooded depressions, called *dambo* (Roberts, 1976). The Soli and Lenje used a variety of farming practices, but a variation on the northern Zambian *citimene* system often predominated. It entailed coppicing *miombo* tree branches, gathering the branches, burning them, and scattering the ash. This provided a stronger nutrient base to crop plants than that which was naturally present in the soils—in *miombo* and *munga* woodlands, like many tropical forest biomes, nutrients are often stored in the biomass, not the ground. In low densities, with sufficient fallow periods, farming in this manner could be sustainable, but there was little about the 19th century in present-day Zambia that could be described as sustainable (Moore and Vaughan, 1994). Thus, by the time Lusaaka's village greeted the British train line being built to the Copperbelt, the *miombo* and *munga* had already begun to recede from what would soon become the cityscape. The Soli and Lenje—both relatively small ethnic groups by comparison with the Bemba, Tonga, Lamba, Kaonde, Nsenga, Luvale, Chewa, Bisa, or Lozi who dominate the country—would also rather quickly become minority ethnic groups as the city grew.

While in Lusaka, "the imported values of the colonial power were translated into the physical form of a city," in reality, the colonial urban project of the 1930s was something of a flop (Collins, 1977: 227). In the first of his two memoirs, the last colonial-era mayor of Lusaka, Richard Sampson (1971: 69), cites a visiting British architect in 1952, who argued that "in twenty-eight years of planning I've never seen a town—let alone a capital—like this. It represents all that should not be done. 'Horrific' would not be too strong a word." The *Central African Post* in 1955 (cited in Richards, 1971: 69) proclaimed that Lusaka was "a town which even its fondest son could never call beautiful." The city grew slowly, and it grew in shapes and patterns completely unintended by its planners. As of 1928, prior to the capital construction, the official population of white people and Africans was less than 2,000; by 1946, the population was still under 20,000, with fewer than 8,000 African residents in formal employment. Bowling and Dutton's plan had included only a Governor's Village as a model settlement and a village for the African servants of government officials; both were highly controlled, surveilled, and under-serviced settlements of tiny, round (rondavel) huts. Dutton's aim in these areas from a design standpoint was to preserve "what is best in the traditional plan of the African village" (Bradley, 1935: 47). Yet, both areas were carefully situated; the Governor's Village was wedged in next to the military barracks, and the personal servants' compound was placed across the railroad tracks and on the down-slope from the Ridgeway, where the main capital buildings were to be built. Crucially, the planned garden city provided no other lands for African residential construction, when the city's African population was already in 1935 far larger than that of its white settler community (Myers, 2003: 66).

The first real burst of growth occurred after the Second World War, with the population, almost all of it African, reaching nearly 200,000 by independence in 1964 (Hansen, 1997; Myers, 2003). Thereafter, the growth rate became dramatically higher, with more than a half-million city residents by 1980, just under a million 10 years later, and 1.7 million by 2010. The spatial frame of the capital area remained largely as planned, as did the architecture of government buildings. Planned, formerly white-only suburban townships of spacious homes on sizeable lots persisted outside the capital zone to its east and north. Almost nothing remains now, however, of the two planned African areas, except for a tiny segment of round huts that long served, ironically, as a government-sponsored "cultural village" for tourists (Myers, 2003: 67). The rest of Lusaka's people—approximately two thirds, coming from all over the country—came to reside in informal neighborhoods that the colonial regime had designated as "unauthorized areas" (Myers, 2006: 293). The colonial roots of Lusaka's deeply bifurcated spatial form spilled over into the contemporary setting for a variety of reasons, some unique to Lusaka, and others common across post-colonial Africa.

Even after the post-independence burst of population growth, Lusaka, like many African cities, largely failed to grow economically (Potts, 2004). Most of Zambia's economy has revolved around mining on the Copperbelt since Northern Rhodesia was created. Lusaka has had a comparably small industrial base of light manufacturing, cement, and agro-processing; it is essentially a government town— the Ridgeway government area is a more impressive center than the drab Central Business District (CBD), as it was planned to be. Most of Lusaka's residents reside on land that had been designated as belonging to white-owned commercial farms or industrial sites outside of the restricted colonial capital site. Since most of the white settlers' economic ventures were modest, they rented land to Africans for the construction of homes. Technically, since the only Africans who were allowed to live in such areas were the employees of the white settlers (who were authorized to house their employees on their so-called compounds), such neighborhoods were unauthorized at their origins. This explains the unique designation of Lusaka's informal settlements as "compounds," and it explains why so many of these settlements, to this day, bear the first names, surnames, nicknames, or family members' names of those white settlers.

As these unauthorized compound areas were outside the legal boundaries of the colonial government's official planning area for the capital in the 1930s, by the 1950s, they were given the additional moniker of "peri-urban" areas, even when some were, in fact, just next to downtown Lusaka. Colonial and post-colonial government attempts to replace the unauthorized, informal, peri-urban compounds with planned neighborhoods of government housing repeatedly fell far short in their goals, with new informal housing areas continuing to grow far more rapidly than the formal areas and the subsidence of planned areas into a state of informality (Myers, 2005a, 2011). Lusaka essentially subsists in a post-colonial hangover state as a largely "unauthorized" city (Myers, 2006). The green veneer of the garden city mystique still masks what it has always masked: a dusty, inelegant, and largely poor city made up of a checkerboard of large, low-density planned elite townships (massive footprints, low populations) and high- density informal compound areas (*komboni* in Chinyanja, the city's *lingua franca*). Some of the terminology, like compound/*komboni*, may be particular to Lusaka, but a similar bifurcation of the city into broadly formal and informal housing zones that increasingly blur into one another around the poorly managed—indeed, unmanaged—urban edges afflicts the spatial form of many cities in sub-Saharan Africa. How did the planned "garden" environment come to this?

What has become of the garden city?

Dutton learned what he learned about trees and tree-planting in Zambia, leading campaigns for the establishment of village woodlots throughout the colony, hosting and fostering researchers in anthropology from Britain, and orchestrating the compilation of human geographies of every district in the territory. However, any sensitivity and awareness of local conditions was fed through structural racist inequalities and blindered by colonialist thinking. It was, with the exception of the "shadowy meaningfulness" of the Ridgeway's avenue trees, more or less doomed to fail. However, where, in other senses, might this project linger in Lusaka's environment?

Robert Pullan (1986: 278) began his pioneering study of the urban biogeography of Lusaka with a contention that it was not an exception to patterns in "most tropical African cities," which he considered to be "recent creations, owing much to foreign architectural ideas and developments." Its biogeography manifested this in the "exotic plants and animals which dominate" there, as in Lubumbashi, Nairobi, Harare, or other cities of white settler regions. The *miombo* and *munga* woodlands were largely removed by 1935, and so the ways in which exotic trees were used, in particular, gave "the city part of its perceived character" as a "garden city" (Pullan, 1986: 281). He distinguished Lusaka's "European" and "colonial" treescape, though, from West African cities, where trees—and particular indigenous trees—had other central significance. In Chapter Three, I discuss the significance of indigenous Swahili tree names in the neighborhood place-names in Zanzibar. By contrast, trees make almost no appearances in Lusaka's place-names, outside of a handful of names in English for colonial

Figure 2.3: Walls and exotic trees of Kalundu, an elite neighborhood of Lusaka

neighborhoods—Thorn Park, Twin Palms, or Woodlands—that had been built for white people. The vast majority of Lusaka's population came to the city from other parts of Zambia or from abroad. Although Chinyanja serves as the *lingua franca* for many of its residents, English is increasingly a second such common language among Lusaka people. There are a few places with Soli or Lenje names (like Chi*lenje* [place of the Lenje], which is one of its oldest African areas, and, of course, Lusaka itself, alongside Soli place-names like Chainda ["it has passed"] or Kalingalinga ["headless snake"]). However, most of the city sits on the landscape like an outsider, toponymically. The newer areas labeled as "overspill area number 1, 2, 3," and so forth, or "extension," or "south extension," add to this sense.

Walking or driving around the planned capital area of Lusaka in the 2010s, one still sees the trees of the 1930s, or individuals of the same species that replaced the originals. In the neighborhoods known as Rhodes Park and Ridgeway, to this day, fig, toon, jacaranda, red mahogany, cassia, flamboyant, ficus, and tulip trees predominate as the avenue trees; the densest concentration of original "garden city" trees in the city are along the end of Addis Ababa Road in these neighborhoods. Larger ornamental shade trees like these originals can also be found in some of the older middle- and upper-class neighborhoods of Lusaka, but most of these are inside the property walls of nicer homes, or just outside them on the plots of these owners. In newer private residential developments for elites or even for the middle class, there is no effort to create avenue trees; the only trees present at all are those planted on plots, inside walls, and this largely happens only in the most well-to-do areas. The plaster model of the Silverest Gardens planned suburb that sat in the central indoor square at the Manda Hall Mall throughout 2013 showed a lot of trees, including avenue trees, but in actuality, these are not a part of the Chinese-origin Henan-Guoji Development Company's plan for building the neighborhood (Cornhill, 2013; Myers, 2015a).

Jones and Cloke (2002: 2, 20) tell us that the "fate of trees is often emblematic of the wider environment," including the political-economic environment, since "tree-landscapes are bound up with all manner of powerful cultural constructions, not least national identity." Keil and Graham (1998: 119) argue that "in the post-Fordist city, nature has become a major discursive element in the production of urban space," and trees—perhaps especially avenue trees—are a key element of this. Do the arguments of Jones and Cloke or Keil and Graham carry over to Lusaka? To some extent, in modified form (ie it is probably not relevant to think of Lusaka as a "post-Fordist" city), I see their claims as relevant. Trees were certainly essential agents in the colonial plan for Lusaka, and the links to the broader agenda of cultural and colonial-national identity and discourse endured well beyond Dutton's departure. Writing in his gardening guide for white settlers to Northern Rhodesia at the end of the colonial era, James (1961: 1) noted that:

> trees are so much a part of our lives that we should all have some knowledge of what they are and how they should be cared for and cultured.... In Central Africa, with its swift spread of civilization, the need for proper appreciation of trees is more urgent than ever.

James's book was one of several guidebooks to trees and shrubs published for Northern Rhodesian white people more than 20 years after the capital project had completed (eg Fanshawe, 1962).

In the creation of Lusaka as a supposed garden city, Dutton brought trees and shrubs from around the world into the already-disturbed *miombo* and *munga*, and oversaw their planting on the streets of Lusaka. Some 60 species of trees and shrubs were imported from Australia, with another 35 coming from the agricultural research station at Amani in northern Tanganyika, eight from Kenya, and three from the Belgian

Congo. Still others came from India, Brazil, or South-east Asia. African trees utilized included a few species native to Northern Rhodesia, too, such as the black wattle, African tulip tree, *khaya* (African Mahogany), or flame tree. However, toon trees, jacarandas, and various species of cassia and fig became by far the most prominent trees of the capital area's public face. The avenue trees were crucial to the overall political and cultural purposes of the garden city plan. Dutton brought his very British aesthetics into the work, arguing that "a little extra care makes all the difference between an unsightly avenue and a beautiful one" and "should a tree in a street begin to languish a whole avenue may be spoilt" (Dutton, 1937: 31). The practical purpose of the avenue trees, for Dutton (1937: 43), lay in their work as windbreaks, protecting settlers from the "nerve-wracking winds" of Northern Rhodesia even as the trees added "to the appearance of the town."

At the same time, Dutton (1937: iii) also sought to expand the tree culture of Britain more broadly in the colony in white settlers' private gardens and yards, "in the belief that the planting of ornamental trees and shrubs is of great importance to young townships, as well as to individuals, and should be encouraged in every way." This use of trees was fundamentally bound up with the importance of private landed property, albeit at a smaller scale than the lordly estates of Yorkshire that Dutton grew up around. In discussing the creation of open home gardens without hedges or fences, as an apparent trend of the time in Southern Africa, Dutton sought to emphatically undercut it: "It is a matter of opinion, but my own vote goes to a hedge, as high and as impenetrable as possible" to mark the property and the boundary of the garden.

In 2013, the 100th year of Lusaka and the 78th year after its royal opening ceremony, in collaboration with two colleagues, I sought to see what legacies remain in Lusaka of this colonial garden mindset, and whether or not the bifurcated mentality of the city extended into different "tree cultures" today. The colonial mentality about trees and gardens, of landscaping for aesthetic beauty, has only taken root in the wealthiest parts of Lusaka. In the colonial-era planned African areas and zones of colonial government housing for Africans, by contrast, there is precious little tree cover, aside from an occasional hedge or fruit tree. Around the grounds of the Dutton-era Munali High School, Zambia's first secondary school for Africans, the plantings that Dutton supervised remain, in places—mulberry hedges around the teachers' quarters, for example. However, in most compound areas, only trees with economic value can be found, and these are planted more sparingly the farther down the income scale a neighborhood is. The city council has, for a number of years, had a program for planting seedlings from the nursery in compound areas or overspill developments without tree cover. The chief gardener for the city council put it this way:

> "in the rainy season, we would go to Kamwala South, Chilenje South, places like this, to plant trees. But you see, these people have not been sensitized, so they see these trees and they say, 'Oh, these belong to the city council,' so they don't care what happens to them, they may just drive right over them, the children break them, or do whatever to them. We want to give them trees, any trees—that is better than no trees—but they rarely have any sense of ownership unless it is a fruit tree." (Nyirenda, 2013)

The city council has faced so many cuts, particularly of staff from its payroll, that it no longer has enough staff for maintaining the trees of the garden city. The Parks and Gardens Department had 450 employees in 1988, toward the end of the era when the country was led by President Kenneth Kaunda (1964–1990); by 2010, there were 28 (the late President Michael Sata, who was claimed to have been an inveterate tree-lover, had subsequently increased the staff in 2013 back to 80, but this was still less than one fifth of what it had been). In some areas, they had turned to private landscaping companies by the 2000s to manage the avenue trees. These companies both used the spaces to advertise their businesses, lease advertising space to others, and, occasionally, allow for petty street trade in their privatized shade. Such street traders were even more common in 2013 in the stretches that the government still claimed to be maintaining. As the chief gardener argued:

> "In the 1970s, Lusaka was a very beautiful place; it was still a garden city. But we can no longer enforce the codes which say that if someone is planning to cut a tree, they must first get a permit, or ... rules against crops in residential areas. In the high density areas, people may attack you, with violence, if you try to prevent them from farming maize." (Nyirenda, 2013)

The government's commitment to the colonial vision of a garden city has withered in other ways, too, in the years of neoliberal transcendence. This is evident most graphically in the de-gazetting of both the Lusaka North and Lusaka East Forest Reserves so that land may be sold for residential development in areas of Lusaka Province outside of the city council's boundaries. However, even within the Parks and Gardens Department and the staff of the city's forest nursery in Woodlands from which many of the colonial seedlings came, Zambians have consciously adjusted that colonial vision. For example, Zambian gardeners have seen that indigenous trees like *khaya* (the local mahogany) have been hardier (termite-resistant) and long-lasting, and less damaging to streets and sidewalks; exotic species like jacarandas (which frequently die young in Lusaka's climate), toons, and figs (the roots for which sprawl out along the surface and damage pavement or cement) have fallen out of favor with staff. The chief gardener reserved special disdain for palm species: "it is a pretty tree with a nice architecture, but it doesn't have the economic or environmental benefits of other trees…. In terms of leaf litter, or oxygen production, or climate change mitigation, a palm does nothing for us" (Nyirenda, 2013). Yet, palm species are among the most popular trees in elite areas of Lusaka.

"At the end of the day," chief gardener Nyirenda (2013) told us, "this [Parks and Gardens] is a political office, and we need to satisfy the politicians." I would extend Nyirenda's claim to include pleasing the city's economic elites, for, as the Zambian geographer Evaristo Kapungwe (2013) put it, in Lusaka, "the landscaping and biogeography reflect the inequalities." Lusaka's bifurcation into the leafy elite sorts of suburban areas like Kabulonga or Roma and the unauthorized compound areas like Misisi or Chibolya has long been inseparable from biogeography and landscape architecture (Pullan, 1986). In the city's newest gated communities and planned extensions, the dominant tree and flowering plant species are ornamental exotics, mirroring the plantings of formerly white-only townships like Kabulonga. In the older unplanned settlements or semi-planned lower-income areas, such trees as one finds are nearly entirely fruit trees—even the hedge plants are typically fruit-bearing—along with food crop plants. In the poorest and newest squatter settlements, there are no trees, and barely any plants at all. Of all properties in the elite suburban area of Kalundu in 2013, 96% had a cement wall around the property, and most had either trees or hedge plants outside that wall. Only 22% of the properties in the older peri-urban compound of Kalingalinga had cement walls to mark the property boundary, and just 11% in the more recent informal settlement of Misisi had such cement walls. While 47% of Kalingalinga residents at least had a hedge to mark the edges of their properties, scarcely 15% of Misisi properties did; two thirds had no marking at all for the property borders (Myers and Subulwa, 2014).

For all that private planned suburbs and gated communities purportedly offer something new now in Lusaka, much remains similar to the colonial era. Tait (1997: 162) noted that "perhaps more than in other former colonial cities, the contemporary process of urbanization in Lusaka and its administrative framework remains rooted in the structures underpinning its historical expansion." Rakodi (1986: 213) cited the "structures, attitudes and feelings" of colonial planning, and the "underlying ideologies of separate development" for the supposed garden city as crucial, tangible aspects of the colonial legacy in the city. Despite the appearances of so many distinctions—widespread middle- and upper-class high-standard private sector housing development, considered a major step of progress for mainstream economists (Collier and Venables, 2015), might be seen as the largest distinction of all— one can make the case that continuities with colonialism in structures, attitudes, and feelings, and in a reformulated ideology of separate development, still anchor the new trends.

First, Lusaka remains a city with graphic spatial injustices, and the new wealthy housing areas on its outskirts only exacerbate these. Colonialism's influx controls and white-only townships are officially gone, but they are replaced with walls. At the edges of town, we find walls around new gated communities and walls around the new homes inside them, or gates at the edges of neighborhoods. The mirror-opposite communities, Lusaka's poor compounds, face barriers of a different sort. As new walls surround elite estates and new or improved roads serve to link them, compound areas are increasingly cut off from pedestrian routes through elite areas and further distanced from the road network. The exception to this is in the recently approved plan for a ring road around greater Lusaka as a part of the latest master plan, but if built according to plan, this road will displace compound residents in "unauthorized" locations and bisect contiguous compound communities as it slices its way around the city.

Lusaka's formal road grid has always been as much a spatial manifestation of its coloniality as its exotic avenue trees. When one is inside a planned pod, the roads follow a mix of grid and curvilinear logic, with all roads bearing names and street signs. In the unauthorized compounds and in government-planned areas for the poor that have re-informalized, such as Mtendere or Kaunda Square, roads seldom follow a regularized form, or have tarmac, names, or signs. The commercially produced street map available for purchase at the Manda Hill Mall would be useless for navigating the areas where two thirds of the city's population resides, since nearly all peri-urban compound areas are actually covered by the map's advertisements. Public transport mini-bus routes dump passengers from every compound into downtown Lusaka—there are no routes that connect from compound to compound across the city east to west or north to south.

These patterns of disconnection and invisibility are not likely to be redressed through the 2013 master plan. In its six-year gestation period from 2007 to 2013, the Japan International Cooperation Agency's plan for Lusaka built little goodwill in the compounds. In Chibolya and Misisi, for example, residents heard the Lusaka district commissioner, at a 2012 news conference on the master plan, declare that in the plan's implementation, their compounds would be demolished without compensation: "You can't have a city with such types of houses meters away from the Central Business District, those houses will have to go," he remarked (Zambian Watchdog, 2012). While other officials quickly contradicted the district commissioner, and no demolitions had occurred as of June 2013, it remains the case that the planned ring road calls for significant demolition of compound areas and the relocation of residents to land to be allocated in Chongwe District, east of the city and far from the existing road grid and the lives and livelihoods of these residents. This is a pattern of planning practice with deep roots in the "structures, attitudes, and feelings" of colonial cities across Africa, as cited earlier, regenerated for the 21st century.

Second, despite the evidently successful transition to multiparty liberal democracy in Zambia, it is highly questionable how much of a voice the people from compounds such as the seemingly doomed neighborhoods of Misisi or Chibolya have in any urban development. Indeed, despite the disappearance long ago of racial barriers in the city, many of the real powers or key stakeholders in the city, including major landholders, are foreigners, white people, South Africans, Chinese, or mixed-heritage Zambians. The barriers that once existed to popular participation in local politics built around race or property were technically wiped away at the end of colonialism (Myers, 2006). Symbolically and almost metaphysically, they still hold sway, perhaps nowhere more starkly than in the office of then Vice President of Zambia Guy Scott; in 2013, before he became (for a few months) Zambia's interim president upon Michael Sata's death, Scott was occupying the Lusaka City Council Nursery offices in Woodlands, just beyond the Golf Club, at the old colonial city boundary—the nursery where many of the seedlings for the colonial garden city avenue trees were grown.

Thus, in both symbolic and material ways, the contemporary city reproduces the colonial one in political biogeography and the bifurcation of tree cultures. This is a re-creation of the "garden city, but of a very different nature" that Jaeger and Huckabay (1986: 267–8) identified, wherein more than half of all compound households 30 years ago had vegetable gardens to feed themselves. Our 2013 survey showed the clear evidence for distinctions in the species composition and boundary biogeography of five different Lusaka neighborhoods on a continuum from wealthiest to poorest. Dutton's preference for walls and hedges to mark private property has not just become the norm, but done so to an extreme degree, in wealthy areas of Lusaka, including the many new gated or semi-gated communities being constructed; but in the poorest areas, nothing marks the boundary for the majority of plots. We found an ingenious assortment of makeshift hedges here and there—those comprised of the original form of the planned African areas (thatch or mulberry hedges), but equally common were boundaries formed by asbestos, rubber sheets, burlap or plastic bags, and, in one case, the burned out chassis of a car. We also found, though, that the newest neighborhoods of Lusaka's elite and middle classes, the various forms of gated communities and planned suburbs now being built, largely lack the vision of avenue trees that came with the original British capital. Instead, the treed landscape here is virtually entirely within the walls of each plot.

The stories the powerful people want to tell with trees have remained rather similar for nearly 80 years, figuratively exoticizing the cityscape, while ordering Africa into a European box of beauty. In the latest form of this story, the elite suburban plot, what we are seeing is the privatization of the cityscape, where each plot contains within its ever-higher walls a forest of wealth. Colonial elements remain in the stubborn manner in which the failure of the garden city and the gross injustices of it stab the eyes of visitors and residents alike. One need only think of the central compound of Garden, with its gloriously ironic place-name, a poor, largely treeless informal settlement built in the field planned as the outfall area of the city's sewage treatment plant. Other stories of this urban socio-nature are often quite hidden. One has to work to even enter Misisi compound other than on foot since it is essentially off even an informal road grid despite being within a kilometer of downtown. What greets you at its entrance in any direction is not a garden, an allée, or a stand of trees; it is piles of rotting garbage.

Conclusion

Each city in Africa presents its unique histories. There are many that parallel Lusaka in adhering to colonial inequalities and divided environments even while adjusting these legacies. In Nairobi in 2012, for example, one could open any newspaper and see advertisements for luxury estates like those being built on the outskirts of Lusaka: the ad for Buffalo Hills, a "leisure and golf village" in suburban Thika, promoted its vision of the new environment with a photograph of a white man playing golf. Inevitably, any sort of neo-colonial urban imagery would be much more circumscribed in West Africa. Ouakem, a pre-colonial Lebou settlement encircled by modern Dakar, celebrated its cultural vibrancy in 2013 with a multifaceted festival of the arts that highlighted environmental issues in the quarter and lacked any observable element of neo-colonialism, beyond perhaps its European funding base. The "deep-seated relationship between the Dogon people and the desert plateau" (Dainese, 2014: 897) in Bandiagara, Mali, was changed by French colonialism and intrusions of legal culture surrounding land, but the settlement structure and environment bear little of the sort of colonial impress that we see in Lusaka.

Might indigenous, pre-colonial practices of urban environmental management like those of the Dogon provide a means for decolonizing Africa's urban environments, particularly in such less-impacted settings? Njoh (forthcoming) argues that "it is not enough to simply extol or advocate a return to tradition." Yet, his own empirical study in north-western Cameroon led to the conclusion that "indigenous systems" of urban management and governance were "markedly outperforming their modern counterparts." I would certainly say the same of Jongowe, on Tumbatu Island in Zanzibar. However, extrapolating from the small examples to much larger cities and polities is, for me, much harder to envision being enacted.

Why is the past so important to any overarching political reading of Africa's urban environments of today? In this chapter, I have made an effort to highlight three ways: pre-colonial variations, colonial exploitation, and colonial neglect. To this, we might add early post-independence processes, now largely the stuff of history given that most African countries have been independent for more than a half-century. There are, then, many themes in the past beyond those that I have stressed. The key point is to recognize that the urban environments of 21st-century Africa have been shaped by forces that often reach far back in time. This means that when we approach the tangible environmental issues of today, including air pollution, water pollution, environmental services provisioning, environmental hazard risk, climate change threat, and so on, as a part of an interactionist UPE approach, we cannot do so as if these issues or problems have no politicized past. They are what they are as a result of historical forces.

THREE

The cityscape

Introduction

Beyond his four books and his unpublished memoir, the British colonialist Eric Dutton (1949) also wrote an extended "Introduction" to *The useful and ornamental plants of Zanzibar and Pemba* (Williams, R.O., 1949). His Introduction to that guide provides a kind of foil for taking African cultural practice seriously in developing ideas from Africa about African cityscapes and urban environments. As a city in the 21st century, Zanzibar depends heavily upon a tourist economy, much of which relies on the preservation and promulgation of a historical cultural imaginary; the environment is central to both tourism and the imagination. Yet, there is a lack of substantive research linking the image and the reality, particularly for the urban environment. Dutton (1949: 32) claimed that "in Zanzibar trees hold a very particular place in the thoughts and acts of the people" so that "tree worship is universal." When we follow this colonialist claim through to the contemporary context in a deeper engagement with Zanzibari cultures, what emerges is not "tree worship" at all, but rather a complex stew of socio-natures, where the urban society and the urban environment reproduce one another.

In Chapter One, I focused on understanding expert perspectives on urban environments in Africa as a part of an interactionist urban political ecology (UPE), with a focus on environmental planning in Nairobi; in Chapter Two, I argued that Africa's urban environments and the politics of environmental issues in the continent's cities need to be seen in a deeper historical context in UPE, illustrating this with a concentration on Lusaka. In this chapter, I center on the actual physical-natural substances of African urban environments, but also on the imaginary—the symbolic and spiritual conceptualizations of those landscapes—with Zanzibar as my featured city. Although I pay particular attention to trees, I discuss other components of the natural and spiritual setting as well.

Urban political ecology, landscapes, and structures of feeling

Conceptually, I take my cues in this chapter both from African studies scholarship and from what was once called the "new" cultural geography. As geographer Denis Cosgrove (1989) put it long ago: "the many-layered meanings of symbolic landscapes await geographical decoding." They still do. Working from the Gramscian ideas of Raymond Williams, Cosgrove suggested the possibilities of a decoding framework that would identify dominant, residual, emergent, and excluded landscapes. In this framework, the dominant landscapes manifested the hegemonic group's projections of power, while the residual landscapes expressed "experiences, meanings and values ... lived and practiced on the basis of the residue ... of some previous social and cultural institution or formation" (Williams, 1977: 122). The emergent forms manifested new meanings, values, practices, or relationships that were "continually being created" (Williams, 1977: 123). Cosgrove (1989) added to Williams' original triad of terms (dominant, residual, emergent) the notion of hidden or excluded landscape forms and formation processes to account for the landscapes of marginalized people in society.

Since Cosgrove's essay did not really aim at methodological rigor, one might do this decoding with methods suggested by James Duncan (1990) in *The city as text*. Duncan's (1990: 17) work was crucial in turning geographers toward the analysis of "landscape as a signifying system." His analysis rested on hermeneutic scholarly interpretation of "what a landscape signifies to those who produce, reproduce or transform it" (Duncan, 1990: 17). In doing so, Duncan (1990: 20) examined the "tropes which allow a landscape to act as a sign system" through *allegory* (wherein "people, particularly powerful people, tell morally charged stories about themselves, the social relations within their community, and their relations to a divine order"), *synecdoche* ("the employment of a part to stand for the whole or the whole to stand for the part"), *metonymy* (where "a word or an icon stands for something else"), or simple *repetition*. In this chapter, I discuss the signs in the socio-nature and place-names of Africa's urban environments—the voice, if you will, of the cityscape itself—with a case study of Zanzibar.

Cosgrove and other new cultural geographers were strongly influenced by Williams, who sought to "construct materialist cultural analysis without reductionism and determinism" (Jackson, 1989: 33). Although the new cultural geographers were sometimes critiqued for shortchanging the natural or the material at the expense of the symbolic or iconographic, their roots in Williams' work make the reassertion of physical environmental factors within their approaches actually rather easy. For example, let us take Williams' many essays on nature, and his notion of the "structure of feeling" as "the particular quality of social experience and relationship … which gives the sense of a generation or a period" (Jackson, 1989: 39). Although his discussion of "nature" in *Keywords* (his dictionary "of culture and society") is built around Western thought, his reminder that the word carries three *related* senses—the "character of something," the "inherent force" directing the world, and "the material world itself" (Williams, 1976: 184)—can be usefully paired with common indigenous conceptualizations of the environment in Africa that do not immediately separate out the physical and metaphysical world (Mamabolo, 2012; Mawere, 2014a). Williams elaborated further on this in "Ideas of nature," where he traced the increasing "separation between [hu]man and nature" as a function of "increasing real interaction," which became "really problematic" in urban, modern, industrial society (Williams, 1980: 83). In the now ever-more "complex dealings with the physical world," human societies become, in a sense, natural "products" (Williams, 1980: 83):

> the pollution of industrial society is to be found not only in the water and in the air but in the slums, the traffic jams, and not these only as physical objects but as ourselves in them and in relation to them. (Williams, 1980: 83)

In other words, for as much as Western urban cultures claim a distance and separation from nature, their actions in nature reacted back upon them, tying them into rather complicated structures of feeling. Mawere (2014a) and Okoyea (2014) have made similar arguments about nature–culture relations in Africa under conditions of urbanization.

Williams (1977: 132) distinguished "structures of feeling" from concepts like "world-view" or "ideology" because of his concern with "meanings and values as they are actively lived and felt," or the "practical consciousness of a present kind, in a living and inter-relating continuity." However, he was not just concerned with belief systems and institutions as lived. The structures of feeling also included "elements of social and *material (physical or natural)* experience which may lie beyond, or be uncovered or imperfectly covered by, the elsewhere recognizable systematic elements" (Williams, 1977: 133, emphasis added). The structures of feeling tie into politics, and, more pertinently, environmental politics, through the contestation for hegemony, the power of the ruling group to make its representation of the landscape—

including the "imperfectly covered" physical landscape—the reality for everyone else.

Analyzing the semiotic or discursive dimensions of the cityscape is also critical, though, in part because the dangers of determinism lurk nearby to any other sort of claim to a "voice" for a cityscape. On one hand, environmental determinism of the oldest variety runs deep in the study of environmental problems in Africa. Colonialist writings were rife with it—in Dutton's (1925: 18) first book on the people of Basutoland (Lesotho), he claimed that the physical environment itself "made Basutoland the asylum of the weaker races." Even the contemporary turn to "geography" in analysis of African economic development bears the touch of determinism. For example, the *World development report 2009*, with its subtitle, "Reshaping economic geography," was roundly critiqued for its deterministic understanding of geography, which followed on from simplistic understandings of how certain latitudes are "bad" for development (Rigg et al, 2009; World Bank, 2009; Hart, 2010; Lawson, 2010).

On the other hand, UPE has had a tinge of a different sort of deterministic reasoning to it on occasion, particularly in its structural-Marxist urban geography roots, which has the potential to be misinterpreted in a deterministic manner. By assuming that it is "historical process[es] of capital accumulation" that produce "distinct socio-natural landscapes such as cities," UPE can run smack into the very real problem of the highly uneven and unclear penetration of capital or formation of class structures in urban Africa as it seeks to unpack those socio-natural landscapes (Lawhon et al, 2014: 500). As Lawhon et al (2014, 2015) have argued, UPE must recognize the plurality of many of its fundamental notions, whether of the historical materialist sorts or the post-structuralist sorts (such as "cyborg," as I have discussed in the Introduction), and situate its analysis in the everyday realities of particular socio-natures and cityscapes.

Situating UPE in Africa means moving beyond economic determinism, and it means conceiving of multiple sources of determination. However, given the multiplicity of semiotic, symbolic, and spiritual interpretations of the cityscape in Africa, it is also the case that an understanding of the non-human or the more-than-human in urban environments in Africa requires the broadening of appreciation for what the non-human and the more-than-human actants *are* in these settings. UPE commonly analyzes water technologies, and urban metabolic flows, in its engagement with the non-human and more-than-human. In most sub-Saharan African cities, spiritual and symbolic agency is a far more significant player in urban environmental dynamics.

I do not simply refer to the extremely important role of formal religious institutions and practices (by Christians, Muslims, and others) in shaping urban spaces and urban natures (Mamabolo, 2012). Human settlements of all sizes across the continent are full of sacred groves, land shrines, water spirits, and living stones, where the metaphysical meets the physical (Tangwa, 2010). Plants and animals, and even inanimate objects, take on powerful social meaning, without which a full scholarly understanding of urban environments is impossible. Urban political ecologists, importantly, have drawn scholarly attention to the co-production of nature and society, but UPE has yet to grapple with the environmental philosophies and socio-natural constructions of African urban communities that bring these complicated, ethereal things to life, literally and figuratively. Examination of African urban perspectives on material-and-symbolic cityscapes, as a means for fostering further understanding of the rhetorical flows in the urban landscape, can thus produce a valuable contribution to the pluralization of UPE.

There is also the matter of nuances for the political in landscape interpretation in an interactionist UPE. Lawhon et al (2015) argue that scholars need to pay "more attention to explicitly political struggles—the contingent, messy and ever shifting politics and possibilities that engage and confront unjust dynamics"—in the urban environments of Africa. They further contend that "politicization occurs when antagonisms are made visible, hearable or sensed." However, precisely because politics are "contingent, messy and ever shifting," it is not enough to focus in on polarization, injustice, or inequality, the forms of unevenness generally central to UPE. On a political level, what emerges from a pluralization of the map of agency is too often simplistically rendered as a clash between official and non-official discourses of landscape representation (Shirlow, 2009). However, there needs to be a more nuanced sense of the spectrum of discourses, at the very least across what Cosgrove would have called the dominant, residual, emergent, and excluded voices of the cityscapes of Africa. Consider Bekker and Therborn's (2012: 1) study of capital cities in Africa, both in their analysis of how "the nation state projects its power through the urban landscape and spatial layout of the capital city", as well as its "architecture ... public monuments and the names of its streets and public spaces," and in their exploration of what they call "counter-power." These are important starting places for the political interpretation of symbolic landscapes, but the clashes of "power" and "counter-power" must be seen in all of the multilayered socio-environmental character that an interactionist UPE helps to elucidate.

Concepts from the old new cultural geography might be put to work for UPE, too, by linking them with political theories regarding states and nationalism in urban landscapes. In *Seeing like a state*, James Scott (1998: 55) examined how modern states sought to overcome the "spatial unintelligibility" of organically developed medieval cities in order to "make urban geography transparently legible." Empires, like the British Empire in urban Africa, would "find it symbolically useful to have ... camps and towns laid out according to formula as a stamp of [the empires'] order and authority" (Scott, 1998: 55). Scott (1998: 77) argued that little had changed from medieval and colonial times in the drive of states for this legibility in contemporary cities, at least as far as motivations go. What he called the state's "project of legibility" would, he contended, never be "fully realized" because of the "resistance of its subjects." I argue that Williams' and Cosgrove's refraction of alternatives to the dominant project of legibility, or hegemony, into residual, emergent, and excluded landscapes provides a more nuanced understanding of the terrain of public and popular responses to the dominant project—responses that one can see in the tools for analyzing the rhetoric of landscape that Duncan provided, and by also extending to a more-than-human socio-natural (or psycho-natural) terrain.

Like Scott, Benedict Anderson (1991 [1983]) "draws attention to the need for regular cultural practices to produce and reproduce the significance of national identities" (as discussed by Painter and Jeffrey, 2009: 154) in shaping what he famously termed the imagined communities of nationalism projects. However, there are regular cultural practices that counter this agenda. Homi Bhabha (1994: 149) noted that "counter-narratives of the nation that continually evoke and erase its totalizing boundaries—both actual and conceptual—disturb those ideological manoeuvres through which 'imagined communities' are given essentialist identities." Moreover, many of these disturbances are, in fact, mundane, everyday, and banal; rather than strictly harbingers of resistance, cultural practices such as place-naming or imbuing trees with cultural significance (potentially, but not exclusively, through place names) are often basic manifestations of the production of cultural landscapes in dominant, residual, emergent, or hidden forms.

Approaching the cityscape politically, but attending to greater nuances and to the mundane or the everyday, then brings us round to religion and spirituality in African cities. Religious groups are "probably the most widespread form of associational life in African cities" shaping the everyday cityscapes of urbanites (Rakodi, 2014: 90). Most analysis of religion in urban Africa stresses "unusual, dramatic or threatening" religious practice, such the work of movements like the Islamist extremist group Boko Haram in north-eastern Nigeria and surrounding states, "rather than the everyday and routine" (Rakodi, 2014: 93). Mosques and churches are frequently prominent and central features of African cityscapes, and these two world religions have enormous influences, through their varied (and sometimes conflicting) teachings, on human relationships with urban environments, in thoroughly politicized but utterly everyday ways. Both religions hold the potential for mobilizing greater consciousness for environmental protection, but, at the same time, from other scripture or interpretations of it, for environmental exploitation. It is impossible to see either religion as uniformly shaping urban environments for the better or worse, as uniformly for the dominant groups or against them. Moreover, in much of urban Africa, both Christian and Islamic religious practices have continued to be heavily influenced by African traditional religions, particularly in terms of a cosmology in which "the visible and invisible worlds are interconnected—invisible forces are thought to control life events" and the physical environment (Rakodi, 2014: 95).

In his analysis of the changing patterns of relationships between rural and urban settings in *The country and the city*, Williams (1973: 289) cautioned us to be wary of the reduction of the "historical variety of the forms" to mere "symbols or archetypes," thinking only of their "psychological or metaphysical status." This is worth remembering, but the larger point is that for many urban Africans, the urban environment or cityscape is *both* physical *and* metaphysical. The structures of feeling embedded and contested in the cityscapes of the continent likewise often come with that multiplicity.

Cityscapes in Africa in physical and metaphysical contexts

Cities in Africa can be found in all sorts of environmental settings. Large urban agglomerations exist from the deserts to the tropical moist forests, and from sea level to the highest highlands. Climate extremes and biome diversity have to be the starting point for any classification attempts for Africa's urban environments. At the same time, there are some generally common patterns in terms of physical settings. For many scientists, scholars, and planners, perhaps the largest overarching theme for these physical settings is *risk*.

Exactly half (35) of the 70 cities on the continent estimated to have more than 750,000 people as of 2014 are within 50 miles of the coast. Of the other half, another handful (including some of the largest cities of all, such as Cairo, Kinshasa, Khartoum, and Brazzaville) are entirely or substantially in low-lying riverine areas highly vulnerable to flooding. UN Habitat considers 19 big cities (those with more than 1 million people), 10 intermediate cities (500,000 to 1 million residents), and 62 small cities (100,000–500,000 people) on the continent to be at risk due to rising sea levels, including Zanzibar. More than 20% of the entire population of 11 countries (Benin, Djibouti, Egypt, Equatorial Guinea, The Gambia, Guinea, Guinea-Bissau, Liberia, Mozambique, Senegal, and Tunisia) resides in Low-Elevation Coastal Zones (LECZs) (UN Habitat, 2014: 45).

Urban vulnerabilities from climate change do not stop with sea-level risk, however. Many of Africa's cities outside of the LECZs are in arid and semi-arid areas facing increased water stress and declining agricultural yields—meaning potential food and water shortages in these cities. Still others are in steeply sloped settings prone to increased erosion that also threatens food security, or to greater flood risks. Some cities face all of these risks, and more—again, including Zanzibar. According to the latest projections of the Intergovernmental Panel on Climate Change (IPCC), cities in Africa face: increased freshwater shortages; increased waterborne disease threats (including the spread of malaria into East African highland cities that were previously malaria-free, such as Addis Ababa or Kigali); and dramatic decreases in agricultural yields, especially from rain-fed agriculture, leading to widespread urban food shortages. The most severe threats of freshwater shortages, unsurprisingly, appear to be in cities in arid and semi-arid areas such as the Sahel.

In combining a range of risks, the Climate Change Vulnerability Index (CCVI) for 2014 ranks many African cities as among the most vulnerable places on the planet. According to the CCVI 2014, the Democratic Republic of Congo (DRC), Ethiopia, Guinea-Bissau, Nigeria, Sierra Leone, and South Sudan comprise six of the 10 most vulnerable countries, with extreme risk; of the continent's 10 largest cities, seven (Abidjan, Johannesburg, Kano, Khartoum, Kinshasa, Lagos, and Nairobi) fall within high or extreme risk zones, and the exceptions here (Cairo, Dar es Salaam, and Cape Town) would clearly be on other scientists' maps for extreme risk, from sea-level rise alone.

Assessing these physical environments merely as sites of risk misses seeing cities as wellsprings of environmental opportunities. After all, so many cities in Africa are on coasts or navigable rivers because of trade opportunities that continue to rise. African cities are among the leading cities in the world for the practice of urban agriculture; parks, preserves, forested areas, and natural open spaces are also widespread, despite stereotypes of African cities as "cities of slums" (on a "planet of slums," a la Davis, 2006). Centers of higher learning across the continent tend to be urban, as do higher literacy rates, and the curricula in many countries feature environmental education lessons from primary levels onward; environmental awareness-raising programs and environmental activism are on the rise across the continent, especially in urban areas.

The environment *matters* to urban Africans. As I suggest in Chapters Four and Five, this is often most in evidence with artists, writers, musicians, or, obviously, grassroots environmental activists. Of course, as I argued in the Introduction to this book, there are many urban Africans for whom the environment does not matter, or does not seem to matter. However, even in these cases, my contention in this chapter is that the urban environments in which Africans reside are constructed or produced—both physically (in terms of both the built environment and the natural environment) and socially (in terms of meaning and symbolism)—and that that socio-natural construction of the cityscape matters to all.

Let me further explain a few key water-related examples since water figures so frequently in UPE. For the Ga peoples whose pre-colonial hunting grounds were in the vicinity of today's Accra, the Korle Lagoon at that city's center is considered a sacred site, with a dedicated shrine (Grant, 2009: 115–16); more recently, ecologists have recognized the lagoon's important role in maintaining and improving the water quality for Accra through groundwater recharge and the removal of toxic pollutants. Despite a multimillion dollar, US-funded effort to restore the lagoon in the 2000s, by 2012, the Ghanaian Environmental Protection Agency had declared the lagoon "virtually dead" (*Daily Guide*, 2012). Both resident leaders of the Old Fadama and Agbogbloshie slums, nicknamed Sodom and Gomorrah, which surround the lagoon, and captains of polluting industries in Accra argue that they have nothing to do with polluting the lagoon. However, in reality, everyone in Accra suffers from the death of the lagoon, and its spirit, and causes of its death are found in all sectors of the city: Accra's groundwater becomes more polluted as a result, and all human health is thus negatively impacted.

Along the Congo River in Kinshasa, the project to create two artificial islands in the river and to develop them as a new *Cité du Fleuve* was nearing the completion of its first phases by 2015; eventually, the new suburb aims to have 10,000 luxury apartments (for sale at a beginning price of US$175,000, with a minimum deposit of US$50,000) and a few hundred mansions (CORES, 2015). This wealthy neighborhood sits on the river next to a sprawling mega-cityscape constructed largely by its desperately poor (with a per capita income of US$280 per year), deeply religious majority; hundreds of fisherfolk and wetlands farmers were forcibly removed to make the new city-of-the-river possible (Kushner, 2013). They join the massive numbers of residents already in Kinshasa's informal slums, but instead of overwhelming bitterness, De Boeck (2011: 278) found the displaced envisioning "a new heterotopia, a new space that escapes from the real order of things ... a mythic Kinshasa." He reminds us that Kinshasa is a city "where the Holy Spirit manifests itself at every moment of the day in the form of glossolalia [speaking in tongues], and where the trancelike prayers of the faithful are continuously charged with the power of the Divine" (De Boeck, 2011: 280). On Mangenge Mountain, a "holy place within Kinshasa's spiritual geography," where the Bateke people worshipped their ancestors in pre-colonial times, De Boeck (2011: 281) found a "rudimentary prayer camp," where residents of the "spectral" city across a variety of Christian denominations were praying:

> to retreat and cleanse oneself from the urban pool of sin, its temptations, its problems and its disillusions; to momentarily exorcise Kinshasa from one's body and mind, to be stronger to confront it afterward, and to be able to insert oneself once more into this omnivorous giant that is rapidly approaching the foot of the mountain, engulfing the once empty sandy plains, dotting it with thousands of small rectangular rudimentary housing constructions, the color of their cement brick walls barely visible against the plain's gray sand, their sheets of corrugated iron roof glistening in the sun.

From the many variations on the *mami wata* water spirits across Western, Central, and Southern African towns, to the *zar* spiritualist groups of cities in Egypt and Sudan, there are many manifestations of the sort of intersection between spirituality and the physical construction of the cityscape that De Boeck describes here, and which concerns believers and non-believers alike.

For some, this discussion of spiritualism and the supernatural fits perfectly with stereotypes of African society. It is very far from my intent to contribute to such stereotypes. Supernatural and spiritual impacts on the socio-natures or structures of feeling of Western cities are just as significant, or more so (Pile, 2005). In the US, one almost never finds a 13th floor in any building with more than 12 stories because the number is associated with bad luck; books, television shows, and movies about vampires, zombies, and werewolves dominate the popular consciousness of US cities from Atlanta, New York, and New Orleans to Seattle and San Francisco. Pile (2005: 1) starts straight from the mouth of the canon of urban studies, with the words of Robert Park of the Chicago School, in arguing that the cityscape is much more than its built environment, "institutions and administrative devices," and instead is a "state of mind, a body of customs and traditions, and of the organized attitudes and sentiments that inhere" in those. Yet, urbanists rarely contemplate talking about US cities as realms of the supernatural, of the "shadows, irrationalities, feelings, utopianisms and urban imaginaries" that go into the "structures of feeling" (Pile, 2005: 2; see also Donald, 1999). My effort here to highlight the importance of religion and spirituality in African cityscapes is not about further exoticizing urbanism on the continent. Instead, I argue that this is a crucial space for using insights from UPE in African contexts to speak back to UPE in other parts of the world, a potential new direction for analysis, globally (Myers, 2016).

Within African studies, there is, of course, a massive literature on spirits and the supernatural, often touching on cities and urban settings (Nel, 2014). The most influential work for me in this regard has come from the anthropologist John Janzen (1978, 1992). Janzen focused much of his career on the intersections of religion and healing in what he termed, following Turner (1968: 15–16), "rituals or cults of affliction," within which "misfortune" is interpreted "in terms of domination by a specific non-human agent, and the attempt to come to terms with the misfortune" entails "the afflicted individual, under the guidance of a 'doctor' of that mode, joining the cult association venerating that specific agent." Janzen, Turner, and a number of the "Copperbelt" anthropologists (eg Mitchell, 1956) were responsible for the development of broader understandings of rituals of affliction (often referred to as *ngoma*, Swahili for drum or dance, since most rituals center around drumming and dancing) in their urban contexts in Central and Southern Africa (from the Congo basin into South Africa). Other scholarship has extended the conceptualization to cover its various manifestations in Eastern, Western, and Northern Africa over the last few decades.

Janzen (1992) specifically set out to examine *ngoma* groups and practices in Kinshasa, Dar es Salaam, Mbabane-Manzini (Swaziland), and Cape Town. He documented how the assortment of cults that he studied were both maintained and transformed by their urbanization. In Kinshasa, for instance, Janzen (1992: 11) found "enormous suburban villagelike settlements" even in his fieldwork during the early 1980s (long before De Boeck's [2011, 2012] recent work), where the massive scale and rapid pace of urbanization brought a great many *ngoma* groups from all over DRC and beyond together in one setting. Since these were originally rural spirits, new manifestations and remedies had to be sought in this new context, perhaps embodied in "smooth stones or lumps of coral resin found in appropriate streambeds"; ritual healers had to adapt to the city's multiculturalism and density by becoming more "generic urban healers" (Janzen, 1992: 13–14). Some healers resorted to such extreme generalization in the quest for income that they opened themselves to charges of charlatanism that would have been rare in the rural areas from which they came (Janzen, 1992: 20). Spirits known to afflict individuals in one culture group came to afflict those of other ethnic origins in Kinshasa's diverse context; "plants or materials called for in the recipes" or ritual treatments for spiritual afflictions were often "not available in the city," necessitating the development of "substitutes ... based on the dictates of underlying principles" (Janzen, 1992: 20). He found variations on these adjustments in each of the other three urban areas under study. Liebs et al (2013) show that a great many of Janzen's findings in Kinshasa remained relevant 30 years after his fieldwork, and their practices expanded many times over, like the city around them.

Luise White (2000) took on the task of confronting the misapprehension of "African superstition" head on in her masterful analysis of stories about vampires, bloodsuckers, and cannibals from colonial-era Kenya, Zambia, Tanganyika, Uganda, and the DRC. Her chapters on Kampala and Nairobi use narratives, rumor, and gossip about vampires to provide what she baldly calls "accurate depictions of life" in those cities. She sees the stories as comprising a "formula," in its ancient sense as a "group of words that expressed an essential idea" (White, 2000: 8). She shows, for colonial Nairobi in the interwar years, how tales of bloodsuckers were women's and men's reinterpretations of the challenges that women faced in the process of becoming urban property-holders. The stories that women and men interviewees told to her were redolent with specific psycho-environmental consciousnesses and geographies. In Nairobi in the 1920s, specific places came to be identifiable as sites of danger for women or men to be taken for their blood by "firemen" bloodsuckers—women were "most vulnerable" near Kileleshwa and its new arboretum, and Kibera was a site where the firemen vampires buried their victims (White, 2000: 162). It was often in "specific places that were beyond African control," such as those two parcels of Crown Lands (ie technically owned by the English King) and all the stretches of forest lands that "separated the nascent white suburbs from the central city," where vampire abductions were said to take place (White, 2000: 164–5). In Pumwani, the first formally planned, legal African area of the city (Myers, 2003), the specific neighborhood of Mashimoni (In the Pits) earned its name not from physical holes in the ground from quarrying or naturally occurring pits in the cityscape, but "because so many of the men who went there [to visit prostitutes] in the 1920s were never seen again," according to White's (2000: 168) informants. Men fell into trap holes that the prostitutes dug in the homes that they owned there, and they were then collected by the (white) firemen vampires.

Of course, as White (2000: 169) acknowledges, such pits "did not exist." They were allegories about property possession and dispossession. The use of the landscape feature of a pit (*shimo* in Swahili) as a sign of property connects to Dorobo (Okiek) and Kikuyu property boundary-making through pit-digging in the Nairobi vicinity during the pre-colonial era. Furthermore:

> when Africans told stories about clever white men digging pits in public places or African women digging pits in their rented rooms, they were not only describing the expropriation of land by Europeans and women, but their expropriation of African men's rights to limit that expropriation. (White, 2000: 171)

A great many related examples besides those of Janzen, White, or De Boeck have been vividly brought to life in the work of urban historians, anthropologists, and occasionally geographers, whether we consider Ndjio's (2006) analysis of the *feyman* spirits of Douala, Cameroon, or Bastian's (2001) work on the vultures, witches, and spirit children of Onitsha, Nigeria. For a full sense of the structures of feeling, or of the range of dominant, residual, emergent, or excluded cityscapes, in urban Africa, it is imperative to work through both the physical register and this metaphysical register through which the landscapes are also interpreted, as I seek to do in the following for Zanzibar.

Zanzibar's cityscape and socio-natural structures of feeling

In a somewhat delusional manner, Eric Dutton fancied himself a keen observer of African cultural geography and landscape, and his writings suggest an apparently dramatic contrast in the urban environments of the two African cities that he most impacted. In Lusaka, as we have seen in Chapter Two, he strategized that trees had agency, as a way of hiding a "multitude of sins" (Dutton, 1937), or as a moral imposition on a "land of flies and want" (Dutton, 1983). Northern Rhodesia's people, white and black, apparently needed instruction in every aspect of tree cultivation, as much as they needed a cityscape that would remind them of the Empire's might, an "answer in bricks and mortar," in Dutton's view (Myers, 2003). In Zanzibar, by contrast, he claimed that trees were so important that the people "worshipped" them. His introduction to the guidebook to plants there, which he commissioned, was meant for newly arriving officials; Zanzibaris already knew what they were doing with trees and shrubs, as far as Dutton saw it, because of their "worship."

In his examination—and his production—of cultural geographies on the continent, Dutton also paid careful attention to toponymy. As a principal mountaineer in what was nearly the second recorded ascent of Mount Kenya in the 1920s, he gave official names to many of the mountain's features as a part of his unsuccessful attempt on the summit (Dutton, 1929; Myers, 2002a). In Zanzibar, he used names for places—buildings, streets, or neighborhoods—to construct his vision of the political culture of British colonialism in Africa (Myers, 2009). Oddly enough, though, Dutton's love of and interest in trees never met, at least in print, with his love of and interest in toponymy. Alas, his "unashamed colonialist" mindset would have narrowed the insights he might have been capable of in that intersection (Dutton, 1983). One sees this mindset, for instance, in the patronizing tone of the very phrase "tree worship is universal in Zanzibar," when, of course, he would have known that in religious terms, over 90% of Zanzibar's population were Muslims, and even the rest—Christians, Hindus, and a few Sikhs—would have hardly "worshipped" trees in the manner his phrase implied.

In this section of the chapter, I want to dig into Dutton's claim about trees in Zanzibar, and to test it against the realities of the actually lived and produced socio-environments of the city into the contemporary context, with a not-entirely-exclusive focus on the city's rapidly urbanizing peri-urban West District areas. Since that is obviously a massive undertaking, I warn at the outset that the chapter segment is merely suggestive of a great many avenues for further deployment of the conceptual tools of Williams, Cosgrove, or Duncan within the African environmental philosophy of Mawere and others. Before we can unpack the environmental philosophies or socio-natural perspectives of ordinary West District (or Urban District) urbanites, though, we need a thorough physical grounding in the cityscape, and then in its toponymy as my key empirical lens on the cityscape (see Figure 3.1).

Figure 3.1: Map of Zanzibar

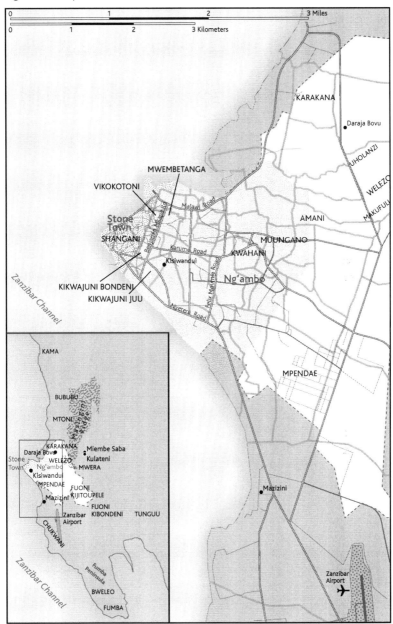

Unguja Island, on which Zanzibar city is located, was once described by Zanzibari novelist Muhamed Said Abdulla (1976: 39) as neatly "divided into only two segments, that's it: 'mjini' and 'shamba' [town and plantation]." A contemporary Zanzibari urban planner explained to me the commonly held sentiment that "the sense of belonging to the city is very weak for Africans. I am from Muyuni [a rural town in Southern Unguja] and I came to the city in 1974 but I would never say I am 'from the city'" (Mwalimu, 2006). However, in reality, the distinctions blur, most obviously in contemporary West District, the peri-urban or suburban zone that rings Urban District. It is impossible to separate the city from the entire rest of the island, in both physical and human geography—in part, because it is a fairly small island after all, about 80 kilometers long and less than 40 kilometers wide. It is all one landscape, and all part of the same structures of feeling.

Physical geographers actually separate Unguja into two major segments, too—the fertile plantation uplands (this is Abdulla's *shamba*) of the north-west quadrant, and lowland coral bush thicket everywhere else (Piggott, 1961). Zanzibaris themselves further subdivide the coral lowlands between true bush thicket and the stony flats nearest the shore that have historically held some taller (tropical dry) forest (*uwanda* and *maweni*, respectively). The island's bedrock is sedimentary, but impacted everywhere by ancient reefal limestone. The north-west quadrant has some modest undulation and several zones of extensive soil formation that are considered quite fertile (hence, the *shamba*, those plantation forests of coconuts, cloves, and other tree crops). The yellow sandy loams under much of the city and its surroundings have long been utilized for coconut plantations, while red loams have been used for growing cloves, oranges, and other tree crops. However, virtually the whole southern half of the island, its entire east side, and the islets around it—two thirds of Unguja's land surface—are poor for farming (this is the *uwanda* and *maweni*; see Myers, 1999). There are a few stretches of meager riverine lowland environments (*mabonde*) that were converted to large-scale collectivized rice or sugar production after Zanzibar's 1964 socialist revolution, but these have steadily declined in productivity and economic significance. *Mabonde* closest to the city have been slowly filling in with informal settlements, as some of the last urbanizing pieces of the checkerboard of West District.

The city (*mjini*) began in the thin-soil coral flatlands (*maweni*) of the Shangani peninsula in the 1690s as the capital of Oman's empire on the East African coast, and from then until the end of the British colonial era (1890–1963), its built environment spread only to the western edge of the uplands, the foot of the Masingini Ridge, where today's West District begins; unlike the *uwanda* or *maweni* areas, though, all of the urban areas beyond the rocky Shangani peninsula itself (today's historic Stone Town) have yellow sandy loam soils (*changa*) that are suitable for farming, with patches of even richer red loams (*kidongo chekundu*—which is a contemporary neighborhood name). Hence, on the other side of the historic Pwani Ndogo tidal creek that separated Stone Town from the rest of the island, the area known as Ng'ambo (literally, "The Other Side"), became home to the *viunga* (sing. *kiunga*, "the attached thing," often translated as suburb) plantations of Zanzibar's 19th-century Omani royalty and elite (Myers, 2003). By the 1940s, most of Ng'ambo within the colonial-era border had been urbanized as the African and Swahili peasant and working poor heart of the city (Fair, 2001), but the rest of today's Urban District east of that old border to the first upland hill was farmland even into the 1970s.

A majority of Unguja's urban residents now reside outside of Urban District, though, in West District, the northerly two thirds of which consists largely of fertile *shamba* lands (most of it planted predominantly in coconuts and other fruit or spice trees even into the 1990s). As more and more fertile farmland has been urbanized, the government has slowly sought to shift further development toward the south, into the *uwanda* and *maweni* lands of southern West District's Fumba Peninsula and the planned satellite town at Tunguu that straddles the West District border with Central District. (In mid-2015, in fact, the Tanzanian government divided West District into two, creating West A and West B Districts, with the dividing line owing much to this distinction of an increasingly densely populated southern zone and more fertile, still somewhat wooded, northern zone; since all government data and fieldwork data is based on the old, unified West District, I keep to that older geographic designation here.) Tunguu has been planned and built since 2005 in part for food security and the preservation of agriculture. However, this is also an effort to preserve *shamba* forest lands because these figure in the tourist economy both literally (in the form of "spice tours" of West District spice plantations revitalized in the 2000s specifically as a tourist attraction) and symbolically (since the Zanzibar tourism industry markets the place as the "Spice Islands").

Maweni literally means "on the rocks" in Kiswahili, and refers to land where soils are extremely thin or non-existent. Pockets of relatively deep black-brown soils rich in organic material exist in *maweni* areas, though, giving rise to a few widely scattered forests or woodlands that are home to several endemic or endangered species of plants and animals. These coral forests comprised only about 4% of Unguja's land surface by the late 1990s, and less than 2% in the 2010s. Most of that forest land is now contained within Jozani-Chwaka Bay National Park (JCBCA) (where the dominant tree species, outside of the coastal mangroves, is actually red mahogany planted under Dutton's directive as part of a sawmill operation for the city's construction and furniture needs in the 1940s). Otherwise, *maweni* lands are markedly bereft of cultivable stretches; hence, these areas have historically had low human population densities, except along the coastline. Most of the marine zone around the *maweni* areas is rimmed by coral reefs. Relatively small mangrove stands are found in the inlets and coves of the island and its islets, but the coastal geomorphology does not favor mangrove development as much on Unguja as it does to the north on Pemba Island, Zanzibar's other main island. Thin, sandy beaches are present all along east-coast *maweni* lands.

Uwanda land refers to areas with slightly more soil development in general, and is often translated into English as "coral bush thicket" since the vegetative cover there is dense with shrubs, but it is as often covered with grasslands. *Uwanda* areas are also generally not intensively cultivated or densely populated away from the coastline, although cultivation via rotational bush fallowing has increased dramatically in the past 20 years with the rise of tourism on the east coast. *Uwanda* and mangrove areas on the western side of the island are prime extraction zones for sand used in urban construction (Myers, 1999). Since the *uwanda* lands are, in most cases, closer to the city of Zanzibar and more easily accessible to it than the *maweni*, it is also there that most (but by no means all) coral limestone quarrying activity has taken place during the expansion of the urban area across most of West District.

Much of Unguja's east coast became the domain of foreign-owned beach resorts during the 1990s, decimating the remaining *maweni* forests outside of JCBNP, and leading to a dramatic increase in farming intensity in *uwanda* lands. Tourist visitors had already climbed above 100,000 in 1998, from nearly zero in 1978 (Honey, 1999); more than 100,000 international tourist arrivals were documented for the first six months alone in 2014, suggesting a doubling of numbers in just 16 years, even amid the uncertainties and insecurities of East African coastal tourism in the shadow of the Global War on Terror. Ecotourism became prominent within Zanzibari tourism early in the 21st century, with conservation, sustainability, and nature as central features of the rubric of tourist promotion (Myers, 2002b; ZATI, 2014).

Stefan Gössling's (2001, 2002a, 2002b) work on the political ecology of tourism in Zanzibar documented, more than a decade ago, the commodification of nature and images of the environment in Zanzibar. The years since have only sped this process further. Gössling (2002a: 19) showed tourism as both an indirect and "direct agent in the degradation of local environments." This "local" agency extended beyond the immediate settlements on east-coast beaches near to the preponderance of international hotels. Tourism disrupted economic backward and forward linkages in agriculture, fishing, and forestry throughout the islands and totally transformed the ethnic and demographic character of every community on Unguja and Pemba, to varying degrees (Myers, 2002b, 2005b). With the country in the city and the city in the country, it is increasingly impossible—if, indeed, it ever was possible—to carve out different and distinct rural and urban political ecologies.

Mji wa Kusadikika (city of make-believe)

I have spent more than a quarter-century researching and writing about Zanzibar. In the Kenyan writer Binyavanga Wainaina's (2005: 92) brilliant, acerbic editorial "How to write about Africa," published a decade ago in *Granta* magazine (including advice like this: "never have the picture of a well-adjusted African on the cover of your book, or in it, unless that African has won the Nobel Prize"), "Zanzibar" is suggested as a useful subtitle as long as you have "'Africa' or 'Darkness' or 'Safari' in your title." Wainaina lands startlingly close to the truth of most outsiders' deployments of stereotypes about Africa and Zanzibar. As I was writing this chapter, the *New York Times* travel section published what seems like its semi-annual article on Zanzibar (Doyle, 2014: TR9), which opened with this: "The name Zanzibar conjures up visions of sultan's palaces, paradisiacal beaches and winding alleyways," beyond its "cocoa-fringed shore of purest white"—despite the fact that cocoa trees have never been even a marginal part of the forest cover.

After more than 25 years of research, Zanzibar "conjures up" none of these exoticized visions, despite its many inevitable (And legitimate!) appearances in the subtitles of my publications. For me, it is a city and an island archipelago that lacks adequate solid waste management or effective implementation of urban environmental governance, and which overthrew an oppressive oligarchic Omani sultanate only to endure more than a half-century of a different sort of suffocating misrule as the nominal capital of a semi-sovereign part of the United Republic of Tanzania under revolutionary socialist control. Energetic and enthusiastic planners and activists in Zanzibar have attempted several generations of ambitious, transformative urban environmental plans, with only very modest positive impacts given that political context. It is a place where I have watched my friends of all backgrounds be forced into exile, or be ground down by whatever the latest falsehood masquerading as a government may be. (Multiparty politics returned to the islands in 1992 and to the electoral process in 1995, but the ruling Revolutionary Party [CCM, for Chama cha Mapinduzi, its KiSwahili name] manipulated the results to claim dubious, narrow victories in the first four Zanzibar elections of this new era over the Civic United Front [CUF].) However, it is also an urban environment profoundly alive to the people who live in it, on multiple dimensions, beyond the perceptions of outside observers like me.

One of the ways that Zanzibaris have talked with me about their city is in relationship to the great Swahili novel of the Tanzanian mainland writer Shaaban Robert (1991 [1951]), *Kusadikika* (translation: *Land of make-believe* or *Imaginary land*). *Kusadikika* has some narrative parallels with Swift's *Gulliver's travels*, as Robert tells the satirical tale of Kusadikika, a country that floats in the heavens, and its misrule. Robert first published the novel in 1951, and it is typically taken as a parable about colonial oppression. Many Zanzibaris read it in contemporary times as a fable about the misdeeds of the pirates and tyrants who have ruled the islands since the 1964 socialist revolution. The sense of Zanzibar as an island state unmoored, floating in space, an imaginary, nightmarish land, also hits home for Zanzibaris for reasons beyond the 51 years of revolutionary misdeeds. Zanzibari society, like many societies in urban Africa, is richly and deeply spiritual—and not just in the religious sense, though, indeed, the overwhelming majority of Zanzibaris are extremely religious. This religiosity intersects every day, as it does in many parts of the continent, with the supernatural, imaginary world. Indeed, in religion and in their daily lives, "people dwell in proximity with spirits" (Larsen, 2014a: 6).

Norwegian anthropologist Kjersti Larsen (2014a: 6) has argued that for many Zanzibaris, "the human world as it appears to most people seems rather unpredictable and chaotic while the world of spirits, in contrast, is seen as stable and predictable." This stable or predictable world of spirits inevitably plays a central, intrinsic role in conceptualizing environments in urban Zanzibar, even in its basic elements, since "the spirits are beings of the air and created from fire" (Larsen, 2014a: 7). Spirits most forcefully enter Zanzibar's socio-nature by occupying human bodies—Larsen prefers the term "embodiment" to the more common, and overly misused, "possession." Varieties of incense from Zanzibari or Eastern African wood (eg aloe wood and gum copal) are utilized to try to appease or shape the behavior of the embodying spirits by the embodied humans (Larsen, 2014b).

Spirits are "spatially grounded"; many of them "originate from different places beyond Zanzibar itself, such as Madagascar," but in Zanzibar itself, these spirits become associated with certain places and environments (Larsen, 2014b: 17). For example, the neighborhood in which I resided in 1991–92 has been strongly associated with spirits of Malagasy origin (*kibuki*); a (human) ritual leader for this spirit group lived two doors down, and many of my neighbors occasionally "possessed" or embodied this spirit. Since spirits have much longer life spans than humans, they are often more strongly rooted in Zanzibar's history than the humans occupying the space. Hence Kisiwandui ("Island of Smallpox," formerly an island in the Pwani Ndogo creek upon which all Africans entering Stone Town from Ng'ambo for work had to be tested for smallpox in the early colonial era), where I lived, and neighboring Vikokotoni ("On the Gravel"), had been home to Comorian-Malagasy communities in the mid-19th century, at the very beginning of Ng'ambo, and the *kibuki* ritual performances still prominently involve showcasing rare Maria Theresa *thalers* (dollars), the principal accepted currency of the western Indian Ocean trade more than 200 years ago (Larsen, 2014b).

One of the landscape settings "where humans and spirits meet" (Larsen, 2005) is in the karst caves of *uwanda* and *maweni* areas. On the Fumba Peninsula in southern West District (ie post-2015's West B District), for example, limestone cavities around the settlements of Bweleo, Bwefum, and Fumba have a long association with Giningi, the spirit world, along with many wells in this landscape. Healers often bring offerings or burn incense in the caves. The two protected forests left on Unguja (Jozani-Chwaka Bay National Park and the government's Masingini forest reserve, slowly disappearing from the ridge just east of Urban District) provide another zone commonly associated with spirits. The Jozani Forest, in which no island leopard has been sighted since 1999, is still associated with leopards by residents of nearby Chwaka Bay communities, and local healers and practitioners of spiritualism are regularly reported to be keepers of leopards. In 1999, several Chwaka residents informed me that one of these spiritualists was capable of embodying a leopard. A third major setting is actually at sea since indigenous cultures on the island recognize the presence of a number of vital spirits in the ocean. Certain passages in the ocean and the channels around the island are particularly alive to spirit–earth interaction, such as the waters near to Mwana-wa-Mwana islet just north of Tumbatu Island—adjacent to the site of the horrific 2011 sinking of the ferry boat, MV Spice Islander, when more than 1,500 Zanzibaris drowned. Few Zanzibaris would ever dispute that the incompetence and incapacity of the marine vessel inspection agency of the islands' government had much to do with the ferry disaster, but a great many would also not hesitate to locate the non-human agency at work at that location in the ocean.

Back on land, perhaps the most significant zone for the physical and metaphysical shaping of the structures of feeling that dominate 21st-century Zanzibar is that of peri-urban West District. In Tanzania's 2012 census, Urban-West Region (Mjini-Magharibi) had 593,678 people, with just over 223,000 in Urban District (Wilaya ya Mjini) and just over 370,000 in West District (Wilaya ya Magharibi). More than 45% of the total population of Zanzibar (1.3 million) resided in Mjini-Magharibi, and three in 10 Zanzibaris are in the Magharibi (West) side of that region. This West District cityscape is woefully under-examined by comparison to that of Urban District, and most especially the Stone Town (home to less than 5% of the region's population and yet most of its scholarly research projects over the last 30 years). In 2006–10, I engaged in a research project examining the increasingly urban character of West District, and the environmental impacts of its urbanization. Some of this work has been published elsewhere (Myers, 2008, 2010, 2011). Here, let me examine the socio-nature and structure of feeling of West District (incorporating to a lesser extent parts of Urban District) that emerged from that research, beginning with place-names, which can be characterized as part of dominant, residual, emergent, or excluded landscapes, whether through allegory, synecdoche, metonymy, or repetition.

Place-names, trees, socio-nature, and structures of feeling in Zanzibar

Although there are fascinating characteristics to the naming of monuments or streets, the strongest and most enlightening base for rigorous analysis lies with neighborhood names. I developed a sample of 122 official and commonly deployed names for neighborhoods in contemporary Urban-West Region. The dominant bloc of post-1964 Zanzibar certainly makes its presence known. We still see neighborhoods that were named or renamed in a bout of revolutionary fervor in the 1960s. Several honor allied states of the Zanzibar Revolution of 1964, allies in the fight against apartheid South Africa, or the socialist revolution itself and subsequent union with Tanganyika: Angola, Russia (Urusi), or Mozambique (Msumbiji), Muungano (The Union), and Nyerere (first President of that Union). Revolutionary Zanzibar, particularly under its first president, Abeid Amani Karume (1964–72), was a staunchly socialist police state when neighborhoods like Urusi, Muungano, Msumbiji, or Nyerere were built, down to the menacing operations of the ruling Afro-Shirazi Party and its secret Security (Usalama) apparatus in those and other neighborhoods.

Karume honored his son, Amani (who later served as Zanzibar's president from 2000 to 2010), in naming the new national stadium for him in the early revolutionary era, and the neighborhood that grew around it took that name (with its double meaning since Amani is also simply "Peace").

Dominant-bloc place-names are much more prominent in street names and landmarks (like the Amani Stadium) than they are in neighborhood names. The shifts in the dominant bloc's narratives on the landscape from the colonial era to a revolutionary socialist one, and slowly now to a more nuanced form, is best embodied in the main city hospital: built under Dutton's post-war development plan as Karimjee Hospital (named for its Stone Town elite benefactor, Hassanali Karimjee), it became V.I. Lenin Hospital after the 1964 Revolution, but was renamed again in the late 1990s as *Mnazimmoja* (One Coconut Palm Tree) Hospital. Yet, it is often in toponymic repetition where the dominant landscape is commonly reinforced: revolutionary socialist and Tanzanian-union themes are repeated all over Unguja and Pemba in street names and landmarks, and these repeat, like an echo, the same street names and landmark names of mainland Tanzania under CCM.

One is much more likely to find neighborhoods named by their residents for the physical features present there, the trees planted there, and the human economic activities for which that neighborhood came to be known. These largely represent the residual landscapes of the city, but not in the political sense as names representing previously dominant groups. Zanzibar has been and remains overwhelmingly an indigenous African-Swahili urbanism; it pre-dates the British colonial period by 200 years as a city, and by six centuries as a settlement of some sort. The British imposition toponymically is virtually non-existent. Only Dutton's synecdoche in the creation of the Swahili neighborhood name Raha Leo (Happiness Today) (for the area of what was once the Ng'ambo Civic Centre from 1946 to 1964, political centerpiece of the Ten-Year Post-War Development Plan that he led) has stood the test of time as a European-imposed neighborhood name. Ironically, the tiny neighborhood known as Mitiulaya (European Trees) designates a stately *allée* along both sides of the small street at the neighborhood's center; although the trees were planted during the British colonial period, the chief officers in charge of tree planting in the 1930s were Goanese, and the trees, Saman or Summer Rain Trees, are spectacular and massive South-east Asian shade trees. There are a few references in neighborhood names to Omani or Indian landowners—Kulateni (Qulatein family), Kijambia (the Omani ceremonial knife), Kwahani (Land of Khan), or Kwaalinatoo (Land of Ali Nathoo)—but the long dominance of Swahili working-class and peasant communities in the city and its suburbs is very evident in the place-names.

About one third of the neighborhoods take their name from their physical features, whether a soil type (like the Kidongo Chekundu example mentioned earlier), a rock formation (Bweleo), a river (Mtoni), or a spring (Bububu). Moreover, nearly 25% of all neighborhoods in Zanzibar have a tree in the name. The plentiful array of trees represented in the city's indigenous names for neighborhoods surely betray a great significance for trees in the local urban culture as it developed. Mango, baobab, Indian almond, jackfruit, banana, kapok, wild kapok, neem, rambutan, saman, tamarind, Mandarin orange—tree after tree is a part or all of about one quarter of all neighborhood names.

Zanzibar has a full assortment of trees and tree-based place-names. When we look inside those neighborhood tree names a little, though, we see the everyday life of working-class and peasant urban communities. First of all, nearly every tree named in a Zanzibar neighborhood is also an exotic species, one brought either by the British or by other European, Indian, or Arab traders over the centuries. Many of these—and varieties of palms or mangoes, most notably—have grown in such abundance, with many species and subspecies among these families present in the isles for so many years, that most urbanites would have found these trees *in situ* upon their arrival to the town even in the 18th or 19th century.

Ten Zanzibari neighborhood names have mango trees in them. Mango trees grow tall and broad, providing extensive shade; they thus become focal points for cultural and economic activity. Mango trees (Mwembe; plural Miembe) that had shade areas for sail-mending (Mwembe-tanga), advice-giving (Mwembe-shauri), coir-rope-making (Mwembe-makumbi), small-scale sales of groundnuts (Mwembe-njugu), fish (Kiembe-samaki), sweets (Mwembe-ladu), and pregnant women to rest by the maternity hospital (Mwembe-mimba) appear in neighborhood names. Most other trees named in neighborhood toponymy are likewise large shade trees (kapok, baobab, jackfruit, and Indian almond, or even medium-height trees known for shade, like neem/mwarubaini), where people would gather. This is exactly what urban political ecologists mean by "socio-nature": the trees and the culture are co-produced, and co-*re*produced. However, this culture–nature interface also points us toward a key commonalty between the Zanzibar case and other cities in Africa, and something that is, as yet, very much absent from the UPE literature in reference to Africa: the prominence of residual indigenous cultural-historical narratives in neighborhood naming.

Zanzibaris have produced many neighborhood names out of African cultural processes, events, rituals, or stories. In some cases, the origin of these has been lost to the residents in them, but others are marks of culture and local society embedded in the character of the community, or clear statements of profound meaning. The memorialization of the everyday shines through in many Zanzibari names, as with the many tree-based names where a tree is paired with the activity under it. There is also a Piece of a Road Ballast (Baraste Kipande), Lucky Coconut Pudding (Bumbwisudi), a Place to be Carried (Chukwani), a Place for Moonshine Liquor (Gongoni), a place to play Hide and Go Seek (Kajificheni), and a place You Have to Love (Mpendae). Places of work and community activity are frequently named for the work or activity: Sokomuhogo (Cassava Market), Gulioni (At the Market), Karakana (Workshop), Kama (Milking), Mazizini (At the Cattle Pens), Fuoni (At the Clothes-washing Place), or Kinuni (At the Grinding Mill).

A great many of the activities memorialized in those names are gone from the neighborhoods in question—there is no cassava market in Sokomuhogo, no cattle pens in Mazizini, no workshop in Karakana. Most of the trees memorialized in the names have been cut down— the neem tree of Mwarubaini was chopped down in the 1990s to make way for an official CCM gathering place, and the seven mango trees of Miembe Saba made way for the city water tanks and pipes on Welezo Hill a few years later. In the urban and suburban residential neighborhoods that have displaced these features, perhaps the prevailing social ethos that has, in a parallel fashion, displaced the patronage systems, faith-based neighborliness, and customary interdependence that had often previously defined life there is best captured in the Swahili word "*fitina*", or discord. This *fitina* is especially prominent in West District's more recently urbanized areas.

One clear feature of the emergent landscape/structure of feeling of *fitina* is the sharp political commentary enmeshed in some names, as in Daraja Bovu (Broken or Rotten Bridge, adjacent to a frequently flooded bridge structure), Uholanzi (Holland, named because of frequent flooding), or Sogea (Pack It In, a dense informal settlement). It is hard to miss the allegory, synecdoche, or metonymy in these names, particularly in those deployed informally, and in how the names are performed. In the Welezo area, one stop on the mini-bus route—at least from 2006 to 2010—was known as "Baghdad," and the neighborhood around it took on this name as well. Many homes in the valley just below that minibus stop were demolished in 2005–06 on the order of the Tanzanian Army, who claimed that the homes encroached on the land of their base, which actually begins on the other side of the road.

The enduring *fitina* in "Baghdad" went together with the commonly deployed name for the entire strip of West District neighborhoods along the edge of Urban District, from Mtoni south to Chukwani: the "Gaza Strip."

No official map will ever tell you where this Gaza Strip is, or Baghdad, so that some of the emerging landscape blends into hidden or excluded storyscapes. These are even clearer in their performative dimensions. For instance, from 2006 to 2010, touts for another minibus route, from Amani to Daraja Bovu, would call out "Amani Bovu" when seeking passengers—on one level, they were just making their call shorter, but, of course, they also knew that they were saying that the Zanzibari President at the time, Amani Karume, was rotten. Other excluded stories are often quite literally hidden. The two minibus stops on the Mwera line informally known as Royal Camp and Usalama ("Security") in the subdivision of Mwera called Regezamwendo (Reduce Your Speed) hide both a historical and a contemporary feature to the local environment that goes unspoken in Mwera: this was once a country retreat villa for the Omani sultan, but when his land was nationalized after the revolution, it was secretly distributed to officers in the internal security service (CID; Central Intelligence Directorate). Even in 2006–2010, 14 to 18 years after the end of the single-party political system, Mwera residents spoke only in hushed tones about "Usalama" and walked by the Usalama stop with their eyes averted from that part of the neighborhood lest they face harassment from the CID. Notoriously fast minibus drivers reduce their speed here with the same fear in mind—hence the area's name, Regezamwendo.

West District's main source of *fitina* lies with land distribution (see Figure 3.2). After the revolution, the first President Karume, Amani's father, nationalized all land and seized the plantations of Arab, Indian, and Swahili landholders who had supported the Sultanate; although a handful remained in Zanzibar, many of these landowners were killed in the revolution or fled into exile. What became West District was the primary zone for land seizures. These fertile plantation lands were redistributed in Karume's *Eka Tatu* (Three Acre) Program (so called despite the fact that most parcels varied in size from one to five acres). These *eka tatu* lands have been the areas of West District most heavily urbanized since the 1980s, and the patterns of settlement have produced dramatic socio-natural diversity in a short time (Myers, 2010). Older, farming communities around and amid the *eka tatu* areas have been inundated with Pemba islanders, mainlanders, and fellow Ungujans, and the resulting tensions are further compounded by the enduring political strife in Zanzibar between CCM and CUF (Myers, 2008).

The "Gaza Strip" has long been seen as strongly in favor of the CUF, and even in the height of tension and violence in and around the elections of 1995, 2000, and 2005, CUF's trademark light-blue, red, and white banners (or just ribbons with these colors) were ubiquitous inside Gaza Strip neighborhoods.

Figure 3.2: West District *shamba* lands becoming urban plots, Zanzibar

Many aspects of the *fitina* over land remain part of the hidden or excluded cityscape, though—one does not see the banners flying that announce them. It is in quiet conversations, or in the dying end of an interview out of earshot of the government minder, where one hears from a mainlander whose families have been squatters in the area since the 1940s about the Arab families' wells that were "poisoned" by the dead bodies that revolutionaries threw down them in 1964, or from the Arab patriarch decrying the mainlander Christian churches that have been given plots in his neighborhood to promote "devil worship." Other Swahilis in a focus group laugh at a story of two mainlander boys who drowned swimming in the seasonal flood zone of a West District informal settlement, reciting for me the perverse Zanzibari saying "A death in the family is a wedding (for someone else)." It was only after a month of interviews in Welezo and Baghdad that my Zanzibari research assistant and I learned that we ourselves had been the subjects of a rampant rumor about home demolitions for the major water project with which, in fact, we had nothing to do. Nearly half of the 62 residents we interviewed recommended the demolition of their own neighborhoods to maintain agricultural land; the loss of trees—the currency by which land is valued in the informal market remains the number and type of trees on it when it is sold—is paramount within this concern. One interviewee explained this with the Swahili riddle "When the monkey is finished with the trees, he will come for your body" because the loss of trees signaled broader danger to her, of increased theft and social violence (Anonymous A, 2007). Interviewees stressed their despair at the loss of tree crops for their financial and food security, even while recognizing that it was impossible to really envision any program for starting the urbanization process over again in West District:

> "We have a saying in Swahili, 'Work the clay while it is wet.'
> If you want to make a sculpture, if the clay is wet you can
> make a crocodile, and then change it into a lion, or a cow.
> If it is already dry, forget it. Do you see what I am saying?
> The clay is dry here." (Anonymous B, 2007)

For many West District residents, the allegory of dry clay stands for the whole landscape of *fitina* that has become the predominant structure of feeling in Zanzibar city and its suburbs. The 2010 elections were carried out peacefully—for the first time in the islands' electoral history—and a "government of national unity" was established between the ruling CCM and its opposition partner, CUF (Myers and Muhajir, 2013). However, tensions have ratcheted upward again in the 2015 election season. Furthermore, in places like West District, the *fitina* has never been simply about political parties. It is about ghosts in wells, drowned children, invisible vampire bats (who made their appearance in the 1995 and 2000 elections especially), devil worship, and dispossession. It is about workshops without work, *kraals* without cattle, and treeless neighborhoods called Seven Mango Trees. It is about clay that has dried.

Conclusion

When we return to Duncan's idea of landscape as a signifying system, with Cosgrove's variations on Williams and Mawere's take on African conceptions of sustainable development in mind, we see that much more than just a rhetoric of "power versus counter-power" is at play in this structure of feeling in Zanzibar. State projects of legibility there have clearly involved toponymy and constructed nature. However, residual, emergent, and excluded "rewritings" of these projects are quite evident in all of their shades of nuance. There is a need to attend to the mundane and the banal, rather than seeing all naming as part of a grand, essentialist contestation.

For over a decade, scholars have stressed the need for greater analysis of African "cities as places which are socially as well as physically constructed" (Rakodi, 2006: 312). This analysis of cities as "socially constructed" or produced landscapes needs to extend to the spiritual and symbolic realms out of which many urban Africans conceive those constructed environments. At the same time, analysis of the construction of Africa's cities ought to take into account the physical environment and the broader ecological links of cityscapes with their hinterlands. I began the chapter with Dutton's claims for "tree worship" in Zanzibar, and I tested and decoded that to see the much more complicated stew of socio-natures that exist and are contested in that city. I believe a similar approach is useful across the continent's cityscapes.

I have aimed in this chapter at pluralizing UPE by opening it up to exploration of the genuinely "everyday" environmentalism of a broad array of urban residents in Africa, as expressed in naming practices and the performativity of the landscape, and to a sense of the non-human agency present in spiritualism and religious belief on the continent. Seeing African cityscapes as environments where the visible and invisible, or the physical and the metaphysical, worlds meet is an essential step in moving beyond various forms of determinism to get at the structures of feeling in those cityscapes.

The development of a critical analysis of environmental politics requires recognition of the depths of complexity in socio-environmental conflicts. There is more at work than a clash of classes, or of forms of rationality. There is more than just risk in the physical city environments. There are also worlds of opportunity. For every cityscape that seems to be "dry clay," in other ways, we find urban Africans hard at work with the "wet clay." Chapters Four and Five of the book take us through the agency of two interrelated groups of voices in the multi-vocality of African urban environments: the artists (Chapter Four) and the activists at the grassroots (Chapter Five).

FOUR

The artists

Introduction

In the late Senegalese filmmaker-novelist Ousmane Sembene's (1970) novel *God's bits of wood*, the history of a 1947–48 workers' strike against the colonial operators of French West Africa's Dakar–Niger railroad is retold through the stories of the social networks of the strike's organizers, activists, and opponents along the line of rail at three urban junctures: Dakar, Thiés, and Bamako. Sembene connects the cities, and the countryside between them, in a kind of produced socio-nature of resistance to colonial rule and its consequences. As Sembene does in nearly all of his works in print and film, in *God's bits of wood*, he places women at the center of the narrative, and he emphasizes their roles in the production and re-production of the cultural and physical cityscape. It is one of the strongest African novels for linking the urban and the environmental in firmly political ways. However, there are, in fact, hundreds of African novels that do so, and those novels are only a thin sliver of the body of works by African artists that are, in effect, works of urban political ecology (UPE).

Since political artistic visions of urban environments come in many forms of art, it is totally impossible to do justice to the whole panoply. In this chapter, I examine the visions of environments and environmentalism in art largely with novels, but extend in the end to popular music and, to a lesser extent, institutions of the arts. (All of these visions provide some connective tissue with Chapter Five, on the grassroots, and thus my discussion of them overlaps into that chapter.) Artists, writers, and artistic institutions obviously also cover the map of the continent, and while I take examples from a variety of settings, I acknowledge the utter impossibility of covering that whole map. In keeping with my approach in the previous three chapters, each of which has a main focus city, here, my concentration lies with Dakar, as a city alive with visual, musical, performing, and written arts that have been influential around the world—and specifically with its satellite city of Pikine—as well as the environmental issues surrounding waste, water, and urban floods.

Theoretically, I take the scholarly field of postcolonial ecocriticism as my base point in the chapter. Ecocriticism can perhaps most simply be boiled down to analysis of "ecologically sensitive writing and criticism" (Ojaide, 2013: v), and postcolonial forms of this scholarship link analysis of that ecologically sensitive writing with cultural circumstances in societies living with the aftermath of European colonialism. Ecocriticism arguably exists in Africa as a means of challenging Western-centered ecocriticism while, at the same time, engaging with the field of postcolonial studies from environmental perspectives (Caminero-Santangelo, 2014: 9–15). Ecocritical scholarship joins a growing list of works on cultural production and the arts in urban Africa with political-environmental emphases. Musicians, hip-hop artists, photographers, painters, sculptors, dancers, and theatrical artists, often in collaboration with writers and poets, offer a crucial array of voices on urban environments. An interactionist UPE needs to account for those voices, specifically because they have often provided tangible rallying points for environmental politics in Africa's cities.

Ecocriticism and Africa's urban environments

In a way parallel to what I suggest in the Introduction and Chapter One regarding UPE, literature scholars inspired by the emerging work in ecological criticism have debated how applicable the Western-derived theoretical lens is in Africa and whether there should be an "African" form of ecocriticism. Ecocritical work in Africa has also often had a fairly strong—though not exclusive—emphasis on South African (and often white) writers and a similar palette of rural environmental issues to those that have preoccupied political ecologists in Africa, thus creating challenges comparable to those for the literature of UPE. The recent volume on African ecocriticism that Byron Caminero-Santangelo and I co-edited is a case in point—seven of its 11 chapters deal with white writings from Africa and six-and-a-half chapters focus on Southern Africa (Caminero-Santangelo and Myers, 2011). Only two chapters have any substantively urban dimension, but even here the urban is not the only or main focus (Nixon, 2011b; Vital, 2011). Although there is a growing Nigerian literature of ecocriticism, it is also often built around rural analysis, with the Niger delta, oil, and Ken Saro-Wiwa or the poet Tanure Ojaide as the main focus (Okuyade, 2013; Caminero-Santangelo, 2014). This is not to discount such work—indeed, as I have argued in the Introduction, one key insight from African settings for UPE is the blurring of urban–rural distinctions, and, potentially, a similar theme can be discerned in ecocritical work.

For an Africa-based ecocriticism to thrive, though, it must identify and interrogate still more non-South African writers and find ways of analyzing urban environments in the continent's literature without falling into an easy and uncritical championing of the disadvantaged, particularly because even a nominally comprehensive look at African writers shows great variation in the conceptualization or deployment of environmental themes. For that reason, postcolonial ecocriticism has the potential to be very helpful in furthering the interactionist framework for UPE around which I have built this book. African writers offer an amazing and surprising array of environmental voices on the urban dynamics of the continent. The voices of writers and artists can therefore be part of a vehicle for creating an interactionist UPE situated in Africa.

Ecocriticism has, like UPE, emerged largely out of Western academia (Buell, 1995; Glotfelty and Fromm, 1996). Analyses of its appropriateness or applicability in African literary studies are still at the beginning stage, leading at least one critic to claim, mistakenly, that African literature offers little of substance for ecocriticism (Slaymaker, 2001). However, even if few works explicitly labeled as ecocritical have appeared in African literature beyond white South African literature, it is plainly the case that "there has been some form of eco-criticism in African scholarship long before it became vogue in the Western academy" and that "traditional African literature has ... been sensitive to nature and the environment in many ways" (Ojaide, 2013: vii; see also Obiechina, 1975; Caminero-Santangelo, 2014). Ecocritical writings from or on Africa often argue for strong connections between questions of human rights or social justice and the environment. Rob Nixon (2011a) recently brought the notion of "slow violence" into the analysis of African ecocriticism as a means of reading the atrocious decline of global environments in terms of their devastating and unjust impacts on the world's poorest people. He brilliantly parallels Kenyan socio-environmental activist Wangari Maathai's (2006) autobiography with the work of Rachel Carson in the US in this regard (Nixon, 2011b).

Yet, even as the literature of African ecocriticism expands, little of it explicitly addresses urban environments outside of South Africa. Nixon (2011b) does make note of the important junctures at which Maathai engaged in activism to preserve both Karura Forest and Uhuru Park in Nairobi, but he only touches briefly on the urban environmental implications of Maathai's work (see also Njeru, 2010). In the path-breaking recent collection edited by Ogaga Okuyade (2013), *Eco-critical literature: regreening African landscapes*, there are many chapters that develop a way of seeing African writers as critiquing the role of humans in the destruction of the environment, and some that move beyond that to environmental justice activism and analysis thereof. Although there is a huge emphasis on the Niger Delta, there are effective efforts to tie the particulars of the setting into dialogue with other African settings and with literary criticism and ecocriticism around the world. However, there is very little that is explicitly urban in the book, and nothing that makes reference to political ecology, let alone to its urban variations. Of 18 content chapters, only three place any notable emphasis on urban environments; two thirds of the chapters are all or in part about the Niger Delta. Admittedly, this is an industrial landscape, but the sites of oil extraction, routes of pipelines, and damages to indigenous livelihoods are largely rural environments, and the chapter authors are much more concerned with rural matters and rural natural environments. Six chapters are all or in part about Tenure Ojaide, and only one of these chapters really deals with the urban dynamics of Ojaide's poems.

The actual urban analysis of these few urban chapters might help build toward seeing the rural and urban divide in blurry terms, but, in fact, the possibility for that from this volume is limited. Obari Gomba (2013: 247) offers a fascinating reading of Ojaide's uses of urban symbolism in his poetry, such as the repeated dystopian depiction of the Delta city of Warri or the insertion of Nigeria's capital city of Abuja ("where the national flag covers a cesspool") as the oppressor of the Niger Delta. Sunny Awhefeada (2013: 103) similarly shows how Kaine Agary uses Port Harcourt as the setting for the decline and fall of a rural migrant woman in *Yellow-Yellow* as she is "overwhelmed by the glitz and glamour" of the city. Ifeyinwa Okolo's (2013: 15) rich analysis of Ngugi wa Thiong'o's *Wizard of the crow* suggests that Ngugi, like other contemporary African novelists writing about urbanization, tends to "point the cities back to their rural roots for correction" as a sort of effort to "regreen the disappearing ecosystems." In all three cases, though, the trope of the urban as the *opposite* of nature emerges—and this is, in fact, the opposite of what much UPE theory, by contrast, claims to seek.

When we include a broader group of writers, geographically, temporally, and otherwise, I argue that we see many *different* voices on the urban environment in African literature that can potentially contribute to an interactionist UPE. To be sure, simplistic visions of a rural pastoral pitted against evil belching urbanization are there in African writing, but so are the sorts of revolutionary movements that someone of a radical ideological persuasion would champion, and quite a number of voices in between. Caminero-Santangelo (2014: 3) has offered a powerful rebuttal to common Western thinking about Africa and the environment that portrays "Africans as lacking the proper environmental sensibility and knowledge to take care of precious biodiversity hot spots," and which is thereby essentially "suggesting that environmentalist efforts in Africa need to be conceived and led by non-Africans." African authors and artists have produced a similar rebuttal to outsider ideas that African residents have little environmental sensibility when it comes to urban environmental issues. There are many possible authors or cities to use to illustrate that point; regardless of the authors chosen, I am arguing that in literary analysis, it is worthwhile to move beyond some of the more expected writers whose urban environmentalism might be more obvious to find the urban political-ecological in more unexpected, and yet, strangely everyday, literary moments across the continent and across a political spectrum.

Caminero-Santangelo (2014) has taken an ecocritical lens to a valuable array of African authors. In *Different shades of green*, he analyzes the struggles against environmental injustice in East, West, and South Africa through interrogations of some familiar authors (Maathai, Saro-Wiwa, Ojaide, and Nadine Gordimer) but also a host of other writers previously unexamined or under-examined in an ecocritical light: Okot p'Bitek, Ngugi, Camara Laye, Nuruddin Farah, Alan Paton, Bessie Head, Zakes Mda, and Chinua Achebe. Moreover, he explicitly addresses the heretofore buried tethers between ecocriticism and both the political-ecology and environmental justice literatures. He argues that "in political ecology (as in postcolonial ecocriticism) the framing of environmental transformation as a problem (or not) is always inflected by social struggle" (Caminero-Santangelo, 2014: 33).

At the same time, and crucially for my deployment of his ideas in building ties between an interactionist UPE and ecocriticism, Caminero-Santangelo (2014: 33–4) is wide awake to the "varying degrees" to which African writers address environmental justice or political-ecology themes, and to how "limiting and misguided" it would be to analyze "only the commonalities" between these ways of thinking (political ecology and ecocriticism). The key to his analysis of the literary texts in the book lies in "putting the texts in dialogue" and in "critical consideration of different ways of imagining relationships across scale" (Caminero-Santangelo, 2014: 33–4). This leads him to see political ecology as "offering the tools for unearthing the socioecological unconscious of naturalizing, romantic representations of community and resistance in African environmentalist writing" (Caminero-Santangelo, 2014: 35). However, it can be equally valuable in analyzing writing that sees those romantic representations as "suspect or useless" (Caminero-Santangelo, 2014: 35). In other words, it is crucial to see the diversity across the continent and over time, to acknowledge "the varied landscapes of African environmentalist writing and environmentalism in Africa but also resist closure in the imagining of effective ways to move toward a more equitable, sustainable future" (Caminero-Santangelo, 2014: 35). This approach enables him to critique the mythic pastoral and idyllic environmental imagery of many African writers (who often idealize indigenous or pre-colonial rural African cultures' relations with nature), including Ngugi, Maathai, p'Bitek, Saro-Wiwa, and Laye, but also the counter-narrative to that romanticism in Farah's novels. Throughout the book, what Caminero-Santangelo (2014: 74, 184) offers are "contrapuntal" (or polyphonic) readings that "foster multivoiced, open approaches to environmental consciousness and action" cognizant of the "profoundly heterogeneous" character of Africa.

Waste and the city

With the slight exception of his analysis of Ojaide's poetry on the Niger Delta, Caminero-Santangelo (2014: 174) does not really deal with urban themes or settings in the book; however, his approach is easily adapted to analysis of works by African writers that are urban-based narratives. The following section of this chapter gives a few suggestions of how that could be done, with a contrapuntal reading that compares the deployment of urban waste themes in several key ways in the narratives of four books—Ayi-Kwei Armah's (1977 [1968]) *The Beautyful ones are not yet born*, Chris Abani's (2004) *GraceLand*, and Farah's (2011) *Crossbones*, as well as *God's bits of wood*.

Waste is an ideal focus for Africa-based urban ecocriticism, in part, because it has been a key discursive realm for what stands as essentially the fullest existing Africa-based urban ecocriticism, the work of South African literary scholar Anthony Vital (2008, 2011, 2015). Much of Vital's conceptualization is drawn up, like Caminero-Santangelo's, in dialogue with Western UPE, and, interestingly, considering what I have discussed in Chapter Three, Raymond Williams. He reminds us that "cities have never existed 'outside' of nature" and they are sometimes networked into and enmeshed in nature on a "planetary scale" (Vital, 2015: 4). Vital argues that a focus on waste as a broader concept, for example, in his reading of J.M. Coetzee's novel *Age of iron* (1990), enables us to see the city (in this case, Cape Town) as "a world of waste, of what is cast out for being useless, unable to support a flourishing life" (Vital, 2011: 187).

Waste is also a valuable focus beyond the literary, discursive properties of the word, precisely because it is such an important ecological, material, fluid encapsulation of African urban dynamics (Myers, 2005a; Adama, 2007). It is difficult, and perhaps dangerous, to overgeneralize across all of Africa on urban waste issues. Some cities or countries appear to have dynamics at work that distinguish their waste issues or policy implementation from those of neighboring cities or countries (Karani and Jewasikiewitz, 2007; Nahman and Godfrey, 2010; Oteng-Ababio, 2010; Lawhon, 2012; Nzeadibe, 2013; Bjerkli, 2015). There are several common themes that pertain for waste issues in most of the region's cities, though, where each cascades from the next. The majority of residential waste, in particular, goes uncollected, especially in informal settlements. Landfills are overflowing and unsanitary, and the provision of waste services has been highly uneven, with wealthier and central city commercial areas receiving more effective services than poorer areas (Nchito and Myers, 2004; Parrot et al, 2009; Adama, 2012).

The incapacity to collect and deposit waste creates new environmental health hazards, especially in the increasing prevalence of waterborne diseases emanating from a greater presence of standing water as a result of uncollected trash clogging storm-water drains in many neighborhoods. Management technologies have not kept pace with the needs for more sophisticated equipment or processes, leaving landfills more susceptible to contamination or spontaneous combustion and waste workers more vulnerable to toxic wastes. Efforts to replace government-led urban solid waste management delivery services with private-sector and public–private–popular partnerships have had mixed results, at best, across the continent (Nchito and Myers, 2004; Hampwaye, 2005; Kassim and Ali, 2006; Oteng-Ababio, 2010; Salim, 2010; Tukahirwa et al, 2010). Finally, while draconian or authoritarian waste management strategies like those in Rwanda discussed in Chapter One may occasion short-term increases in the percentage of waste making it to a landfill, more effective policies over the longer term seem to entail more participatory, grassroots, popular, and activist engagement with waste issues, from consciousness-raising to deposition and recycling (Cissé, 1996; Imam et al, 2008; Fredericks, 2009). Even with this relatively progressive sort of engagement, solid waste management remains a significant challenge in most cities of sub-Saharan Africa, as it is in Dakar, for all of the reasons just listed. However, this is precisely where the writers and artists come into the picture, as I seek to show in this chapter.

Four visions of urban wastes

Early in *The beautyful ones are not yet born*, Armah (1977 [1968]: 7) has a long discourse on "what seemed to be a small pile of earth with a sort of signboard standing nonsensically on top of it" on the streets of an unnamed city in Ghana. As a character in the book approaches this pile, he realizes that the signboard is a waste box emblazoned with an exhortation from the government to "Keep your country clean by keeping your city clean"—and yet the pile is the waste that has overflowed from it, a situation that was replicated across the city at these receptacles (Armah, 1977 [1968]: 7). "People did not have to go up to the boxes any more," Armah (1977 [1968]: 8) wrote, "From a distance they aimed their rubbish at the growing heap, and a good amount of juicy offal hit the face and sides of the box."

More than 40 years later, I wrote of a similar, but non-fictional, scene in Lusaka, where a 2004 city council sign read "Please Keep Lusaka Clean: Otherwise the Pirates Will Get You," and a pile of garbage crowded the base posts of the sign (Myers, 2011: 21–2). Comparable scenes of the visceral and defiant presence of waste and filth can be gleaned from the fiction and the non-fiction of urban Africa. In his coming-of-age tragicomedy *GraceLand*, Abani (2004: 4) wrote of Lagos as a place where "the smell of garbage from refuse dumps, unflushed toilets and stale bodies was still overwhelming." Many other urbanists and novelists enliven their writings by filling our nostrils with the stenches of garbage-strewn African cities (Davis, 2006). Rampant and pervasive waste has clearly become a trope in representations of cities in Africa, particularly where it combines with flooding and poor sanitation to produce putrid standing water.

One can place a standardized cause alongside this perception of the waste problem: government mismanagement. The Armah (1977 [1968]: 7–8) novel drips with contempt for the "latest campaign to rid the town of its filth" with which the waste boxes were associated. It was an "impressive" political charade, where the newspapers and the radio lined up a succession of "big shots" to warn of the "evil effects of uncleanliness," but the "magnificent campaign" was a spectacular failure. Similar failures haunt common perceptions in urban writings. However, *The beautyful ones* is ultimately a narrow, largely nationalist, and thoroughly depressing critique of the post-colonial state. This, then, is one common way in which urban waste figures in African novels politically, as an allegorical reference point to urban failures. Filth, rot, waste, and shit appear on nearly every page of Armah's novel.

By contrast, more recent and decidedly post-colonial and transnational novelists like Abani in *GraceLand* often voice more complicated understandings of urban environments and a broader or more nuanced deployment of waste as a discursive tactic in the text. Abani celebrates the postmodern absurdism of an Elvis impersonator and some-time cross-dresser caught up in urban resistance in Maroko, Lagos's floating slum. A squatter's rebellion there is crushed, but akin with real youth movements like Dakar's (waste-management-oriented) Set-Setal movement of the 1980 and 1990s, we get a sense of the spontaneous and inspirational rebels' forms of pirate action (Fredericks, 2009).

In *GraceLand*, Abani produces a visceral portrait of place, time, and character that easily lends itself to a UPE interpretation. As the literary theorist Dustin Crowley (2015: 183) puts it, in *GraceLand* as in other Abani writings:

> [the] main characters struggle—and generally fail—to ground themselves in fluid, disruptive, and often unjust cityscapes; yet at the same time, Abani portrays ... marginalized urban spaces as places of vitality and value, engendering possibilities for alterity that exist alongside of—and perhaps arise out of—the hardships of city life.

The parts of the story set in Lagos in 1983, and, in particular, the Maroko scenes, jump out with a lively, complex political-ecological consciousness, cognizant of socio-environmental injustice. "People who didn't live in Lagos only saw postcards of skyscrapers, sweeping flyovers, beaches and hotels" and "one-third of the city seemed transplanted from the rich suburbs of the west," Abani (2004: 7) writes. For the rest, the folks like Elvis, his friend Redemption, and the King of Beggars, Lagos, especially Maroko, is far from the postcards of paradise. Elvis thinks that:

> nothing prepared you for Maroko. Half of the town was built of a confused mix of clapboard, wood, cement and zinc sheets, raised above a swamp by means of stilts and wooden walkways. The other half, built on solid ground reclaimed from the sea, seemed to be clawing its way out of the primordial swamp, attempting to become something else. (Abani, 2004: 48)

Yet, for every attempt to become something else, there are moments like the one that immediately follows this vision from Elvis: "a man squatted on a plank walkway outside his house, defecating into the swamp below, where a dog lapped up the feces before they hit the ground," and Elvis looks the other way, only to see a boy fishing in the same water (Abani, 2004: 48).

In the uprising's attempt to save Maroko from the army's bulldozers in what is called "Operation Clean the Nation," Abani's ragtag rebels—with glorious names like Sunday, Joshua, Freedom, and Confidence—literally become the rubbish that the urban renewal plan sees as being in the way. Despite their solidarity and engagement, the bulldozers win, and a child dies. Licking their wounds in a calm moment in the middle of the standoff, the rebels wonder:

> Had it been worth it? Was any of this worth any principle? Sunday was not so sure anymore. Sighing, he walked past Freedom and Confidence into the tenement. Behind him, children were playing a new dare game: who could jump over the still-burning barricade. (Abani, 2004: 272)

After the defeat and Elvis's stint in a prison torture chamber, though, we have several moments of—literally and figuratively—redemption: the King of the Beggars dies stabbing the Colonel who led the forces crushing the rebels, on camera, and he is "deified, turned into a prophet, an advance guard, like John the Baptist, for arrival of the Messiah" (Abani, 2004: 303). Elvis, ironically, survived the massacre of the rebels while he was being tortured in prison. He recovers his soul in Bridge City, and then his friend Redemption gives Elvis his identity and name to get a plane ticket to America. The novel ends with Elvis responding to his unfamiliar new name when it is called at the airport departure gate: yes, he says, "this is Redemption."

This cheeky "redemption" at the end of *GraceLand* is not some sort of universal African UPE map to solutions for urban problems, but the novel does use waste and rubbish, phoenix-like, as vehicles for redemption, in marked contrast to the hopelessness of *The beautyful ones*. Further, the array of outcomes in the end of the narrative is exemplary of the multiplexity of urban life in Africa. There is no way to coax a unified single voice out of the political-ecological setting of Maroko. This is quite similar to the ambivalent and multifaceted end to Farah's *Crossbones*, which is, arguably, the bleakest work Farah has yet produced—and it, too, is still not as bleak as *The beautyful ones*.

As the title hints, *Crossbones* is a novel concerned with piracy off the Somali coast, and piracy of various kinds in Somalia, told largely through the contrasting narratives of two Somali brothers returning from North America. The one, Ahl, heads to a port city in the autonomous region of Puntland, Bosaso, to attempt to find and rescue his stepson from Minneapolis from the Islamist militants he is suspected of having fled to; the other, Malik, is a journalist, and he heads to Mogadishu to write stories on the civil war. Waste is deployed discursively in a number of ways. The dumping of toxic wastes in Somalia's offshore waters is the first way, and it provides the first form of piracy, as foreign companies exploit the unmanaged shores as illegal dumping grounds. (The first acts of "piracy" by Somalis were, as it is argued here and elsewhere, seizures of ships dumping toxic wastes or illegally fishing in Somalia's territorial waters after the collapse of the national government—and with it, the coast guard [see Samatar et al, 2010; Gilmer, 2014].) As with nearly every Farah novel, much of the action in the book takes place in Mogadishu; however, the most intriguing uses of waste discourse in the novel come in and around the newly emerging pirate town in Puntland, Bosaso.

Despite how "Puntlanders in the diaspora have talked up Bosaso, describing it as a booming coastal city brimming with ideas, its gung-ho, on-the-go residents making pots of money," Farah's (2011: 94) protagonist here, Ahl, is unimpressed: the city's streets "look to be assembled ad hoc," and the majority of its buildings are "little more than upgraded shacks." Garbage is everywhere, with "discarded polyethylene bags ... hanging, as if for dear life, from the electric wires" (Farah, 2011: 95) even around the few fancy homes in the town. When Ahl asks his host if the city has "always been like this," the host acknowledges the "disorderliness" and "beleaguered nature of the city," and tells Ahl that human trafficking and piracy "attract all sorts of riffraff" (Farah, 2011: 94). Indeed, the primary "waste" of Bosaso in the novel is this human riffraff—pirates, human smugglers, and the desperate migrants they exploit. In Bosaso, as one character puts it, we see "a recipe for deceit, double-dealing, and counterfeiting. And we [ordinary Somalis] are the marquee pawns of the greatest dupe" (Farah, 2011: 104).

In Mogadishu and throughout the rest of Somalia during the time period of the novel (December 2006), maritime pirates, the Islamic Courts Union (ICU) that ruled Mogadishu at the time, the extremist Islamic militants of al-Shabaab, and the Ethiopian army that chases the ICU out of the city join the bandit tycoons of Bosaso in cooking up this "recipe," where ordinary Somalis "receive little from the takings" (Farah, 2011: 217). In Mogadishu, all is "ruin" and "rubble" (Farah,

2011: 235); in Bosaso, houses are made from "course matting," zinc, and "packing material," with cloth doors (Farah, 2011: 256). In despair, Malik, the journalist brother in Mogadishu, writes that his country is "in a terrible mess. The entire nation is caught up in a spiraling degeneracy that a near stranger like me cannot make full sense of. It is all a fib, that is what it is, a fib" (Farah, 2011: 300). At the same time, in Bosaso, a companion of Ahl's says that this fib is really a case of "self-hate," and Somalia is a "nation murdering itself" and a "death culture" (Farah, 2011: 315). As if to prove this, Malik comes across a crowd of youths in Mogadishu demonstrating against the Ethiopian army's invasion, burning major figures in effigy, and "stamping on a corpse in uniform," a captured Ethiopian soldier (Farah, 2011: 331).

Malik survives a roadside bomb, and Ahl is able to locate and retrieve his stepson before he has embarked on a suicide bombing mission. However, the novel has little of the "redemption" of *GraceLand*. Instead, we are reminded of the wasting of humans that is recurring continually in Mogadishu, Bosaso, and other Somali urban areas: "piracy" of any kind "does not work for Somalis" (Farah, 2011: 367). It is a tremendous waste, of humans, of resources, of potential, of the environment. At the novel's end, Ahl and his stepson reach Djibouti, on their eventual way home to Minneapolis, but their status is deemed "purgatorial." Upon hearing this, their friend from Mogadishu, Cambara, says, "I think I know what purgation is: the discharge of waste matter from the body, isn't that right?" (Farah, 2011: 385). Her colleague, Jeebleh, agrees, and says that Ahl and his stepson faced an inferno in Bosaso, and now "each will rid himself of all defilement" (Farah, 2011: 385). The storyline thus becomes a tale of purgation, of ridding oneself of waste.

Crossbones is vastly different in time and place to *God's bits of wood*, but Sembene's novel is, like the Farah book, very much a comparative urban geography of purgation. Each chapter title begins with its urban setting: nine are entitled "Thiés," six "Dakar," four "Bamako," and one "Between Thiés and Dakar: the march of the women." Although, at first pass, it may seem less explicitly an example of environmental writing than *Crossbones*, a deeper reading picks up its ecocritical dimensions throughout. It is, like *Crossbones*, thoroughly political—it is one of the most nuanced readings of African urban politics in the entire library of African literature, about ridding Senegal (and West Africa) of the waste that was French colonialism.

In the novel, a dichotomy is created between clean and dirty, in people and environs. Sembene's empathy lies largely with the unclean. The prettier or more prettified the people or more luxurious the surroundings, the more contemptuously they are drawn in the novel.

Dirt arises from labor. Sweat covers the heroic. Nature is *produced*. Even the "God's bits of wood" of the title has nothing to do with trees; instead, it is a metaphor for children, and ultimately for all people (Sembene, 1970: 84). The literary allusion makes this historical novel the story of the people, of any age, along the line of rail from Dakar to Bamako.

Both Sembene's love for and empathy with humanity and his subtle sense of humor shine throughout the novel and help to keep it from becoming overly romantic, ideological, or didactic; it tells a rich story. Although it is often seen as a revolutionary anti-colonial novel, as Wendy Belcher (2007: 80) has argued, "the text has more to say about indirect resistance than is obvious at a first glance." Indeed, it has much more to offer than that first glance suggests, on many levels. It is full of complex people and their difficult relations with one another and with the socio-environment through the heart of the 1947–48 rail strike along the Senegal–Niger Railway that linked French West Africa and cemented Dakar's central political and economic role in the region. The railway was approved as a project in 1879 but only completed along its entire length from Bamako to Dakar in 1924. It was built entirely by forced labor. In combination with the campaigns of forced conscription by the French in both world wars and an early rail strike in 1938, by the onset of the strike in 1947, conditions were ripe for widespread labor unrest along that entire line of rail and beyond in French West Africa, as a key building block of anti-colonialism (Boahen, 1970).

God's bits of wood has been critiqued for evident, deliberate historical inaccuracies; however, first of all, it is a work of *fiction*, and, second, my interests are strictly in analyzing the book as a piece of *ecocriticism*. Nature and culture are intertwined, but often in combat, in the novel. The "land of the machine" of colonial modernity is naturalized in the form of the train, which is itself frequently referred to as the "smoke of the savanna" (Sembene, 1970: 132; see also Aguiar, 2003). The breakdown of pre-colonial understandings of nature–society relations—although these are not really idealized or romanticized in the novel—is a crucial part of the struggle, both against colonialism and against its ecological consequences. A Bamako elder, Fa Keita, voices this sentiment at several junctures (Sembene, 1970: 157):

> A long time ago. Before any of you were born, everything that happened happened within a framework, an order that was our own, and the existence of that order was of great importance in our lives. Today, no such framework exists. There are no castes among people, no difference in

the quality of grain or of the bread that is made from the grain; there are no weavers, no artisans in metal, no makers of fine shoes.

This break is symbolized in the novel in the courtyard where Fa Keita lives with his wife, Niakoro: the "old mortar in Niakoro's courtyard had been a tree; its roots were still sunk deep in the earth," (Sembene, 1970:162) but the mortar is cracking now from the drought.

Although the urban political ecologies of Bamako and Dakar play roles in the novel, the central urbanism of the book is actually Thiés. Thiés is regularly described as "the city," despite being the smallest of the three even at the time in which the novel is set (it had an estimated 24,000 people as of 1945; see Boahen, 1970: 26). The first Thiés chapter is even entitled just "Thiés: the city." Its very beginning makes plain the uses of waste in Sembene's (1970: 49) ecocritical vision:

> Hovels. A few rickety shacks, some upturned tombs, walls of bamboo or millet stalks, iron barbs, and rotting fences. Thiés: a vast, uncertain plain where all the rot of the city has gathered—stakes and crossties, locomotive wheels, rusty shafts, knocked-in jerry cans, old mattress springs, bruised and lacerated sheets of steel. And then, a little farther on, on the goat path that leads to the Bambara quarter, piles of old tin cans, heaps of excrement, little mountains of broken pottery and cooking tools, dismantled railway cars, skeletons of motors buried in the dust, and the tiny remains of cats, of rats, of chickens, disputed by the birds.... Thiés: a place where everyone—man, woman, and child—had a face the color of the earth.

As Adu Boahen (1970: 26) put it in his introduction to the English edition of the novel, in French West Africa, "the towns were often also divided into European and African areas in which the opulence and neatness of the former stood in sharp contrast to the poverty and squalor of the latter." Sembene plays this up in Thiés, with the white enclave of "The Vatican" contrasted with the hovels of its "native quarters." Sembene (1970 249) describes the Vatican as having:

> well-kept lawns, graveled walks and ... houses painted in clear, light colors. In the gardens at the rear, rose bushes and borders of daisies and snapdragons made vivid areas of color, shaded from the tropical sun by giant bougainvilleas.... Life

was easy in "the Vatican" [by contrast with the African areas].

The "old hand" French officials become defensive in explaining this to a newly arrived colonial officer, arguing that:

It's their own fault if they [Africans] live in places like that…. Twenty years ago there was nothing here but an arid wilderness. We built this city. Now they have hospitals, schools, and trains, but if we ever leave they're finished—the brush will take it all back. There wouldn't be anything left. (Sembene, 1970: 251)

Bamako (with an estimated population at the time of the strike of around 37,000; see Boahen, 1970: 26) is not spared the dichotomies: its railroad station is described as a rubbish pit or a cesspool:

The walls and floors were covered with dripping, spreading stains of spit, dyed red from the chewing of cola nuts, or black from plugs of tobacco. Clouds of flies swarmed over gourds which still held some remnant of food…. The station looked like the camp of a conquered army, carrying with it its plunder, its wounded, its dead, and its limitless vermin. (Sembene, 1970: 140–1)

However, Dakar's contrasts are arguably the most extreme in the novel, in what was actually far more of a city at the time of the rail strike: after being named the capital for all of French West Africa and the terminus of the railway, Dakar shot up from a population of less than 20,000 in 1916 to over 132,000 by 1945 (Boahen, 1970: 26). In the novel, the Dakar neighborhood at the center of the action has an African-area shop that is defined by "the dirt that pervaded everything in it" (Sembene, 1970: 85). The French and the elites in Dakar, such as the sell-out Imam and the "chief of the district," El Hadji Mabigue, are clean, brightly colored, surrounded by luxury (Sembene, 1970: 196). When he is first introduced, El Hadji Mabigue is wearing "soft Turkish slippers [that] were yellow, and he was protected from the sun by an umbrella of iridescent pink" (Sembene, 1970: 88–9).

In all three cities, besides waste, the other key ecological discourse concerns water, or its lack. In Dakar's African areas, there is no water from the pipes—the French have shut it off as an anti-strike tactic. As with the splintered urbanism of waste, the continuous contrasts of well-watered European quarters and arid, sandy, and thirsty African areas are not at all natural factors for Sembene, but deliberate, political ones. As one of the Dakar women characters puts it: "real misfortune is not just a matter of being hungry and thirsty; it is a matter of knowing that there are people who want you to be hungry and thirsty" (Sembene, 1970: 101). Another woman in Dakar, waiting in a long line at a barren public standpipe, says, "the *toubabs* [white people] are trying to kill us, little by little. There isn't a drop of water from here to Pikine," and Sembene (1970: 117) writes that the women recognized that the "white men could shut off [the water] whenever they wished. The whole system belonged to them, from the water-purification plant through the labyrinth of pipes to the faucet on the fountain itself." At a later point, this injustice narrative returns as yet one more Dakar woman says to the French police officer, "I am sure it is not written in the mother of all books of the law that honest people should be deprived of water and starved and killed" (Sembene, 1970: 181).

Unlike the bleak, despairing, or allegorical deployment of waste, floods, or drought in the other novels I have discussed, in *God's bits of wood*, the Senegalese and Malian characters actively use the waste and the environment at their disposal as parts of their weaponry and strategy in the strike and in the cause of socio-environmental justice. The women in the Dakar segment defend their neighborhood with weapons made from bottles filled with sand (Sembene, 1970: 177), and they burn rubbish to scare the police's horse brigade (Sembene, 1970: 123). In that latter battle, the women drag a platoon leader off his horse "to a little ditch where people of the neighborhood relieved themselves at night and thrust his head in the accumulated filth" (Sembene, 1970: 183). Most profoundly and symbolically, the strike leader's young daughter, Adjibidji, finally solves her grandmother's riddle to her (Sembene, 1970: 166) about what it is that "washes the water," since water washes everything else, by seeing that it is the human spirit that washes the water and purifies it.

However, ultimately, there are no clear winners in the socio-natural struggles of these three cities. At one point, rats devour the watchman in the Thiés train yards, and it seems at first a fitting consequence of his having crossed the picket line. Yet, a bit later, two of the young apprentices in Thiés, heroes of the strikers for their bird-hunting prowess during the drought/strike, are shot and killed by one of the French railroad officials for allegedly stealing chickens from "The Vatican" (Sembene, 1970: 248). Near the novel's conclusion, the women who are supporting the strikers' demands in a brutal march from Thiés to Dakar are attacked by a mysterious whirlwind. Perhaps most tragically, in attempting to defend against the horse platoon in Dakar, when the women fight back with the rubbish fire, their fire inadvertently burns almost the whole neighborhood, with its houses made from "sheets of tarpaper"—and the fact that the French had shut the water off means that it is impossible to fight the fire. As one of the young women surveys the scene the next day, Sembene (1970: 185) tells us that "she was walking in a black dust littered with charred and shapeless refuse." She has a vision then of what the neighborhood could be: "houses painted in clear, fresh colors, of gardens filled with flowers, and children in European clothes playing in tidy courtyards" (Sembene, 1970: 186).

A public health officer chatting with the police after the fire wonders: "Why doesn't the public health service move them all out of the city and settle them in the outskirts, the way they do in South Africa and the Belgian Congo?" (Sembene, 1970: 187). In fact, the French did attempt to do almost exactly this in the creation of Pikine in 1952—which Sembene, of course, knew as he wrote that line in 1960. Furthermore, contemporary Pikine, which is home to the "Trash Mountain" of Mbeubeuss, is both symbolically and physically a city of waste. As with the strikers in God's bits of wood, though, the Pikinois of today's Dakar use waste as a literal and figurative weapon of self-reliance and liberation, as I discuss later.

These four very different novels took on political-environmental stories in different cities at very different times. There is no uniform ecocritical or political-ecological reading of them. Rather, I have read their uses of urban waste imagery contrapuntally to suggest the dialogues between them in ecocritical terms. Instead of immobilizing conceptual development by producing a cacophony of perspectives, I argue that such a reading enriches the effort to find and build common ground between an interactionist UPE and postcolonial ecocritical work on the continent. The effort to see how literary voices can contribute to a broadened UPE and ecocritical approaches that "resist closure in the imagining of effective ways to move toward a more equitable, sustainable future" (Caminero-Santangelo, 2014: 35) in African urban studies can be strengthened immeasurably by widening the range of novels and writers examined. However, it also depends on connecting literary and artistic visions of urban environments to tangible, complex, contemporary realities, as I seek to do for Dakar in the chapter's final segment.

Dakar

Dakar, one of the three urban settings of *God's bits of wood*, is far and away the largest city in Senegal, with an estimated population of 2.9 million in 2010 that the UN expects to reach 4.2 million by 2020. It is a city of glaring contrasts, even at the physical level (see Figure 4.1). Its downtown area, Le Plateau, "compares easily with any European city" in terms of its built environment, form, and level of environmental services (Myers et al, 2012: 362). This core of the city began from French occupation of the Cap Vert peninsula in 1857 and the first French planned layout of 1862 (Bigon, 2009, 2014). As one moves up that narrow peninsula from the Plateau and "Dakar-ville" of that 1862 plan, it widens through the area known as the Medina, a high-density working-class area planned and laid out in 1914 for Africans (mainly the Lebou culture group) that the French displaced from the Plateau and Dakar-ville areas, and into Grand Dakar. At lower elevations farther away from the Plateau lie the *bidonvilles* (informal settlements—but, literally, "tin-can cities") like Grand Yoff (which is no longer really a "*bidonville*") and the historic Lebou settlement at Ouakem, the only one of the original 11 Lebou villages to fully escape demolition.

The most recent master plan for Dakar seeks to more successfully link up these areas just beyond the downtown and Grand Dakar, what the plan calls the Derkle–Kharyalla–Liberté (DKL) Triangle, into a new growth pole for the city (Gridoux, 2012). Indeed, many of the outer areas of Dakar itself, like Yoff, Ngor, Sicap, or Liberté VI, have been sites for gentrification, or a close relative to it, as Senegalese traders in the diaspora build an ever-increasing set of "nearly always unfinished and ... often uninhabited" structures that Caroline Melly (2010: 38) calls "not-yet houses." The speculation boom set in motion by the construction, even as the houses remain largely unoccupied, has increased housing prices in Dakar dramatically, pushing marginalized people farther out of the city.

Farther out, they come to Pikine. Although a number of settlements and about 8,000 residents were present in its contemporary boundaries, Pikine's planned urban existence formally began in 1952. Marc Verniere (1973: 107) characterized Pikine as a case of "pseudo-urbanization" that had "sprung from nothing" because of the degree to which, even early on, its informal settlements outnumbered its planned areas. By 1973, the population exceeded 140,000, and by the 2002 census, Pikine's three *arrondissements* (Dagoudane, Niayes, and Thiaroye) had a combined population of nearly 800,000 people. During 2012–13 fieldwork, most officials and experts estimated the population to be

The artists

Figure 4.1: Map of Dakar

131

more than 1 million in this alleged "pseudo-"city, the overwhelming majority residing outside of formally planned parts of Pikine. Each of Pikine's four largest *communes d'arrondissement* (Djidah Thiaroye Kao, Yeumbeul Nord, Yeumbeul Sud, and Diamaguene Sicap Mbao) had more than 100,000 people, and all but the latter were entirely unplanned settlements. In fact, though, Pikine grew so rapidly because of the combined drivers of Senegalese expelled from replanned areas of Dakar in the segregationist colonial post-war master plan and then droughts and rural poverty after independence (Salem, 1992). Its continuing growth stems in good measure from the speculative boom in real estate in Dakar. The largest and most informal of the *communes d'arrondissement*, especially Djidah Thiaroye Kao, were in low-lying land highly vulnerable to severe seasonal flooding; as these settlements grew, more and more people built in obvious flood zones.

Unlike most cities in Africa, though, Dakar—and even Pikine—is a city that has been managed within an ostensibly democratic political framework from independence onward; while, to some extent, Dakar's local government has been overshadowed by the capital city functions, Dakar has had much more engaged and involved popular local democratic politics than many African cities (Diop, 2012). Moreover, urban management has been central to the furtherance and deepening of democracy, with a specific high point in solid waste management. Activists and artists (writers, musicians, hip-hop artists, sculptors, muralists, DJs, and more) have had especially important roles in Dakar's democratization and its environmental management (Fredericks, 2009, 2014). This has also been the case in Pikine, along with other *banlieue* settlements.

Several of Pikine's communities grew around extant Lebou villages, such as Thiaroye Gare and Yeumbeul, and most area place-names are the Lebou names of former agricultural fields. Even after a 1998 reorganization of local government, these settlements retain some semblance of traditional Lebou leadership. However, most segments of today's Pikine long outgrew the confines of, or just simply overran, Lebou settlement structures and political-environmental management (Chef du Village of Thiaroye Gare, 2013). Despite the lively democratic politics of Pikine and Dakar, many people remain disenfranchised or marginalized, particularly those living on the ecological edges. Electoral democracy and peace have not meant that Pikine has anywhere near remotely adequate urban environmental services, for water, sanitation, and solid waste, in particular. Pikine's municipal government had a budget of 6 billion *Communauté Financière d'Afrique* (CFA) franc, or about US$10 per person, in 2012, and even in the realm of security,

Pikine had one police officer for every 10,000 residents—waste and sanitation services were even further down on the list of municipal priorities, comprising less than 2% of the Pikine city budget (Diouck, 2013). Most residential solid waste is uncollected, and it piles up in empty or abandoned plots. Those who live near the sea or any of the wetland areas or flood ponds of Pikine dump their wastes in the water (see Figure 4.2). Waste and sanitation issues are especially severe in Kiayes (Keur Massar, where the Mbeubuess Trash Mountain is located), but they are rampant throughout Pikine (Cissé, 2012; Diop, 2013).

In the absence of effective environmental services from the state or the private sector, many Pikinois have to make their own plans. Within some of the *communes d'arrondissements*, there is a fairly limited degree of grassroots organizing, or the community groups that do exist have extremely limited authority. With so many residents coming from diverse rural areas mixing with urbanites displaced from Dakar, community organizing has been fraught with potential conflicts or leadership vacuums (Diallo, 2012). Chefs du quartier, for example, have no legal authority to allocate land, but "we find they do it anyway" in most of Pikine, including land allocation in hazardous floodplains (Diallo, 2012). A recent survey in conjunction with home demolitions for highway construction through Pikine found that fewer than 10 of the 125 houses slated for demolition had legal papers or titles for land, houses, or properties (Niang, A., 2013). Donor-funded efforts to regularize land control have barely made a dent (Director, Centre Polyvalent de Thiaroye Gare, 2013). Only six of the 66 neighborhoods in Djidah Thiaroye Kao, for example, belong to "regularized" Pikine—the other 60 are "irregular" settlements (Diouck, 2013).

Artists in urban environmental activism

One of the strongest community institutions that is both invested in the improvement of the urban environment in Pikine and engaged in political-ecological activism is the artists' cooperative known as Africulturban. Based in the Leopold Senghor Center in Pikine West, Africulturban is a cultural center for artists, dancers, musicians, rappers, and other performers. It houses a radio station for the Pikine area, handcrafts center, recording studio, dance studio, art studio, stages, and arts classrooms (Sall, 2013). There is other artist-related activism in affiliation with Thiaroye's Jacque Chirac Centre, for example, but Africulturban has been especially inspirational and influential with Pikine's youth (Diop, 2013). Its founder, and one of its core personalities, the rapper Matador, has gained a significant following in

Pikine and, along with this, political influence in Dakar and in Senegal as a whole, alongside a number of younger rappers (Diouck, 2013). The mayor of Djidah Thiaroye Kao, Alioune Diouck, explained that:

Figure 4.2: Chronic flood, waste, and sanitation issues co-mingle in Pikine

"Pikine has a spirit of revolt. A lot of rap groups give voice to this lack of representation. Hip-hop groups are dynamic organizations that participate in society. They are a good thing…. Government actors have some distance from the reality of people's lives. The hip-hop artists can articulate the underground philosophy of the lower class, like in America, they denounce the lack of schools, health care, and so on." (Diouck, 2013)

Rappers were central to the 2012 election results in Senegal in mobilizing opposition to the incumbent President Abdoulaye Wade's failed attempt to gain a third term as Senegal's president (Fredericks, 2014). Of particular significance was the collective *Y'en a Marre* (*Enough is Enough*, or *We Are Sick of It*), led by a half-dozen or so rappers and one journalist, Fadel Barro, emanating out of the neighborhood of Parcelles Assainies, bordering Pikine (Fredericks, 2014; Mbaye, 2014). However, *Y'en a Marre* and the activism of rappers was always about much more than electoral politics. Fredericks (2014: 132) shows that rappers and young musicians in Pikine, Dakar, and elsewhere created "a locus of political identity formation for youth through offering a language of geographical critique and a spatial practice of alternative placemaking." While hip hop's earliest stars in Senegal were from Dakar, by the 2010s, the dominant voices in the genre belonged to the city's edge, especially Pikine (Fredericks, 2014). Their call to action was wrapped around the lack of urban environmental service provision in their neighborhoods. Hip-hop performance signals a form of "ownership over the neighborhood, a claim to the rights and rewards of the city through occupying its physical space and the space of public dialogue" (Fredericks, 2014: 139).

Hip hop is also, of course, a highly diverse and multi-vocal genre of art, within Dakar/Pikine alone (Mbaye, 2014). However, within what Jenny Mbaye (2014: 399) terms Dakar's "hip hop music with a message," Matador has one of the more prominent voices. Matador hails from Pikine's major informal neighborhood of Thiaroye and was co-founder of the rap group Wa BMG 44. In "Hip hop attitude," Matador raps that "hip hop is a way of living … [that] ain't made for empty minds," and he ends the song arguing that rappers like him are "serving others before oneself/ eradicating stress, uplifting the morale of population, in times we so need it" (Matador, trans Jenny Mbaye, cited in Mbaye, 2014: 400). Along with rappers like Thiat, Foumelade, or Positive Black Soul's Didier Awadi, Matador has fused his music with his politics, but also his geography. In our interview with him,

Matador (2013) said: "if you think people from the US or Europe are going to get you a job or the government is going to provide for you, think again, you have to struggle, build things for yourself." Matador stretched this further in an earlier interview with Mbaye (2014: 402), saying that his group wanted to use hip hop to help young people to be "aware of their surroundings," to "make the youth understand that they should not wait for the state and should act to maintain their own environment."

Matador stressed to Mbaye (2014: 404) that he saw rappers as not just truth-tellers, "but ... also workers and developers." Part of the "developer" side comes with Africulturban, which Fredericks calls "a pioneer in community building" from its founding in Pikine in 2006 (see Figure 4.3). The rapper Foumelade similarly co-founded a community arts center, GHip Hop, in his *banlieue*, Guediawaye, in 2013 (Fredericks, 2014: 139). The rappers in the leadership of the *Y'en a Marre* movement are likewise deeply invested in what Fredericks (2014: 141) calls the "intimate geographies of place-making (not just representing)" in Parcelles.

The *esprits* (spirits) of *Y'en a Marre*, their informal local branches, became enormously influential in electoral politics in 2011–12, but the elections were only a part of their pull. People in the *banlieues* used the *Y'en a Marre* forums to discuss, prominently, "garbage and sanitation" (Fredericks, 2014: 143). One of the movement's most famous (and violent) demonstrations happened in the edge "neighborhood of Cambérène, over the government's inaction in repairing a broken sewer main which flooded the neighborhood" (Fredericks, 2014: 143). Well after the elections of 2012 were done, *Y'en a Marre* "brigades" were engaged to "clean up the city" of waste and refuse.

Some of the environmental activism of hip-hop artists has been related directly to floods. This is especially so for rappers from low-lying Pikine areas. More than 50 years ago, Pikine, and especially the area today known as Djidah Thiaroye Kao, actually supplied drinking water to Dakar, but the groundwater today has become too contaminated. The water table is itself so high in Djidah Thiaroye Kao that one barely has to scratch the surface to get to water, but it is unfit for human consumption. Ironically, Pikine is subjected to what has become an annual cycle of flooding. In 2009, more than 300,000 residents were temporarily displaced. In some parts of Djidah Thiaroye Kao in 2012, more than 8,000 residents were forced to reside in their waterlogged homes because they perceived that they had nowhere to go—in one case, 30 residents of one structure remained in a home that had a half-meter of standing water on its ground floor for more than a month.

Figure 4.3: Graffiti art produced by artists affiliated with Africulturban, Pikine

More than 800 flood-damaged homes stood abandoned in Djidah Thiaroye Kao in January 2013. Hip-hop artists/activists with a major following in Senegal's global diaspora were critical to flood relief in leveraging funds and mobilizing the people in the diaspora (Fall, 2013; Matador, 2013; Sall, 2013).

Conclusion

Hip-hop artists are only one part, albeit a prominent part, of the panoply of artistic voices in Dakar. Graffiti artists, sculptors, visual artists, photographers, playwrights, and many more, such as those who came together in 2012–13's Ouakem arts festival, like the hip-hop artists that I have discussed, have hearkened back to the revolutionary strikers' voices of *God's bits of wood* in their deployments of waste, whether physically or metaphorically, in artistic expressions of empowerment. Furthermore, Dakar is hardly alone in Africa in its incredibly vibrant (visual, performing, and literary) arts scene (Pinther et al, 2012). Nairobi, for instance, has seen the growth of numerous artists' collectives in the last decade or so. The photographer Boniface Mwangi founded the creative space known as PAWA 254 and produced the popular *Picha Mtaani* (Photographs in the Neighborhood) roving exhibition across urban Kenya. In May 2013, he came to much greater prominence as the ringleader of a protest/performance art piece at the Kenya Parliament, entitled M-Pigs, "in which a herd of pigs was unleashed at the Parliament Buildings to highlight the hefty pay rises being demanded by elected officials" (Akugizibwe, 2013: 24). In a provocative interview with Paula Akugizibwe (2013: 24) of the activist magazine *Chronic*, Mwangi claimed that "you have to be spectacular to be noticed"; he wanted to provoke "a revolution of thought" or a "peaceful ballot revolution."

The M-Pigs performance also produced a backlash, including sharp criticism of the unethical treatment of animals and the offence to "religious and cultural sensitivities" incurred with the use of pigs in a city with a sizeable and growing Muslim minority (Mwikya, 2013: 25). Mwangi might be an "acclaimed photographer," the critic Kenne Mwikya (2013: 25) offered, but now that he had "morphed into an activist" producing "in-your-face spectacle," the attention "was on the spectacle" rather than on the root causes of Nairobi's and Kenya's socio-political and environmental crises—which lay in the capitalist economic system, by Mwikya's view. Such criticism, though, misses the ways in which artists and activists have been inseparable throughout Africa's contemporary urban history, and the crucial role of spectacular art/activism in provoking revolutionary thought. Over and over again, around the cities of the continent, activist artists and writers are challenging the received wisdom about urban environments in Africa, as they have been for at least a century.

In this chapter, I have used literature, and other creative arts, to illustrate how the voices and works of artists can (and do) contribute to UPE. My book's theoretical framework bends a bit in the chapter, in that I develop my interpretation in engagement with the literary theory from postcolonial ecocriticism. Despite the fancy terminology often associated with it, in actual fact, this literary theory works well as a part of an interactionist UPE. The chapter needs to be seen in a proverbial toe-in-the-ocean light: my intention is to show that writers and artists are crucial to embroidering the environmental consciousness of urban scientists, scholars, and policymakers, as well as grassroots activists, with complex, imaginative visions of urban environments— both in terms of problems that inhere to them and potential solutions.

At the same time, with Caminero-Santangelo, I am wary of reading artists' and writers' works in a unidirectional way, or as a part of some coherent uniform urban environmental movement; likewise, one must be cautious of a forced marriage of ecocriticism and political ecology— the approaches can have much to share, but they are not one and the same. For this reason, I developed what Caminero-Santangelo terms a contrapuntal reading of four novels, while targeting how each of the novels deals with or deploys urban waste imagery, in settings from Ghana to Nigeria to Somalia to Senegal; however, I also developed a segment of the chapter on actually existing artistic environmentalism in Dakar and its edge city of Pikine as a means of suggesting the threads that often link artistic imaginations with the tangible real (political-environmental) world. The next chapter begins where this one ends since there is much that links artist–activists on urban environmental issues with other urban environmental activists at the grassroots.

FIVE

The grassroots

Introduction

The farthest rural edge of Pikine, just outside Dakar, is home to Senegal's largest solid waste dump, Mbeubeuss, a steaming mountain chain of waste. In Pikine, now a city of over 1 million, residents confront a staggering array of environmental problems on a daily basis, to say nothing of poverty, extreme overcrowding, crime, violence, or social unrest. The urban heart of Pikine experiences chronic, severe seasonal flooding, which leads to lakes of standing water that, in turn, generate a cascade of human and environmental health calamities. One encounters few waste or sanitation services in Pikine; much confronting of environmental crises happens not from government action, but from local initiative. Yet, even this can prove elusive. As Abdurahmane Diallo (2012) has said: "normally initiatives would come from the people, from the ground up, but not necessarily in Pikine."

At the same time, it is unfathomable to have political-environmental action in Pikine that creates meaningful change *without* networks that arise from this "not necessarily" circumstance. In Diallo's (2012) words, in Pikine, "you have to be connected. You have to have relations. Your capital should be in people, not money. If you don't have people, you have nothing. This is where the solidarity works." By contrast, as Alasse Elhadji Diop (Diop, A.E., 2013) of Djidah Thiaroye Kao neighborhood in Pikine put it: "the government basically doesn't give a damn about what happens here." Where the government "doesn't give a damn," people at the grassroots often seek to do so, and we see this on the Trash Mountain. Mbeubeuss has a very entrepreneurial union of informal waste-pickers, Pikine as a whole has an association of informal sector workers and a strong contingent of the *Y'en a marre* movement discussed in Chapter Four, who collaborate in the expression not only of just how "sick of it" Pikinois are, but of how to work together to change it. Yet, they do not necessarily succeed, either in working together or in the changing of their environments.

In Mbeubeuss, the president of the scavengers union (who made the pun about waste as solid gold that I noted at the very beginning of this book) said that this "gold" is the reason why the government wanted to close the Trash Mountain—to control its solid gold instead of leaving it for people like him to survive from. These sorts of sentiments lead to the extraordinary efforts of Pikinois to self-organize, particularly to confront flooding crises, as we saw at the end of Chapter Four. The very formation of organizations is a challenge, though, particularly for women's groups: as Ndeye Niang (2013) said in a January 2013 focus group: "women have a real problem to express themselves in society. Our husbands don't want us to join women's groups because they fear being replaced and losing power over us," but, she said, "some members [of her women's group] lost their sons in that [flood] water," and that spurred them to at least attempt to organize for action.

In this chapter, my goal is to work through the multi-vocality at the grassroots of Africa's urban environments, in places much like Pikine across the continent. There is no doubt in my mind that the grassroots are crucial for addressing urban environmental issues, and the voices of people at the grassroots and the margins are often justifiably pushed to the center in political-ecological analysis. The experts show that there are myriad complex environmental problems in Africa's cities. I have argued: for seeing the beginnings of at least some of these problems in the past; for understanding the cityscape both physically and spiritually as a part of the political-environmental dynamics; and for seeing the problems from ecocritical perspectives, or the literary and artistic imaginations of residents. Now, it is time to turn to what to do, or what is being done, at the grassroots across many cities. The next section surveys some of this terrain, beginning with the intellectual terrain of urban political ecology (UPE), followed by a set of urban contexts on the continent, before moving to an in-depth focus on Cape Town.

The grassroots and the politics of Africa's urban environment

This is an era of what the urbanist Edgar Pieterşe (2013: 12) calls "rogue urbanism" in Africa, an era where "dynamics ... are so unruly, unpredictable, surprising, confounding and yet, pregnant with possibility." The power, creativity, dynamism, and capacity to shape the cityscape at the grassroots are extraordinary in cities of Africa, but so is the possibility for going "rogue" in a negative sense, whether led by rogue states, rogue elites, rogue outsiders, or rogue groups at the grassroots, the uncivil society that runs parallel to the civil society. The implications of this "rogue sensibility" (Pieterse, 2013: 12) for the urban environment are precarious and uncertain. The continent shows us everything from inspiring examples of grassroots organizing that leads to environmentally sustainable development, to violence-ridden paralyzed communities sinking further and further into the mire from incapacitated or fractious grassroots, with multiple stops in between.

Political ecology in Africa has often attended to the margins. Marginalized people and environments are frequently at the center of the analysis, often championed as the wellspring of liberation. Dan Brockington (2002) in *Fortress conservation*, Rod Neumann (1998) in *Imposing wilderness*, and, to some extent, Gudrun Dahl (1979) in *Suffering grass* explicitly or implicitly take the side of the marginalized rural poor in their core arguments, for example. In *urban* political ecology from outside of Africa, the marginalized are there, but often more obtusely. Swyngedouw (1996: 67) saw UPE as a way to tell "the story" of a city's "people, and the socio-ecological processes that produce the urban and its spaces of privilege and exclusion." He says forthrightly that "emancipatory democratic politics" are his principal interest within UPE (Swyngedouw, 2011a). Furthermore, many other UPE scholars, aligned with the political Left, clearly seek ways to combat injustice, promote inclusion, and expand emancipatory politics for the grassroots—surely laudable goals, which I share—yet frequently without entering into the quagmires of actual everyday policy and political realities in cities.

Within Africa, most of the work that calls itself UPE is done in South Africa, and it sometimes bears the influence of UPE work produced in other, mostly Global North, settings, with the theoretical and empirical preoccupations of that work. Alex Loftus (2012: 42) examines how "representations of the urbanization of nature as a sensuous process might lead to the kind of politicized response and the affirmative politics" he claims to see in Amoati in the Inanda area of the eThekwini (Durban) metropolitan area, a "politics born out of desperation and anger." In his Inanda case, he eloquently argues that:

> nature is gradually urbanized and, in the process, residents' relationships to water, the metropole, and the central state have been reconfigured. The environment of the colonial state gave way to a landscape scarred by deepening forms of segregation and racism. This racism was expressed and lived in the very act of collecting water from a standpipe, in the act of drilling a borehole, and in the act of challenging a councilor to provide an improved supply.... Citizens have become consumers through interactions with the flows of urbanized nature in the community: at the same time,

consent to the post-apartheid project has, in part, been secured. (Loftus, 2012: 105)

Loftus (2012: 107) wants to use the ideas of Marxist philosopher Antonio Gramsci to articulate "how a latent volcanic anger might be turned into a coherent and slow-burning rage capable of achieving a lasting transformation of the real world." The problem here is that in South Africa's cities after apartheid, such as in Cape Town, as discussed later in the chapter, the volcanic anger at the grassroots in the post-apartheid era has seldom been "capable of achieving a lasting transformation." Furthermore, the post-apartheid project that Loftus sees as having been "secured" is highly uncertain in that real world, whether considered in terms of the neoliberal ecological modernization part of the "project" that critics such as Bond (2000) or Debbané and Keil (2004) see, or in terms of the populist and progressive delivery of urban services to the poor.

Lawhon et al (2014, 2015) have argued for "provincializing" and "situating" UPE in dialogue with African urban studies because of the difficulties of fitting Western theoretical and empirical fixations on to the cities of Africa. The questions surrounding how we might best approach the grassroots—local, marginalized, poor urban communities—of Africa's cities loom large in this provincializing and situating. UPE's deployment of Marxist theories of power, analysis of networked infrastructure, and critique of capitalism do not mesh comfortably with African urban realities. All three foci imply the shaping of unjust cities that marginalize the poor and working class in particular ways. Less attention goes to the struggle "to identify strategies to improve a more equal distribution of power" in specific policy terms (Bjerkli, 2015: 19). Bjerkli (2015: 20) argues that in African urban contexts like Addis Ababa, where she works, UPE means "exploring everyday practices and processes in which power in its various forms is exercised and negotiated at various scales." However, as Lawhon et al (2014: 502) contend, most UPE has "failed so far to provide critiques which do more than point to the need for change—instead, studies often conclude with non-systemic suggestions for change."

How do we get there, to critical analyses of environmental politics that do more than nod at the need to overthrow capitalism? Lawhon et al (2014, 2015) suggest ways of building from the study of African urbanism to produce situated UPE that can potentially analyze change factors more rigorously, and with an eye toward policy as well as politics. Lawhon (2013: 133), for example, critiques the potential utility of the "reframing of livelihoods struggles into environmental struggles" in studies of South African urban environments, arguing that "this reframing actually limits the potential for grassroots mobilization around such issues," for instance, in the ineffectiveness of South Africa's "environmental justice movement in working with the labor movement." Her argument is that trying to force a conceptualization of the problems that originates from outside of the context ignores the obvious gaps in or misappropriations of the outside concepts. Instead, she argues for thinking from South African urban experience, theorizing the grounds for struggles *from* the particular, situated, and networked environmental movements and senses of place.

Lawhon et al (2014: 506) extend this argument, contending that a situated UPE would still focus on power relationships, but as situated in everyday practices and experiences, as a part of a critique of "city-making," and as part of what they term, borrowing from Pieterse (2008: 6), "radical incrementalism toward recursive empowerment and systemic change." Where most UPE works derived from structural Marxist theorizations of power "leave progressive scholars either depressed at the lack of revolutionary options, or supporting minor changes to the system," they argue that a framework that starts from the "everyday practices" and seeks "radical incrementalism … gives us more hope" (Lawhon et al, 2014: 510). Their vision of radical incrementalism as "a situated, unfolding process which differs over time and across space" (Lawhon et al, 2014: 511) is intriguing and inspiring. Pieterse (2008: 6) defined radical incrementalism as "a disposition and sensibility that believes in deliberate actions of social transformation but through a multiplicity of processes and imaginations," because "we cannot wish into existence an overnight revolution that will make everything all right in the world." I think these authors are on to an extremely important idea, but it also has limitations, some of which Lawhon et al (2014) discuss (eg how exactly those "everyday modalities" *work* "through which ordinary people link together to provide for their urban lives and livelihoods"). Most significantly, it is still crucial to resist the simple, monochromatic lens on the poor and marginalized: the first things we see when we study the everyday modalities at the grassroots in urban African may, indeed, be their dysfunctional character, their fractures, the vast gulf between them, and strategies for radical incrementalism that would result in greater equity, broader socio-economic justice, or deeper democracy. As Pieterse (2008: 173) put it: "radical incrementalism has little prospect if civil society organizations that represent and champion the poor are weak, unorganized and ineffectual." In those all-too-common circumstances, alongside the "quiet encroachment of the ordinary" (Bayat, 2000: 533), we may often find the loud encroachment of discord and debilitating conflict, like the *fitina* discussed in Chapter Three in Zanzibar.

Moreover, grassroots organizations that explicitly focus on the environment are still rare in most African cities: urban grassroots groups are usually focused on other things, like cultural identities or performance, religious communities, political parties, or service provision (though this is often environmental in its thematic elements, even if indirectly). The grassroots can also burn; grassroots groups can be a part of environmentally destructive actions and politically destabilizing agendas—sometimes unwittingly, like the women who burned their own neighborhood down in *God's bits of wood* discussed in Chapter Four, but sometimes willfully, like some Islamist militant groups in Kenya, Somalia, Libya, Mali, Sudan, or Nigeria. It is not the case that the grassroots are always the solution to harmful socio-environments in cities—grassroots groups of all types can work toward development goals that are problematic environmentally. It is highly place- and context-specific, along a wide continuum. The next subsections of the chapter highlight several continental examples across this continuum. Let us begin by returning to Pikine.

The grassroots and the environment in Pikine

Pikine offers a setting where many contradictory factors play out at the grassroots level. Some of the positive aspects of rogue sensibility were quite evident in 2013 in Mbeubeuss, on the Trash Mountain. More than 2,000 scavengers worked as a part of a lively informal union, separating out plastics, bottles, paper, used clothing, tires, and other things for use and reuse. The president of the union told us proudly that everything he was wearing, including his watch, came from the mountain. There were people mining soil from it by a sifting method, other people farming the wetland at its base, and still others building into that wetland. Many of the residents are Senegalese from all over the country, but some Malians and other foreigners are there as well. It is clearly a site of some tensions, but one that also offers inspirational examples of how grassroots organizing might help to improve the quality of life of the marginalized poor and improve the environment at the same time.

South and east from Mbeubeuss, in Thiaroye, there is more that is seething and steaming at the grassroots than the mountains of garbage. The deputy mayor went so far as to claim that:

"the solidarity that is so important to African society is no more [in Thiaroye]. It is now to each his own and God for all…. People are afraid of Thiaroye. If you say you are from here, people are afraid." (Fall, 2013)

One of the leaders of a cooperative of traders in Thiaroye's massive, unruly market said: "every God-given day I hear about somebody getting killed or robbed here, and I never heard of that in the rural areas." The irony for him was that "flooding makes people unite, people really unite as a community. As we are poor, we are obliged to help one another." As to the mayor and the government, "they always promise but they do nothing. There is help but it only goes to those close to the mayor" (Louw, 2013).

The charismatic mayor of nearby Djidah Thiaroye Kao became defensive when told of comments like these from grassroots organizers. In the floods, he said:

"We found more than 8,000 homes abandoned. People get angry. People say the government is not acceptable; they come here to this office and shout it. It is normal; people say negative things about me. I try to communicate with people. I get on the radio and say, 'You need to calm down'…. In 2009, I had the same problem as New Orleans [after Hurricane Katrina]: I'd just been elected and two months later, floods, and more than 800 people flood the mayor's office. The people were shouting. They want me to go to the police, but I said, 'No, the government cannot help us; we need to struggle on our own.' But many of these problems in … *bidonvilles* around the world, where people do whatever they want, well, these problems are the result…. I am very firm in my management of the city. I am the father of the community; then there is the Chef du Quartier, and the other community groups." (Diouck, 2013)

The leaders of these community groups—even those who voted for this mayor—do not see the chain of command or the firmness of order this way. They usually recognize the power of the state, but see things flowing in quite the opposite directions: the grassroots in effect run Pikine, because no one else will, in their eyes. Djibril Djiallo (2013) was the president of a cooperative of dozens of community development groups at the grassroots, *Centre pour des Associations du Developpement et Democratie* (CADD). CADD started over 20 years ago as a response to floods in the 1990s; four different organizations that did not even know each other met through a donor, who convinced them that they should work together, so they united into CADD in 1999–2000. By 2013, CADD-affiliated groups were involved in politics, training, education, and especially women's micro-finance organizations.

At first, people did not trust that the organization would last. Women's organizations became very important to CADD's survival. Djiallo brought the leaders of 20 women's groups, including those with an environmental emphasis, together to discuss issues with us, prefacing the focus group discussion by saying: "if you say you can develop Djidah Thiaroye Kao without women, that is impossible. Women are more reliable with money, with fighting poverty, helping families, and meeting all of the family needs."

Miriam Mbaye, head of the association of women in Djidah Thiaroye Kao and a vice-mayor, interrupted Djiallo, I think because she was sensing that he and the other male head of CADD were attempting to control the focus group:

> "Women are very tired. Very tired of how we are living. If men are tired, then by comparison women are dead! The mayor said to form an organization, so we did. We engage in micro-finance and job training. Women need both. We don't have space, houses or places to make money, places for business, for women to engage in hairdressing, tincture, agro-processing, or a bank that would finance women. If you want to hear about the problems of women you will be here all night. You might have to stay the night."
> (Mbaye, 2013)

This is not to say that grassroots organizing for environmental politics is a failure in Dakar—far from it, in fact. The hip-hop collectives and artists discussed in Chapter Four are obviously a major counter-example. Probably the most famous counter-example of such organizing emerging as a success environmentally and politically belongs to the *Set/Setal* (Be Clean/Make Clean) movement of the 1980s, where a youth clean-up movement impacted Dakar and Senegal in unprecedented ways (Fredericks, 2009: 2). Fredericks (2009: 4) sees in *Set/Setal* and its later echo in 2007 "productive moments in which key political, economic, and social factors crystallize and new configurations of social relations are negotiated." Most significantly, Dakar's trash workers succeeded, from the grassroots, in winning a strong collective bargaining agreement from the Dakar government in

2014 against the trend toward greater cutbacks in support for grassroots groups like theirs (Fredericks, 2016).

Grassroots and rogue urbanism across other African urban environments

Urban Africa in the 21st century has been such a terrain of struggle that such productive moments for grassroots environmental concerns as *Set/Setal* fade into the background. In cities engulfed in war and civil strife in this era, whether for months and years like Tripoli, Benghazi, and Abidjan or, in the case of Mogadishu, for decades, basic questions of urban environmental management like what to do with solid waste or how to handle sanitation, let alone questions about the monitoring of air and water quality, become untenable, or unaskable. The absence or poor quality of urban public health management certainly played a role in making the 2014–15 Ebola outbreak in Guinea, Sierra Leone, and Liberia that much more severe in urban areas there. Yet, even in the worst scenarios imaginable, there are counter-examples available for the knee-jerk Afro-pessimism that often rules the airwaves of the world. The remarkable fact of Ebola's rapid isolation and eradication from Bamako, Dakar, and Lagos—to say nothing of its non-appearance in Abidjan, Lomé, Porto Novo, or Accra—rarely received attention from the world press; these successes were clearly the result of efficient and rigorous management of urban public health in cities where few outside observers would have expected it (Odumosu, 2015; Sy, 2015). Some of that involved active community organizations in collaboration with effective local government—including exactly the women's groups and the *commune* mayor in Pikine discussed earlier. The question seems to be one of how to sustain "productive moments" of dynamic grassroots engagement on the environment that gain state (and sometimes private sector or philanthropic) support—to grow the grassroots, if you will, in a manner that leads to broad environmental justice and long-term socio-environmental sustainability. Across the continent, over and over, what we see instead are "productive moments" that come crashing down far too soon, like the occupation of Maroko's barricades in Abani's (2004) *GraceLand* discussed in Chapter Four. If we start in the north of the continent and move south, the variations on this same theme become evident.

First, there is the extraordinary story of the collaborative grassroots environmental management of Cairo's Tahrir Square by its occupiers throughout Egypt's so-called "Arab Spring" revolution (Prashad, 2015). Demonstrators protesting against the regime of President Hosni

Mubarak occupied the square continually by the tens of thousands in early 2011. Their occupation was a key part of the peaceful exit of Mubarak from power and his replacement by Mohamed Morsi after a free and fair election. The blog site Livable Cities (2011) noted:

> how thousands of Cairenes, strangers to each other, within just a few days peacefully collaborated to build an organized village in the square, with makeshift camp sites in certain areas, toilets, water, rubbish bins, food stalls, clinics, artwork and a kindergarten, and the astonishing way in which after Mubarak's resignation, the people again collaborated to sweep and clean the square.

This should not, in fact, have been so surprising, considering the high levels of cooperation among Cairo's poor in informal settlements long before the uprising (El Mouelhi, 2013).

However, in 2013, Egypt then experienced a military counter-revolution that overthrew the Morsi regime and installed a de facto military dictatorship. Even before that counter-coup, reports began to surface that the occupation of Tahrir Square had a dark side, especially in violence against women. Grassroots groups also formed to protect women, such as Tahrir Bodyguard, but in the final days of the Morsi presidency, demonstrators in favor of the military takeover committed 169 acts of sexual mob crimes against women, including 80 rapes in one day (Kingsley, 2013).

In Tunisia, grassroots groups that helped overthrow that country's dictatorship have struggled under the strains of economic uncertainties, Islamist extremism, and the inefficiencies of the regime they helped to elect. In Morocco, where no revolution occurred, organizers and activists, including the Casablanca-based Arterial Network arts organization, have worked to instill more participatory and deeper democratic practices in the city, but the regime appears to be working away from those more liberatory and sustainable objectives (Essaadani, 2014; Philifert, 2014; Valette and Philifert, 2014). There are "more positive elements" to the grassroots democratization in Tunis, but the overall regional picture is one of growing "doubts on the very interpretation of the capacity of societies to achieve political change through mobilization in the context of strong external influences, and even military interventions" (Bocquet, 2015). Across the northern tier of the continent, the "Arab Spring" seems to have passed fall into its own form of winter, and the glimmers of possibility for grassroots organizing to produce environmentally sustainable, deeply democratic, equitable cityscapes have largely faded (Bayat, 2013). What Asef Bayat (2013: 189) calls the "Refo-lutions" that replaced the blooms of spring led him to offer a rich critique of the mistaken assumption that "there is an urban ecological and cultural affinity between the habitus of the urban poor and militant Islamism." Caught between reactionary, military authoritarianism and Islamist movements that Bayat contends have shown little real convergence with marginalized urban poor communities' agendas, the grassroots of the north have been stifled and scorched.

A "Black Spring" briefly came to Ouagadougou, in Burkina Faso, in late October 2014. Street protests led by a youth activist group that called itself the "Citizen's Broom" modeled on Dakar's *Y'en a Marre* swept long-time dictator President Blaise Compaore from power; a charismatic young rapper, Smockey, helped this "Broom" storm the Parliament (Farge and Felix, 2014). There were certainly echoes of the radical coup of Compaore's predecessor, Thomas Sankara, in the words and sentiments of the Citizen's Broom (Tate, 2015). However, very soon after the broom had swept through, the Burkinabe military stepped in. Although the new interim military president, Isaac Zida, promised an electoral democracy, and he eventually scheduled an October 2015 election, it remains to be seen how much of a "Spring" will genuinely endure in Ouagadougou. The Presidential Guard led an attempted coup against the interim regime and announced the cancellation of the elections a few weeks prior to the planned date, and people poured into the streets again, pushing the army to remove the coup leaders. But at the time of writing, the Black Spring remained rather uncertain.

In Eastern Africa, while there was no such "Spring" in political terms, many cities have seen an upturn in grassroots activism. In Addis Ababa, informal sector recycling workers sought to mobilize the city in a manner not unlike *Set/Setal* in Dakar, and they worked to build relationships with the city administration. Instead, they found themselves ignored, other than when "given empty promises" by the regime at election campaign time (Bjerkli, 2015: 18). Dar es Salaam's grassroots eco-conscious movement for bicyclists' rights, *Uwaba*, allied with hip-hop artists, carved out spaces for populist action for sustainable transport and socio-environmental justice, though in the face of elite disinterest and a long history of government intrusion into (and effort to shape and control) non-governmental organizations (NGOs) in the city (Mbuya, 2014). *Uwaba* has operated bicycle activist caravans to raise consciousness, and it has some notable successes in building alliances with government officials sensitive to cycling as an alternative, eco-friendly form of transportation (Mbuya, 2014). However, the overwhelming emphasis in the transport sector of the city has been heavily top-down, dominated by road-building and mass transit systems implemented with little grassroots input. The slow and rather wobbly roll-out of Dar's Bus Rapid Transit System (BRT) was met with intense protestation from the *daladala* (minibus) transport workers at the grassroots, which successfully forced the government to eschew the World Bank's demand for an international corporate bidding process to run the BRT. Yet, this still left the generally progressive mayor with serious doubts about the capacity of the grassroots to actually *run* the BRT instead of international capital (Massaburi, 2015).

In Nairobi, grassroots activism has been extraordinary, and the environment has been central to many organizations' principles in the city. The community organization Carolina for Kibera has been part of several significant grassroots environmental organizing campaigns. For one notable example, its MapKibera program engaged community leaders elected in its own elections in Kibera's 12 separate villages for a multi-ethnic team that produced interactive community maps for health services, water points, electricity, and safe spaces for women. Carolina for Kibera's co-founder, Salim Mohamed (2015), noted that a 2015 cholera outbreak in Nairobi did not claim victims in Kibera, in part, as a result of the greater grassroots-based environmental health consciousness that his group had been a part of creating. At the same time, Mohamed (2015) was cautious about over-reliance on grassroots organizations for solving Kibera's environmental problems, noting wryly that the settlement had "more NGOs than toilets." This was not just hyperbole—a survey a decade ago found more than 700 NGOs operating in the settlement (Bodewes, 2005). Of course, some of Kibera's NGOs actually *focus* on toilets, and its grassroots produced the entrepreneurial company Ekotoilet, which for the few years of its existence made a profit out of building and running pay-per-use public toilets (Njeru et al, 2014).

Carolina for Kibera, like the Mathare Valley Football Club across the city in another large informal settlement, Mathare, uses sports as a vehicle for galvanizing youth activism. Other Nairobi grassroots organizations, like Kwani Trust, utilize the arts and music, much like we have seen with the organizations in Dakar in Chapter Four, or *Uwaba* in Dar. These grassroots organizations face many challenges. First among these is the relationship with the state. For Wangari Maathai in an earlier, more authoritarian era in Nairobi, the state became a major obstacle to grassroots organizing—or, perhaps, one may say that Maathai became, literally, an obstacle in the way of the state in the interests of environmental defense when she chained herself to a bulldozer to prevent the privatization and further destruction of the Karura Forest in the north end of Nairobi (Njeru, 2010, 2012, 2013). Jeremia Njeru's (2012) study of the factors that motivated a poor community on the forest's edge to join with Maathai's Greenbelt Movement showed how particular spatial and place-based dynamics led to an ephemeral coalition across scales, the loosely aligned Friends of Karura Forest. The confluence of forces that "saved" the forest in actions between 1998 and 2000 worked, in part, because they shaped the narrative about the forest as symbolizing the fight to end authoritarian misrule (Njeru, 2012). When the authoritarian regime left office in 2002, though, the pull of unification around this environmental cause faded—no such movement saved the Ngong Forest from being bisected by a highway, as I have discussed in Chapter One.

In the less authoritarian era since 2002 in Nairobi, grassroots relationships with the state are quite mixed. Projects like MapKibera received financial support from the Bill and Melinda Gates Foundation and Google, Inc., and were at least tolerated by the regime. The government of Uhuru Kenyatta, in power since the 2013 election, has begun work on a sewer line for Kibera and temporarily employed more than 6,000 youths in the settlement to clean its streets and manage its garbage through the National Youth Service. The problem, as organizers like Salim Mohamed (2015) see it, is that "this needs to be more than a six month project," when the government will score some political points for a while and "then move on." Meanwhile, the government's sanitation program in Kibera had already caused several sanitation NGOs there to close doors by early 2015. The fizzled grassroots energy in such circumstances may undo the better intentions of the government on the improvement of the urban environment for the long term on a sustainable basis, and fuel the worst intentions of the state and elites allied to it for land grabbing, gentrification, and the construction of yet more elite shopping malls.

The other cities besides Nairobi and Dakar on which I have focused in earlier chapters, Zanzibar and Lusaka, exhibit markedly less environmental activism at the grassroots. The Zanzibar government's Department of Environment, often in collaboration with the Department of Urban and Rural Planning, has worked more or less informally for several decades to foster greater environmental consciousness among ordinary residents, particularly in the city's informal settlements. Most of the time, though, these are the actions of individuals, operating privately as people who care deeply about the environment and about community politics (Juma, 2014; Jumbe,

2014; Rijal, 2014). Even the 2010 formation of a so-called government of national unity between the ruling *Chama cha Mapinduzi* party and powerful Civic United Front opposition after more than 15 years of *fitina* and political strife in the city has not sparked much in the way of grassroots activism for the environment. Most grassroots organizing is overwhelmingly political or cultural in character, and still built around the contestation for state power; most communities remain reluctant to participate in environmental conservation or sustainability programs, or to initiate their own (Killian, 2008; Muhajir, 2011; Myers, 2011; Shinn, 2015). In Lusaka, community-based groups with an environmental focus also lag far behind political and religious groups in number and significance, and community–state relationships surrounding urban environmental concerns are often conflictual and non-inclusive (Nchito, 2007, 2013; Mulenga, 2013).

One of the more surprising success stories for engagement between the grassroots and the state in the interest of urban environmental management over the last few years in Africa can be found in Zimbabwe. A decade ago, the regime of President Robert Mugabe sought to eradicate opposition strongholds in informal settlements with a brutal and drastic program of demolitions, Operation *Murambatsvina* (Operation Restore Order, or Operation Take out the Garbage), in and around major cities in the country (Potts, 2006). The program took away the homes of 700,000 households, or about two-and-a-half million people, largely in the political interests of the ruling Zimbabwe African National Union-Patriotic Front (ZANU-PF) party: "during the operation, the violence was wanton, symbolic and punitive, signifying ZANU-PF's determination to maintain power and social control" by punishing those who had supported the opposition Movement for Democratic Change (MDC) in the previous election (Muchadenyika, 2015: 3).Yet, over the last few years, programs of participatory planning for sanitation and urban service delivery in Harare and the town of Chinhoyi (about 75 miles north-west of Harare) have been introduced, which, while hardly perfect, have brought the Zimbabwe Dialogue on Shelter, Zimbabwe Homeless Peoples Federation, and local branches of Slum/Shack Dwellers International, among other grassroots community groups, into participatory, inclusive planning relationships with the city of Harare and Chinhoyi's local government for improvements to the urban environment, again with Gates Foundation funding (Banana et al, 2015).

For grassroots urban environmental activism to come to the fore, it seems, there must be an alliance of environmental consciousness with political consciousness; for that grassroots environmental activism to gain political traction, it needs to be able to engage the state (at both local and national levels) and, to some extent, socio-ecologically conscious international capital where it exists (like the Gates Foundation)—in a way that somehow reduces violent confrontation without eliminating the strengths of the "rogue sensibility" that is often present in the activism. This brings us to Cape Town, the focus city for this chapter and a city that, perhaps more than almost any city on the continent, tests these premises.

Cape Town

The metropolitan area of Cape Town was home to an estimated population of 3.5 million as of 2010, and it is expected to pass the 4 million mark by 2020 (UN Habitat, 2014). With an estimated growth rate of 1.71% for 2010–2025, Cape Town is actually now possibly one of the slower-growing major cities on the continent (see Figure 5.1). Yet, its spatial sprawl has accelerated dramatically in the post-apartheid era (since 1994) as its "physically urbanized area increased by 40%" (Dubresson and Jaglin, 2014: 173). Unlike Dakar, Zanzibar, or Lusaka, the cities of focus in the last three chapters, Cape Town was also—like Chapter One's Nairobi—a city studied in the Economist Intelligence Unit's (EIU, 2011) *African green cities index*. Where Nairobi was rated as below-average for green policies and environmental progress, Cape Town emerged in the EIU study as one of the few African cities rated above-average. It even warranted mention as one of the six "best green initiatives" among the cities in Africa studied for the report for its policies toward reducing its carbon footprint (EIU, 2011: 22).

Of course, as a post-apartheid city, 21st-century Cape Town's alleged greenness comes with the immediate caveat of its deeply divided character. As of 2005, Cape Town had a Gini coefficient of income inequality of 0.67, one of the world's most unequal cities in income (UN Habitat, 2014: 242)—albeit lower than the levels of inequality registered in South Africa's two other largest cities, Johannesburg and Durban (eThekwini). Only 14% of Cape Town residents live in informal shack settlements as of 2015, one of the lowest proportions of any city on the continent. However, while many of Cape Town's poor majority lives in formal housing, this hardly means that their conditions of existence or everyday environments are all that much better than for the shack dwellers. In Mark Swilling's (2006: 34) typology of social stratification in Cape Town, 51% of Capetonians occupied the bottom tier of residential spaces, including what was then 15% of the population "below the breadline" in shacks, and another 36% in

Figure 5.1: Map of Cape Town

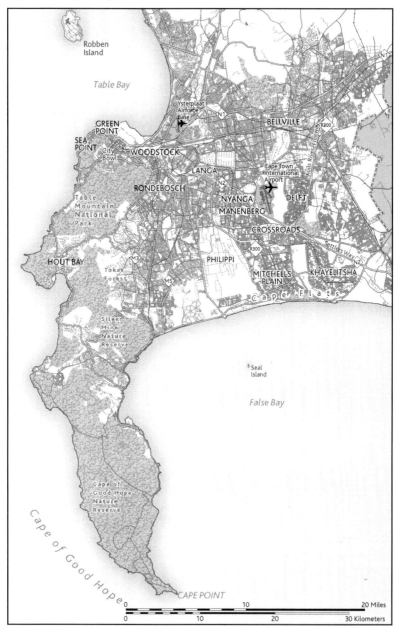

conditions Swilling classified as "township living, towering density, and dire straits." Swilling saw about a third of the city population as part of a struggling middle class, with just 16% of households in elite or upper-middle-class residential spaces.

The environmental politics of Cape Town are similarly stratified. On the one hand, it is a key site for environmentalism built around conventional Western notions of conservation and preservation. Natural spaces visually dominate much of the city, from the beaches through Table Mountain National Park (established in 1998) and Kirstenbosch botanical gardens, to the wineries that hug the outer edge of the metropolitan boundaries—largely in and around formerly white-only residential spaces. "Numerous ecological associations" work to implement "conservation policies keenly supported by rich Capetonians" (Dubresson and Jaglin, 2014: 173). Some 970 square kilometers of the metropolitan area's 2,500 square kilometers (or about 39% of the land surface) are classified as "natural ecosystems," almost half of which lie in formal protected areas, including 24 official nature reserves; since 2010, all of this land is part of the city's Biodiversity Network (Katzschner, 2013: 207). In 2004, the Cape Floristic Region became the world's smallest biodiversity hot spot under United Nations Educational, Scientific, and Cultural Organization (UNESCO) as home to the *fynbos* biome, with its globally significant rate of endemism (SARDC, 1994: 67; Katzschner, 2013; Dubresson and Jaglin, 2014). These natural areas are inelegantly juxtaposed with the Cape Flats area, with its seemingly denaturalized townships, despite the fact that the Flats have their own ecological claims to high rates of endemism (see Figure 5.2).

Cape Town has also been known for decades as a central node globally for protests built around urban service provision, including services for housing, water, sanitation, solid waste, and electricity, with the

Figure 5.2: The new housing in the Cape Flats

townships in the Flats as key arenas for the protests. In 2013, South Africa experienced a community protest against local municipalities for the lack of services provision an average of every other day, with Cape Town as one of the major sites for these protests (Gurney, 2014: 49). Grassroots organizing has been a hallmark of the city's "Colored" and African communities, particularly with the anti-apartheid movement, with its street committees that, by the 1980s, essentially controlled many townships' daily affairs amid waves of violence. Demands for housing, land, water, and services provided the environmental dimensions of this activism, always there around the edges of the violence.

More recently, Cape Town has had "water wars" and "toilet wars"— and the word "war" is not simple hyperbole. The water war in Tafelsig, a section of Mitchell's Plain township, emerged as a community response to the provincial and municipal government's Cape Flats Renewal Strategy (CFRS). The CFRS, which began in 2001, "was intended to combat crime on the Flats" (Samara, 2011: 101). It included economic and social renewal strategies, as well as policing strategies, but the latter gained the upper hand in its implementation. In conjunction with the government's neoliberal initiative for Growth, Employment, and Redistribution (GEAR), the municipality sought "cost recovery" from years of non-payment for water and other urban services, and Tafelsig was an area substantially in arrears—just as it was equally a crime "hot spot" (Samara, 2011: 156). When the city moved in to attempt to cut off water to residents in arrears, they faced barricades of "burning tires.... Police responded with rubber bullets, live ammunition and stun grenades" (Samara, 2011: 156). Although most would consider the water wars to have ended in a stand-off in this case, arguably, the resistance offered in Tafelsig was one instance among many that, taken together, ultimately resulted in the failure to fully privatize water and other urban services in the city (and thus a success for anti-privatization grassroots activists).

Another way of thinking of the phrase "water wars" would be in terms of flooding, since residents run a constant battle with it in the rainy season. As the zone's name suggests, the Cape Flats consist largely of low-lying areas prone to flooding, with poor drainage: "Rapid recent urban development on the Cape Flats ... disrupted natural drainage patterns and increased stormwater run-off" (Smit, 2015: 196). In 2007 and 2012, anywhere from 2,600 to 22,300 households (or an estimated 6,500 to 75,300 people) were displaced annually due to flooding. As Warren Smit (2015: 196) puts it, "this is just the tip of the iceberg" since flooding also has a whole range of other negative impacts on health, property, and livelihoods. While Smit (2015: 197) credits the city with effectiveness in disaster response, he critiques the "attempts to proactively reduce flooding risk in informal settlements." Grassroots groups have felt excluded, contending that "the crisis in flooding in the informal settlements is caused by government's anti-poor policies … not the weather" (Abahlali baseMjondolo, 2009, quoted in Smit, 2015: 199).

The toilet wars have been, perhaps, a bit less violent or displacing, but more materially graphic. In Cape Flats shack settlements, many residents lack adequate sanitation and must walk 10 minutes or more to use community toilets. In many communities, like the Taiwan shack settlement in Khayelitsha, this leaves residents highly vulnerable to attacks; women, in particular, have been victims of robbery and rape on the walk to the toilet—or in journeys at night to relieve themselves elsewhere since the communal toilets are closed from 9 pm to 5 am (Gurney, 2014). Public toilets have a poor record in terms of functionality, and many have features such as broken doors that leave users exposed. Policing and security become environmental issues in a context where people fear communal toilets and where wealthy, largely white, Cape Town neighborhoods have a police–citizen ratio of 1:38 while the ratio in Cape Flats townships is as high as 1 police officer for every 1,700 residents (Samara, 2011; Gurney, 2014).

Protests over the lack of sanitation services in 2013–14 "politicized the toilet, casting it as a cipher of freedom" (Gurney, 2014: 38). The most notable, or notorious, protests of the toilet wars involved activists throwing feces from highway overpasses, at the international airport, and at the provincial legislature. By 2015, shit-throwing had reached the University of Cape Town—this time as part of a much broader protest over the failures of racial reform at the university, and the victim of the feces attack was a prominent statue of Cecil John Rhodes. In the earlier instances, the protestors were making the case, very bluntly, that "the open toilet is a symbol of the violation of dignity that the middle classes understand" (Robins, quoted in Gurney, 2014: 40). As Rustum Kozain (2013: 3) put it: "as a projectile of protest, shit is at the extreme end of a continuum that extends from rotten tomatoes and eggs to bare breasts and arses—all things, in one way or another, considered unsightly or lacking in decorum." The discomfort caused by human waste as a weapon of protest leads to disgust, but also to rapid actions in response to ameliorate the situation!

> It takes the suffering that is usually hidden away as a private shame and makes it a public embarrassment to the government … when this suffering becomes politicized

and collective action can be taken, especially in elite spaces, things really can change. (Kozain, 2013: 3)

Robins (quoted in Gurney, 2014: 40) also sees the emergence of new forms of grassroots activism capable of "more tactical engagement with the state." Kim Gurney cites the example in this regard of Khayelitsha's Social Justice Coalition, which helped force the Western Cape provincial government to create a Commission of Inquiry into policing in the Cape Flats.

Cape Town is thus a valuable setting for comprehending the fragmentation of the grassroots, especially on the environment, across the continent, and yet also a space of hope for what can be accomplished when grassroots and marginalized voices are heard and included in the shaping of environmental policy. It can be a crucial node for "repositioning urban ecology and natural resource management in relation to the promotion of wellbeing of people and their places" (Katzschner, 2013: 202). Even in the Cape Flats, Cape Town exhibits remarkable examples of grassroots environmental activism, and, in many instances, of elites and elite institutions that tolerate, or even seek to empower, those grassroots rather than crush them. For one example, *Cityscapes* magazine, a publication of the University of Cape Town's African Centre for Cities, recently dedicated its entire issue to the everyday lives and environments of 11 ordinary Capetonians, including the remarkable Luzann Isaacs, manager of an environmental reserve, Edith Stephens Wetland Park, in Phillippi, a poor Cape Flats community (Gurney, 2015: 152–64).

Isaacs works for the city of Cape Town, but it is hard to read Kim Gurney's (2015) article about her and not see her as a grassroots activist. Half of South Africa's "critically endangered vegetation types are found in Cape Town," the city has the "highest number of threatened plant species [of any biome] in the world," and some of the most threatened are those in the Cape Flats given the rapid pace at which housing and commercial properties have been developed there since the end of apartheid (Gurney, 2015: 154). Isaacs acknowledged to Gurney (2014: 155) that Hanover Park, Manenburg, Gugulethu, Nyanga, and Phillippi, the working-class townships that surround the park, have issues with putting "food on the table," and the nature reserve—or natural elements around it, like Clicking Stream frogs—can just be a nuisance when hunger, "violence and gang-related trauma" predominate (Gurney, 2015: 161). However, NGOs, youth groups, and schoolchildren who collaborate in projects for conservation at the wetland sanctuary often find the "value of a safe space, the value of space with beauty on it, and the experience" of quiet that the park provides (Gurney, 2015: 161).

In almost every instance, for every measurable success with grassroots movements impacting the urban environment, there are an equal or greater number of narratives of failure. Tania Katzschner (2013: 202) tells the story of the organization and program Cape Flats Nature, which lasted from 2002 to 2010, as a grassroots attempt to re-imagine socio-ecological relations in this zone of "poverty and marginalization." Cape Flats Nature was an initiative of the city of Cape Town's Environmental Management Department and, in fact, included the establishment of on-the-ground management for the Edith Stevens Wetland Park, along with three other reserves (two of which were created by the Cape Flats Nature project) at Wolfgat, Harmony Flats, and Macassar Dunes. Implemented through the South African National Biodiversity Institute, Cape Flats Nature sought to "put people in the middle of nature, put nature in the middle of people and to find a way of forging a relationship between them that is mutually beneficial and self-sustaining" (Peter, quoted in Katzschner, 2013: 209). Katzschner (2013: 209) pronounces its program "both inspirational and naïve ... pioneering and vulnerable" (see also Soal and Van Blerk, 2005; Pitt and Boulle, 2010). The emphases were on building relationships, empowering the community, and consciousness-raising—"growing together," as a book about the project is entitled (Pitt and Boulle, 2010). Although it did not arise from the grassroots, it took marginalized and impoverished people seriously from the beginning. Institutional and financial factors led to the project's failure, even though the city continued employing people like Luzann Isaacs at Edith Stephens Wetland Park (Katzschner, 2013: 224).

Another example of spaces of hope shaped by grassroots activism that productively engages the state is Khayelitsha's project for Violence Prevention through Urban Upgrading (VPUU). This program began in 2005, and it combines a participatory approach to upgrading with an emphasis on community security. Thus, in the Monwabisi area of Khayelitsha, a safe-house community center, a safe toilet facility, a football pitch, and an upgraded communal water point have all resulted from VPUU's collaborative approach with the residents. One tangible outcome for this neighborhood is measured in the increase in water availability for residents—an increase from 60% to 95% of households being covered.

The Victoria Mxenge (VM) Housing Project, while it did not directly address itself to urban environmental issues, was, in fact, all about the urban environment. The Victoria Mxenge Housing Development

Association was an affiliate of the South African Homeless People's Federation (SAHPF), which built more than 5,000 homes between 1992 and the early 2000s (Ismail, 2015). Despite its simultaneous achievements in the tangible improvement of the physical environment, the empowerment of women, and community-building, by the early 21st century, VM had become a part of a "deeply fractured" movement for housing rights (Ismail, 2015: xxv). The SAHPF was under the umbrella of the NGO People's Dialogue (PD), until that folded in 2005. In 2000, SAHPF had split in two, with the original Federation joining the PD and the Utshani Fund in the South African Alliance while a more radical contingent formed the Federation for the Urban Poor (FEDUP). Then, the South African Alliance entered into a partnership in 2001 with the Housing Department of the government, which led to substantial disagreements between the white-dominated PD and the African women of VM. When FEDUP, too, began collaborating with the state, an even more radical housing rights group, *Abahlali baseMjondolo*, came to Cape Town (Ismail, 2015: 132). With the constant, dizzying (In the abbreviations alone!) shifts of alliances and ideological guiding principles, "unresolved issues" continually exacerbate "tensions between organizations and between them and government," resulting in what Salma Ismail (2015: 133) calls a "cocktail of protests" that do not necessarily lead to productive changes, while the state has "betrayed its promises to the poor" (Ismail, 2015: 140).

Perhaps the most comprehensive picture of the possibilities that the grassroots offer comes from an area just outside of Cape Town, in keeping with my book's contention about the blurry boundary of the urban. Mark Swilling and Eva Annecke (2012: xii–xiii) use their experiences in creating and residing in Lynedoch EcoVillage, 30 minutes from Cape Town, as the launching pad for creating what they call "just transitions," creating ways for all people to become "visible in a place" within "the most unequal society in the world." Their sweep is broad, from their tiny suburb out to the whole globe, through five types of transitions toward "just sustainability." They develop an idea of "livable urbanism," dissecting and reassembling the "flows and networks of a city" (Swilling and Annecke, 2012: xx–xxi, 113–14). In Cape Town, they contend, the UN Habitat-style "inclusive urbanism was not enough" because its policies did not produce "bottom-up empowerment" in the city (Swilling and Annecke, 2012: 246). Instead, they offer the "gritty," face-to-face narrative of Lynedoch's livability, modestly achieved through more than a decade of patient and testy collaboration between activists, residents of all income groups and races, and a wide array of people (see also Swilling, 2010, 2013).

Winter 2015 brought a massive wildfire to Cape Town, which burned more than 5,000 hectares of the Cape Peninsula and Table Mountain Reserve—a mind-boggling extent roughly equivalent to the entire downtown "Loop" of Chicago and significant stretches north and south from it, for example—without the loss of a single human life or even of much residential housing. While one segment of Cape Town dealt with fire quite literally in 2015, much of the rest of the city deals with fire figuratively on a constant basis, in the sense of the burning resentments over injustices that flare up into a variety of protests—many of which have the potential for "forming a learning alliance" that can advance socio-ecological understanding and equity (Katzschner, 2013: 224). Lynedoch EcoVillage, the Development Action Group, the various iterations of the Homeless People's Federation, Shack Dwellers International, the Victoria Mxenge Housing Association, Cape Flats Nature, and on and on—Cape Town's vibrant strain of activism has tremendous potential for transforming the city's environment while improving the everyday lives of ordinary people, even if there are also forces that often hold back this potential. Many social movements lose "momentum and dissolve once the issues under protest are resolved" (Ismail, 2015: 122). Others fracture on ideological and personal grounds, such as the split that occurred in the SAHPF discussed earlier. However, they have to be seen, taken as a whole, as precisely the agencies of the "radical incrementalism" that can propel an interactionist UPE forward toward fundamental positive change in the city's socio-environments.

Conclusion

Nkululeko Mabandla (2006: 190) has written that "Cape Town remains a city of contrasts and paradoxes, of mesmerizing physical beauty and grandeur on the one hand and abject poverty and hopelessness on the other. And these side by side, too." It is becoming more cosmopolitan (Brudvig, 2014) and continuing to sprawl, and, in some ways, improving its negotiated relations between communities, and between those communities and the environment. Yet, it remains full of contradictions—the center of the famed "Cape liberalism" and, at the same time, a bastion of reactionary politics (Mabandla, 2006: 187–8); a hearth of grassroots progressive activism and yet a metropolitan area rife with violent gang activity and police brutality; "one of the most startlingly beautiful places on earth" and a "smug and small-minded place, desperately unaware of its modest position in the firmament" (Cartwright, 2006: 203). Somehow, there is a dialectic at work in

Cape Town, though, pulling these contradictory elements toward one another on a continual basis, and this is where the hope resides for a liberatory radical incrementalism. Vijay Prashad (2015: 4) has written, in relation to the complete opposite end of the continent in Cairo's Tahrir Square, that there is a "consistent hope in the Arab political landscape" that this will be (here echoing the words of a Syrian poet) "the generation that will defeat defeat." It does not always feel that way in Cape Town's grassroots environmental politics nor in the similarly situated grassroots across the cities of Africa as a whole; however, without such hope, there is little purpose in a situated, interactionist UPE in the first place.

Power is relational. It operates in networks. These networks are constantly shifting and in tension. At the grassroots in marginalized poor urban communities that constitute the majority in most of the continent of Africa's cities, these networks hold less power in the overt world. Yet, they are ultimately responsible for a great deal of the production of urban space, and therefore for the urbanization of nature and naturalization of the urban. Pieterse (2010) writes: "I have no doubt that the street, the slum, the waste dump, the taxi rank, the mosque and church will become the catalysts of an emancipated African urbanism." From Pikine to Cairo to Addis Ababa to Nairobi to Cape Town, and with many stops in between, we see that marginal communities do have the potential for transformational energies and dynamism that produce radical incrementalism and an "emancipated African urbanism."

However, their successes are often fleeting; the emancipation transitory or ephemeral. Environmental consciousness varies significantly at the grassroots in Africa's cities. Likewise, the degree and character of the politicization of that consciousness varies. The rogue sensibilities that predominate in marginalized-majority urban communities are unpredictable and difficult to harness into revolutionary moments that are sustained. The task ahead is to sustain them. Doing so requires us to remain cognizant of the past, the physical and spiritual cityscape, the literary, artistic, and creative imaginations of urban ecological politics, and the views of experts, planners, and policymakers—and to bring these into the processes of grassroots action, and vice versa.

CONCLUSION

Urban environments, politics, and policies

Introduction

Now, we come to the question of what to do with this interactionist map of reading Africa's urban environments politically. Doing something with this is itself an explicit component of the situatedness of urban political ecology (UPE) in African contexts (Lawhon et al, 2014). The literature on the cities of the Global South and Southern urban planning makes plain that practice and engagement for urban change ought to be constituent elements of any theory (Watson, 2009a, 2009b; Parnell and Oldfield, 2014). Facing the panoply of ideas that an interactionist, multi-vocal approach throws up can be paralyzing. The contrapuntal or polyphonic character of the reading or listening to urban environments has the potential to be debilitating. We might in effect be stopped by what Robinson (forthcoming) refers to as singularities, where each story is unique, and thus might require different theories, or lead to different ideas or solutions to environmental issues (see also Robinson, 2013; Söderström, 2014).

Instead, can we think of these instances, spaces, and realms of urban environments as revisable, contextual, nuanced, and negotiated? Such an approach would commonsensically suggest, instead of an incomparable mess, that in different cities, in different parts of these cities, at different times, with different issues, different approaches are called for, but that, at the same time, seeing and reading the interrelationships of the environmental consciousness (and unconsciousness) of the experts, the past, the cityscape, the artists, and the grassroots in a given place and time may provide opportunities for "better," more socially and environmentally sustainable and liberatory urban development. This lens may thus help produce what Pieterse (2008) calls "radical incrementalism." It is my belief that we can build better bridges between communities and urban environment-and-development when we have in sight and mind the elite or expert analysis of issues, the past of the problem, the physical and metaphysical cityscape context, and the variegated artistic imaginations, along with diverse grassroots voices.

Examples of interactionist urban political ecologies in practice

A great many well-intended programs and policies have been developed for Africa's cities. Whether these have the "aim of ameliorating poverty, rescuing the environment [or] growing local economies," they tend to "come with built-in assumptions about the nature of the city, its people, cultures and possible futures" (Pieterse and Simone, 2009, as cited in Pieterse, 2013: 12). However, there are increasing numbers of institutions, programs, policies, and dialogic processes that mark routes toward radical incrementalism. I have mentioned several of these in different chapters of the book, such as the work of Africulturban and other music and arts institutions in Dakar, Lynedoch EcoVillage, or Carolina for Kibera in Nairobi. Here, let me highlight two more examples for further reflection and elaboration of how they tie into the ideas of radical incrementalism and the constant revisability of urban environments and theories about them: the Kibera Public Space Project in Nairobi and various environmental politics programs and activities associated with the African Centre for Cities (ACC) in Cape Town.

The Kibera Public Space Project is a collaboration of the Kounkuey Design Initiative (KDI) and six Kibera communities. KDI is an international planning/engineering non-profit partnership, registered in California, which began in 2006 with its work in Kibera; it has since developed similar projects in Haiti, Ghana, Morocco, and—using the insights from its work in these Global South contexts—in a trailer park in the Coachella Valley in California. KDI collaborates with local partners at the grassroots to create what it terms "productive public spaces" out of "formerly unusable and sometimes unsafe areas" in poor urban communities (see: http://www.kounkuey.org/about.html). They are "working to generate radical alternatives to slum conditions" in Kibera (Odbert and Mulligan, 2015: 177).

In contrast with most of the hundreds of well-intentioned projects in Kibera, though, KDI's work combines the expertise of technically trained planners with a keen understanding of the past of the place, a rich collaborative conception of both the physical and the spiritual dimensions of the Kibera landscape, an awareness of the artistic and creative capacities of residents, and, obviously, engagement with the complex and nuanced grassroots of Kibera neighborhoods. They aim for "true agency in the decision-making process" for a wide net of partners and stakeholders, avoiding oversimplification and disenfranchisement in building toward "multi-stakeholder participation, sectoral integration and networked change" (Odbert and Mulligan, 2015: 178). The

166

evidence suggests that their work has "mobilized a network of Kibera residents with increased resilience and capacity to effect change" (Odbert and Mulligan, 2015: 189). The participants continue to ask the hard question of "why ... slum conditions persist given significant investments and upgrading efforts" in places like Kibera, and they evaluate the project "not in terms of success or failure, but in terms of new insights" that can incrementally change the "urban realities of growing cities like Nairobi" (Odbert and Mulligan, 2015: 177, 192). Project organizers, of course, do not state that they are producing an incrementalist UPE that is "progressive and redistributional, not only changing the ecology and creating new socio-natures, but also tweaking relations of power and transforming the very meaning of nature in the city and the nature of cities," to recall Benton-Short and Short (2013: 240) from Chapter One. However, that is what the KDI's Kibera Public Space Project is doing.

The urban ecology work out of the University of Cape Town's ACC includes many projects circulating around it and facilitated through it since 2008, some of which are directly related to radically reformulating urban environmental politics incrementally. For example, the CityLab led by Pippin Anderson and research projects coordinated by Henrik Ernstson offer examples of interactionist UPE in action comparable to KDI. This ever-evolving constellation of urban ecology interests seeks to create: research on the historical socio-ecology of the Cape region; a re-conceptualization of the cityscape's ecology as a network of human and non-human agency; artistic expressions of community conservation-and-development political activism through film, dance, and hip hop; and support for indigenous gardening in poor communities of the Cape Town metro area (Anderson, 2015). Like KDI, the ACC's CityLab at least strives to be open to revision, to rethinking its mistakes or missed opportunities. A number of researchers then affiliated with ACC, including Ernstson and Mary Lawhon, among others, created the Web platform Situated Ecologies, which draws on international comparative projects in building toward situated UPE (or SUPE, as this website puts it). One of the collaborators' goals in exploring the meaning of SUPE is to produce and sustain progressive networks of activists around the city region, but both the site and the collective admit to being "a work in progress" (see: http://www.situatedecologies. net/supe).

While the work highlighted on the Situated Ecologies website is often more academic and abstract, in 2015, one of the scholars behind it, Henrik Ernstson, was producing a film entitled "Ways of knowing urban nature," which includes a segment on activists at the "grassroots in Cape Town and their work to rehabilitate the *Princess Vlei* wetland, which has also come to address the city's history and apartheid legacy" (see: http://www.situatedecologies.net/archives/portfolio/ways-of-knowing-the-film). The film presents these activists as, in effect, reinvigorating and defending an indigenous spiritual conceptualization of the Cape Flats cityscape, and the researchers are working to build connections for this work at broader scales. There are certainly possibilities for questioning the representations of the activists as practitioners of indigenous knowledge, but the affirmation of revisability suggests that there is room for this questioning.

ACC affiliates also created a subgroup for Socio-Ecological Movements in Urban Ecosystems (MOVE), which aims at building both ecological knowledge and socio-environmental activism both in Cape Town and in New Orleans. Another of the ongoing projects has been the Cape Town Civic Network Study, a survey that identified the missions of and strengthened ties between more than 130 grassroots organizations in Cape Town from Tokai to Phillippi across the Cape Flats in order to collaborate and work for: "the right to good healthy environments, including parks, soccer fields, recreation areas; the protection of urban nature like vegetation, animals and ecosystems; the lowering of industrial pollution in wetlands, streams and soils; the right to safe and good housing; and the access to electricity, sewage and water" (see: http://www.situatedecologies.net/archives/portfolio/ct-civnet-cape-town). ACC also has or has had further programs and projects that are instances of radical incrementalism manifested in an interactive UPE—including a major research project on urban food security, another on urban impacts of climate change that critically takes into account indigenous knowledge of climates, a third on alcohol's role in urban socio-environmental health concerns, and, indeed, a workshop on the very meaning of "radical incrementalism."

Other related approaches

I am hardly seeking to suggest that these two examples are perfect, or even close to it; nor are these sorts of meldings of theory and praxis the only possible ways forward. There are similar projects, collectives, or institutions cropping up around the continent's cities, fragilely, as the 21st century advances; there are also different routes to implement forms of radical incrementalism, and these increments, too, can go backward as well as forward. Ecological science in urban areas is increasingly open to political analysis; UPE is capable of much greater collaboration than has heretofore been the case with atmospheric, physical, and biological scientists to broaden and strengthen its analysis (Douglas et al, 2008; Douglas and James, 2015). Science and scholarship can take forms that model urban environmental change from more economic lenses than I have in the book, and still arrive at questions quite relevant to urban environmental politics, such as with Turok's use of the concept of resilience in analyses of Africa's cities (Turok, 2013, Turok and Seelinger, 2013; see also Fernandez, 2014).

There are very real, applied concerns in urban environments in Africa for the near future that might make my approach in parts of this book seem secondary. The list is long—feeding people (Crush and Frayne, 2014), dealing with violence, xenophobia, and raw insecurity (Crush and Ramachandran, 2014), the immediate consequences of global climate change (Parnell and Walawage, 2014; Simon and Leck, 2014), fuelwood and household energy shortages (Hiemstra-van der Horst and Hovorka, 2008, 2009), shortages of urban transport and infrastructure (Pirie, 2014; Simone, 2014), and poverty (Satterthwaite, 2014) for starters. Pieterse's (2014) agenda for "tackling African urbanization" begins from acknowledging that there is no way to begin to address all of these in the continent's urban environments without fundamental changes in the power structures to favor civil society and community groups. He calls for a "national commitment to democratization and to the maintenance of functioning political spheres that allow for contestation, negotiation, agreements and oversight of decisions taken," but he sees "very little evidence" of that commitment from the power structures of most countries on the continent (Pieterse, 2014: 205). Still, he offers seven "action fronts" for building "a new urban practice" that starts from "empowering the urban poor," most of which have some bearing on environmental issues (Pieterse, 2014: 207–16): "open-source social infrastructures"; tackling youth unemployment with programs of urban infrastructure and service provisioning; the related notion of "infrastructure-led growth"; innovative but "appropriate" land-use planning; "effective democratic deliberation and accountability" that builds from the grassroots organizations of the urban poor; the related need for building and sustaining "robust institutions, networks and learning"; and "effective data collection and analysis." These may seem mundane, pedantic, or instrumentalist to some, particularly more theoretically minded urbanists, but they are useful proposals for a "realistic and clinical discussion" of how to shape the "never ending construction" that is the city in a manner that is socio-environmentally just, equitable, and sustainable (Pieterse, 2014: 218).

While there are reasons for direct action for change in all of the spheres just mentioned, the realm of the mind cannot be left out of the picture. Without a recalibration of socio-environmental consciousness from both elites, grassroots communities, and those in between, it is hard to imagine that the "never ending construction" will be just, equitable, and sustainable. Some of the work in building or rebuilding that consciousness belongs to the realm of philosophy, and many African philosophers emphasize practice and development in their efforts to reconstruct environmental ethics on the continent. Munyaradzi Mawere (2014a: 46–78), for example, lays out strategies for "reviving interconnections for sustainable development," and his 33 short cases discuss "applications" of indigenous principles, based upon open dialogue, as well as "lessons learnt." While Mawere mostly writes about rural contexts, his dialogic approach, where both Western and African indigenous knowledge are "unconvincing" on their own in the scientific search for principles of sustainability, is both refreshing and very relevant to urban planning and management's impasse over the "clash of rationalities" discussed in my Introduction (Mawere, 2014a: 107). Acceptance of "knowledge pluralism" and multi-vocality is central to Mawere's (2014a: 107) philosophical approach to political ecology, where he finds inspiration across a very interdisciplinary set of literatures—including the work of political ecologists such as Blaikie, James Fairhead, and Melissa Leach. Only "dialogue between different knowledge forms"—a crucial, fundamental tenet of an interactionist UPE—can achieve the "sustainable production of knowledge and advancement of understanding" (Mawere, 2014a: 113).

Mawere is not alone in this exploration of dialogue in African environmental philosophy. While he is less focused on the environment, Cameroonian philosopher Godfrey Tangwa (2010: 58) aligns with Mawere in acknowledging African diversities while calling for "respectful coexistence" of both knowledge forms and cultural groups as bases for a renewed environmental ethics. Tangwa (2010: 67) argues that globalization and the African ramifications of the global environmental crisis highlight the urgency of finding solutions in Africa that build around an "ecobiocentric attitude of live and let live" that he believes can be reconstructed from antecedents in indigenous environmental philosophies on the continent.

Along with Mawere and Tangwa, South African philosopher Matoane Mamabolo has offered a new vision of environmental philosophy for Africa. Mamabolo (2012: 86) considers "Africa's normative responsibility towards the environment" to be among the key "moral and spiritual challenges" facing the continent in this century. "All human beings," he argues, "have a common responsibility to perpetuate other life forms" (Mamabolo, 2012: 88). However, Mamabolo is firmly rooted in real issues for African human beings. Interrogating the "close relationship between technology, society and the environment," human development, food security, inegalitarian trade imbalances, and imbalances in environmental/scientific knowledge acquisition and access are all a part of fostering environmental ethics for Africa for him (Mamabolo, 2012: 89). Kenyan philosopher Odero Oruka and Kenyan environmental scientist Calestous Juma (1994) make a case for an "ecocentric" ethics for Africa that can supplant the anthropocentric and technocentric mindsets inherited from the West. All of these philosophical advances are relevant to the practical deployment of an interactionist UPE.

Transformations in African philosophy and praxis, however, cannot be left in isolation as though Africa is not a thoroughly integrated part of the world. Much more can be done to bring African UPE narratives into the realm of the broader global stories in a manner that is not tokenism (Joseph, 2013; Hou et al, 2015; Sandberg et al, 2015). However, other questions then persist in the realm of politics about where African urban studies fits in the dynamics of global urban studies and global UPE. Let me end this section, then, with some further reflection on my subtitle—a critical perspective on environmental politics.

There has recently been some discussion about what it means to be critical in urban geography (Jonas et al, 2015). For my part, I take it to mean being ready to accept the multi-vocality of an urban society, whether in Africa or anywhere else. I believe African cases offer the necessity of starting from there as a global lesson. If one has read this book to this point, then one is aware that my understanding of politics also stretches much farther than political parties and elections. Again, urban studies in Africa has much to offer to global urban studies in the analysis of the political, and perhaps particularly when it comes to environmental politics. Urban environmental history, studies of urban spirituality, biogeography, hydrology and climatology, and urban ecocriticism—the material of Chapters Two through Four—are all fundamentally politicized, as politicized as the voices and views of the experts and planners of Chapter One and the grassroots activists of Chapter Five.

Some urban geographers have suggested that we have entered a post-political era in the world dominated by the depoliticization of society in the midst of neoliberal good governance (Swyngedouw, 2005, 2009a). There is a related argument concerning the post-democratic wave in urban governance (Swyngedouw, 2011b). Events in a great many cities across the globe have cast doubts on these claims, or recast them as a "return of the political" (Swyngedouw, 2014). Swyngedouw (2014: 133) rightly argues that the key question is that of "what happens when the squares are cleared, the tents removed and the energies dissipate, when the dream is over and the dawn of 'ordinary' everyday life begins again," and that what will have to "happen" will involve:

> painstaking organisation, sustained political action and a committed fidelity to universalising the egalitarian trajectory for the management of the commons; a process that has to consider carefully the persistent obstacles and often-violent strategies of resistance orchestrated by those who wish to hang on to the existing state of the situation.

As I have shown throughout this book, the frames of depoliticization and post-democracy bear limited relevance to contemporary African urban environments. While recognizing that there are many forces seeking to depoliticize urban environmental management and move beyond democratic debate and dissent to technocratic questions (Gilbert et al, 1996), there are countless examples of political and democratic urban environmental activity. Wherever one looks, there is work to be done in the streets and alleys, but also in city council offices to navigate the political in order to craft policies that do not neuter or render mute grassroots activist politics. Being interested in "solutions" does not mean being post-political (Hardoy et al, 2001). Smit and Pieterse (2014: 164) show that there is intense politics surrounding discussion of how the institutional landscape of urban environmental management should be revised, negotiated, and contested to produce "genuine bottom-up interventions."

Conclusion

UPE demands hard work on the most difficult issues facing the world for human and non-human alike. I am arguing for an interactionist UPE that is open to revision, and aware of spaces in between city and countryside, as well as seamless ties across scale (Trefon, 2009; Biersack, 2006; Allen, 2014). It is open to thinking positively about urban environments, rather than thinking solely about problems (Meyer, 2013). It does not shy away from literary, artistic, conceptual, and philosophical discussion, but remains rooted in the progressive and practical realm of a radical incrementalism.

In this book, I have looked at an array of environmental issues in a range of cities from a variety of different perspectives. Each city in Africa has its unique context, its unique combination of experts, histories, cityscapes, artists, and grassroots activists. We may add to this the always-present recognition of the diversity, elasticity, and mutability of urban Africans' environmental consciousness. Despite the multi-vocality and complexity, the diversity of cities and diversity of environments, I have argued that these cities share the hot pot of environmental politics—and that that demands a critical, comparative approach. In the interactionist UPE for which I have argued, there needs to be greater dialogue with the supposedly "rural" political ecology that has been conducted in Africa for several generations, further attention to both postcolonial ecocriticism and analysis of other art in relation to UPE, and an effort to expand the geographical range of inquiry. This will lead to further exploration of possibilities for urban forms of indigenous environmental knowledge to be engaged in radical incrementalism, and a scaling-up of those explorations. With a deeper historical backdrop and a recognition that everyday environmentalism takes many forms in the city, in such a manner, Africanized and pluralized interactionist UPE could genuinely lead to broader ways of rethinking what constitutes a city and a radical re-imagination of possibilities for producing cities around the world that are more just and genuinely socio-environmentally sustainable.

A dozen years ago, Zimmerer and Bassett (2003b: 278) pointed to the work of Pelling (2003) and Swyngedouw (1996, 2003) as offering "future directions" for a UPE in three realms: "environmental justice and politics," risk analysis, and links between rural and urban environments. At the same time, they noted that UPE had barely begun to examine "newly industrialized and developing countries" (Zimmerer and Bassett, 2003a: 7). The field has come a long way in a dozen years, in urban Africa alone, but it still has much farther to go. My hope is that this book can be suggestive of one path for future analysis through an interactionist UPE.

References

Abahlali baseMjondolo (2009) "The City of Cape Town is politicizing flood aid and failing to deal with the structural issues," press release, 16 July. Cape Town: Abahlali baseMjondolo.

Abani, C. (2004) *GraceLand*. New York, NY: Farrar, Straus and Giroux.

Abdulla, M.S. (1976) "Ufafanuzi wa 'shamba'" ["The definition of 'shamba'"], in J. Mbonde (ed) *Uandishi wa Tanzania, kitabu cha kwanza—insha [Tanzanian writing, book one—essays]* Nairobi: East African Literature Board, pp 35–42.

Adama, O. (2007) *Governing from above: solid waste management in Nigeria's new capital city of Abuja*. Stockholm: Stockholm University Press.

Adama, O. (2012) "Governance and spatial inequality in service delivery: a case study of solid waste management in Abuja, Nigeria," *Waste Management & Research*, 30(9): 991–8.

Adams, W., Goudie, A., and Orme, A. (1999) *The physical geography of Africa*. New York, NY: Oxford University Press.

Ademo, M. (2014) "Protests grow over Addis Ababa's expansion," *Think Africa Press*, 26 April. Available at: http://allafrica.com/stories/201405010041.html

Aguiar, M. (2003) "Smoke of the savannah: travelling modernity in Sembene Ousmane's *God's bits of wood*," *Modern Fiction Studies*, 49(2): 284–305.

Akugizibwe, P. (2013) "'Nice nice' will get you nowhere: an interview with Boniface Mwangi," *Chimurenga Chronic*, November, pp 24–5.

Allen, A. (2014) "Peri-urbanization and the political ecology of differential sustainability," in S. Parnell and S. Oldfield (eds) *The Routledge handbook on cities of the Global South*. London and New York, NY: Routledge, pp 523–38.

Amis, P. (2006) "Urban poverty in East Africa: Nairobi and Kampala's comparative trajectories," in D. Bryceson and D. Potts (eds) *African urban economies: viability, vitality or vitiation?* New York, NY: Palgrave Macmillan, pp 169–83.

Anderson, B. (1991 [1983]) *Imagined communities*. London: Verso.

Anderson, P. (2015) "Reimagining ecology in the city of Cape Town: contemporary ecological research and the role of the African Centre for Cities," in L.A. Sandberg, A. Bardekjian, and S. Butt (eds) *Urban forests, trees and greenspace: a political ecology perspective*. New York, NY: Routledge, pp 261–76.

Angelo, H. and Wachsmuth, D. (2015) "Urbanizing urban political ecology: a critique of methodological cityism," *International Journal of Urban and Regional Research*, 39(1): 16–27.

Armah, A.K. (1977 [1968]) *The beautyful ones are not yet born*. London: Heinemann.

Awhefeada, S. (2013) "Degraded environment and destabilized women in Kaine Agary's *Yellow-Yellow*," in O. Okuyade (ed) *Eco-critical literature: regreening African landscapes*. Lagos: African Heritage Press, pp 95–108.

Balogun, I. and Balogun, A. (2014) "Urban heat island and bioclimatological conditions in a hot-humid tropical city: the example of Akure, Nigeria," *Die Erde*, 145(1/2): 3–15.

Banana, E., Chitekwe-Biti, B., and Walnycki, A. (2015) "Co-producing inclusive city-wide sanitation strategies: lessons from Chinhoyi, Zimbabwe," *Environment and Urbanization*, 27(1): 35–54.

Bassett, T. and Crummey, D. (eds) (2003) *African savannas: global narratives & local knowledge of environmental change*. Oxford: James Currey.

Bassett, T. and Koli Bi, Z. (2000) "Environmental discourses and the Ivorian savanna," *Annals of the Association of American Geographers*, 90(1): 67–95.

Bastian, M. (2001) "Vulture men, campus cultists and teenaged witches: modern magics in the Nigerian popular press," in H. Moore and T. Sanders (eds) *Magical interpretations, material realities: modernity, witchcraft and the occult in postcolonial Africa*. London: Routledge, pp 71–96.

Bayat, A. (2000) "From 'dangerous classes' to 'quiet rebels': politics of the urban subaltern in the Global South," *International Sociology*, 15: 533–57.

Bayat, A. (2013) *Life as politics: how ordinary people change the Middle East* (2nd edn). Stanford, CA: Stanford University Press.

BBC (British Broadcasting Corporation) (2015) "Kenya police fire tear gas on playground protest," *BBC Africa News*, 19 January. Available at: http://www.bbc.com/news/world-africa-30879938

Bekker, S. and Fourchard, L. (eds) (2013) *Governing cities in Africa: politics and policies*. Cape Town: HSRC Press.

Bekker, S. and Therborn, G. (eds) (2012) *Capital cities in Africa: power and powerlessness*. Cape Town: HSRC Press.

Belcher, W. (2007) "Indirect resistance: rhetorical strategies for evading power in colonial French West African novels by Camara Laye, Ferdinand Oyono, and Sembene Ousmane," *Lit: Literature Interpretation Theory*, 18(1): 65–87.

Benton-Short, L. and Short, J.R. (2013) *Cities and nature* (2nd edn). London: Routledge.

Bhabha, H. (1994) *The location of culture.* London: Routledge.

Biersack, A. (2006) "Reimagining political ecology: culture/power/history/nature," in A. Biersack and J. Greenberg (eds) *Reimagining political ecology.* Durham, NC: Duke University Press, pp 3–40.

Bigon, L. (2009) "Urban planning, colonial doctrines and street naming in French Dakar and British Lagos, *c.*1850–1930," *Urban History*, 36(3): 426–48.

Bigon, L. (2014) "From metropolitan to colonial planning: Dakar between garden city and cite- jardin," in L. Bigon and Y. Katz (eds) *Garden cities and colonial planning: transnationality and urban ideas in Africa and Palestine.* Manchester: Manchester University Press, pp 50–73.

Bigon, L. (2015) *French colonial Dakar: the morphogenesis of an African regional capital.* Manchester: Manchester University Press.

Bigon, L. and Katz, Y. (eds) (2014) *Garden cities and colonial planning: transnationality of urban ideas in Africa and Palestine.* Manchester: Manchester University Press.

Bjerkli, C. (2015) "Power in waste: conflicting agendas in planning for integrated solid waste management in Addis Ababa, Ethiopia," *Norsk Geografisk Tidsskrift—Norwegian Journal of Geography*, 69(1): 18–27.

Blaikie, P. (1995) "Changing environments or changing views? A political ecology for developing countries," *Geography*, 80(3): 203–14.

Boahen, A.A. (1970) "Introduction," to the novel by A. Armah, *God's bits of wood.* Garden City, NY: Anchor Books, pp 13–32.

Bocquet, D. (2015) "Reflections on public spaces in revolutionary and post-revolutionary Tunis," *Jadiliyya*, 17 April. Available at: http://www.jadaliyya.com/pages/index/21378/ (accessed 21 April 2015).

Bodewes, C. (2005) *Parish transformation in urban slums: voices of Kibera, Kenya.* Nairobi: Paulines Publications Africa.

Bond, P. (2000) *Cities of gold, townships of coal: Essays on South Africa's new urban crisis.* Trenton: Africa World Press.

Bontianti, A., Hungerford, H., Younsa, H., and Nouma, A. (2014) "Fluid experiences: comparing local adaptations to water inaccessibility in two disadvantaged neighborhoods in Niamey, Niger," *Habitat International*, 43: 283–92.

Boone, C. and Modarres, A. (2006) *City and environment.* Philadelphia, PA: Temple University Press.

Bousquet, A. (2010) "Water and the poor in Nairobi: from water apartheid to urban fragmentation—the case of Kibera," in H. Charton-Bigot and D. Rodrigues-Torres (eds) *Nairobi today: the paradox of a fragmented city*. Dar es Salaam: Mkuki na Nyota Publishers, pp 121–48.

Bradley, K. (1935) *Lusaka: the new capital of Northern Rhodesia*. London: Jonathan Cape.

Brockington, D. (2002) *Fortress conservation: the preservation of the Mkomazi Game Reserve Tanzania*. Oxford: James Currey.

Brudvig, I. (2014) *Conviviality in Bellville: an ethnography of space, place, mobility and being in urban South Africa*. Bamenda, Cameroon: Langaa Research & Publishing Common Initiative Group.

Bryceson, D. (2006) "Fragile cities: fundamentals of urban life in East and Southern Africa," in D. Bryceson and D. Potts (eds) *African urban economies: viability, vitality or vitiation?* New York, NY: Palgrave Macmillan, pp 3–38.

Buell, L. (1995) *The environmental imagination*. Cambridge: Belknap.

Bunnell, T. and Maringanti, A. (2010) "Practising urban and regional research beyond metrocentricity," *International Journal of Urban and Regional Research*, 34(2): 415–20.

Burugu, J. (2010) *The county: understanding devolution and governance in Kenya*. Nairobi: CLEAD International.

Caminero-Santangelo, B. (2014) *Different shades of green: African literature, environmental justice, and political ecology*. Charlottesville, VA, and London: University of Virginia Press.

Caminero-Santangelo, B. and Myers, G. (eds) (2011) *Environment at the margins: literary and environmental studies in Africa*. Athens, OH: Ohio University Press.

Cartwright, J. (2006) "The lie of the land," in S. Watson (ed) *Cape Town calling: a city imagined and the meanings of a place*. Johannesburg: Penguin, pp 197–203.

Charton-Bigot, H. (2010) "Preface," in H. Charton-Bigot and D. Rodrigues-Torres (eds) *Nairobi today: the paradox of a fragmented city*. Dar es Salaam: Mkuki na Nyota Publishers, pp ix–xii.

Chef du Village of Thiaroye Gare (2013) Author focus group interview with Chef du Village of Thiaroye Gare Commune d'arrondissement, Municipality of Pikine, Dakar, Senegal, with Tom Hanlon, Alasse Elhadji, four US undergraduate students, and staff of Partners Senegal, 7 January.

Cissé, O. (1996) "Participatory solid waste management: urban community of Dakar, Senegal," in R. Gilbert, D. Stevenson, H. Girardet, and R. Stren (eds) *Making cities work*. London: Earthscan.

Cissé, O. (ed) (2012) *Les décharges d'ordures en Afrique: Mbeubeuss à Dakar au Sénégal*. Paris: Karthala.

Clos, J. (2014) "Foreword," in UN Habitat (ed) *State of African cities report 2014*. Nairobi: UN Habitat, p. 3.

Coetzee, J.M. (1990) *Age of iron*. New York, NY: Random House.

Collier, P. and Venables, A. (2015) "Housing and urbanization in Africa: unleashing a formal market process," in E. Glaeser and A. Joshi-Ghani (eds) *The urban imperative: towards competitive cities*. New York, NY: Oxford University Press, pp 413–35.

Collins, J. (1977) "Lusaka: urban planning in a British colony," in G. Cherry (ed) *Shaping an urban world*. New York, NY: St. Martin's Press, pp 227–41.

Coquery-Vidrovitch, C. (2005) *The history of African cities south of the Sahara: from the origins to colonization*. Princeton, NJ: Markus Wiener.

CORES (Congo Real Estate Service) (2015) "La Cité du Fleuve and CORES announce their new partnership." Available at: http://www.cores.cd/en/la-cite-du-fleuve-and-cores-announce-their-new-partnership/ (accessed 16 February 2015).

Cornhill, L. (2013) Personal communication between author, Mushebe Subulwa, Angela Gray Subulwa, and Loreto Cornhill, sales agent, Silverest Gardens development, 14 June, Lusaka.

Cosgrove, D. (1989) "Geography is everywhere: culture and symbolism in human landscapes," in D. Gregory and R. Walford (eds) *Horizons in human geography*. Basingstoke: Macmillan Education, pp 118–35.

Couth, R. and Trois, C. (2010) "Carbon emissions reduction strategies in Africa from improved waste management: a review," *Waste Management*, 30: 2336–46.

Crowley, D. (2015) *Africa's narrative geographies: charting the intersections of geocriticism and postcolonial studies*. New York, NY: Palgrave Macmillan.

Crush, J. and Frayne, B. (2014) "Feeding African cities: the growing challenge of urban food insecurity," in S. Parnell and E. Pieterse (eds) *Africa's urban revolution*. London: Zed Books, pp 110–32.

Crush, J. and Ramachandran, S. (2014) *Migrant entrepreneurship, collective violence and xenophobia in South Africa*. Cape Town: Southern African Migration Programme.

Dahl, G. (1979) *Suffering grass: subsistence and society of Waso Borana*. Stockholm: Stockholm Studies in Social Anthropology, University of Stockholm.

Dahl, G. and Hjort, A. (1976) *Having herds: pastoral herd growth and household economy*. Stockholm: Stockholm Studies in Social Anthropology, University of Stockholm.

Dahl, G. and Hjort, A. (1979) *Pastoral change and the role of drought.* Stockholm: Swedish Agency for Research Cooperation with Developing Countries.

Daily Guide (2012) "Dying Korle Lagoon," *Daily Guide*, 2 June. Available at: http://www.modernghana.com/news/399206/1/dying-korle-lagoon.html

Dainese, E. (2014) "A new lesson from the territory of Bandiagara, Mali: the Dogon landscape transformation of the cliff," in R. Cavallo, S. Komossa, N. Marzot, M. Berghauser-Pont, and J. Kuijper (eds) *New urban configurations.* Amsterdam: Delft University Press, pp 897–903.

Davis, M. (2006) *Planet of slums.* London: Verso.

Deacon, G. (2012) "Pentecostalism and development in Kibera informal settlement," *Development in Practice*, 22: 663–74.

Debbané, A. and Keil, R. (2004) "Multiple disconnections: environmental justice and urban water in Canada and South Africa," *Space and Polity*, 8(2): 209–25.

De Boeck, F. (2011) "Inhabiting ocular ground: Kinshasa's future in the light of Congo's spectral urban politics," *Cultural Anthropology*, 26: 263–86.

De Boeck, F. (2012) "Spectral Kinshasa: building the city through an architecture of words," in T. Edensor and M. Jayne (eds) *Urban theory beyond the West: a world of cities.* London: Routledge, pp 311–28.

De Smedt, J. (2009) "'No Raila, no peace!' Big man politics and election violence at the Kibera grassroots," *African Affairs*, 108: 581–98.

Diallo, A. (2012) Author focus group interview with Abdourahmane Diallo, US Agency for International Development (with Tom Hanlon and four US undergraduate students), Dakar, 31 December.

Diop, A. (2012) "Dakar," in S. Bekker and G. Therborn (eds) *Capital cities in Africa: power and powerlessness.* Cape Town: HSRC Press, pp 32–44.

Diop, A.E. (2013) Author personal communication with Alasse El-Hadji Diop, Pikine, 4 January 2013.

Diop, B. (2013) Personal communication with Birame Diop, Partners Senegal, Dakar, 4 January.

Diouck A. (2013) Author's focus group interview with Alioune Diouck, Mayor of Djidah Thiaroye Kao Commune d'Arrondissement, City of Pikine, Dakar, with Tom Hanlon, Alasse Elhadji, four US undergraduate students, and staff members of Partners Senegal, 4 January, Pikine, Senegal.

Director, Centre Polyvalent de Thiaroye Gare (2013) Author's focus group interview with the Director of the Centre Polyvalent de Thiaroye Gare, City of Pikine, Dakar, with Tom Hanlon, Alasse Elhadji, four US undergraduate students, and staff members of Partners Senegal, 7 January, Pikine, Senegal.

Djiallo, D. (2013) Author focus group interview with Djibril Djiallo, President of the Djidah Thiaroye Kao coalition of community groups, with Tom Hanlon, Alasse Elhadji, four US undergraduate students, and staff members of Partners Senegal, 9 January, Pikine, Senegal.

Donald, J. (1999) *Imagining the modern city*. London: Athlone Press.

Douglas, I. (2013) *Cities: an environmental history*. London: IB Tauris.

Douglas, I. and James, P. (2015) *Urban ecology: an introduction*. New York, NY: Routledge.

Douglas, I., Alam, K., Maghenda, M., Mcdonnell, Y., McLean, L., and Campbell, J. (2008) "Unjust waters: climate change, flooding and the urban poor in Africa," *Environment and Urbanization*, 20(1): 187–205.

Doyle, R. (2014) "36 hours: Zanzibar, Tanzania," *The New York Times*, 1 May, p. TR9.

Dubresson, A. and Jaglin, S. (2014) "Governing Cape Town: the exhaustion of a negotiated transition," in D. Lorrain (ed) *Governing megacities in emerging countries*. Burlington, VT: Ashgate, pp 153–215.

Duncan, J. (1990) *The city as text*. Cambridge: Cambridge University Press.

Dutton, E. (1925) *The Basuto of Basutoland*. London: Jonathan Cape.

Dutton, E. (1929) *Kenya mountain*. London: Jonathan Cape.

Dutton, E. (1937) *The planting of trees and shrubs, with special reference to Northern Rhodesia*. Lusaka: Government Printers.

Dutton, E. (1949) "Introduction," in R.O. Williams (ed) *The useful and ornamental plants of Zanzibar and Pemba*. Zanzibar: Government of Zanzibar, pp 5–32.

Dutton, E. (1983) *The night of the hyena: memoirs of Eric Aldhelm Torlogh Dutton* (on microfilm). Oxford: Rhodes House Library.

EIU (Economist Intelligence Unit) (2011) *African green cities index: assessing the environmental performance of Africa's major cities*. Munich: Siemens AG.

El Mouelhi, H. (2013) "Culture and identity in Cairo urban development: a case study of Cairo's informal settlements," in A. Seifert (ed) *Global city local identity?* Dar es Salaam: Mkuki na Nyota Publishers, pp 94–107.

Epstein, A.L. (1958) *Politics in an urban African community*. Manchester: Manchester University Press.

Essaadani, A. (2014) Author personal communication with Aadel Essaadani, Steering Committee, Arterial Network, Casablanca, 3 April.

Etale, A. and Drake, D. (2013) "Industrial pollution and food safety in Kigali, Rwanda," *International Journal of Environmental Research*, 7(2): 403–6.

Ettler, V., Mihaljevic, M., Kríbek, B., Majer, V., and Šebek, O. (2011) "Tracing the spatial distribution and mobility of metal/metalloid contaminants in Oxisols in the vicinity of the Nkana copper smelter, Copperbelt province, Zambia," *Geoderma*, 164(1/2): 73–84.

Ettler, V., Kríbek, B., Majer, V., Knesl, I., and Mihaljevic, M. (2012) "Differences in the bioaccessibility of metals/metalloids in soils from mining and smelting areas (Copperbelt, Zambia)," *Journal of Geochemical Exploration*, 113: 68–75.

Ettler, V., Konecný, L., Kovárová, L., Mihaljevic, M., Šebek, O., Kríbek, B., Majer, V., Veselovský, F., Penízek, V., Vanek, A., and Nyambe, I. (2014) "Surprisingly contrasting metal distribution and fractionation patterns in copper smelter-affected tropical soils in forested and grassland areas (Mufulira, Zambian Copperbelt)," *Science of the Total Environment*, 473/474: 117–24.

Fair, L. (2001) *Pastimes and politics: culture, community, and identity in post-abolition urban Zanzibar, 1890–1945*. Athens, OH: Ohio University Press.

Fall, A. (2013) Author's focus group interview with Abdoulaye Fall, Vice-Mayor of Thiaroye Gare Commune d'Arrondissement, City of Pikine, Dakar, with Tom Hanlon, Alasse Elhadji, four US undergraduate students, and staff members of Partners Senegal, 7 January, Pikine, Senegal.

Fanshawe, D. (1962) *Fifty common trees of Northern Rhodesia*. Lusaka: Government Printers.

Farah, N. (2011) *Crossbones*. New York, NY: Penguin.

Farge, E. and Felix, B. (2014) "Beyond Burkina Faso, Africa's 'Black Spring' hopes may be premature," *Reuters*, 6 November. Available at: http://www.reuters.com/article/2014/11/06/us-burkina-politics-africa-analysis-idUSKBN0IQ1ZE20141106

Ferguson, J. (2006) *Global shadows: Africa in the neoliberal world order*. Durham, NC, and London: Duke University Press.

Fernandez, J. (2014) "Urban metabolism of the Global South," in S. Parnell and S. Oldfield (eds) *The Routledge handbook on cities of the Global South*. London and New York, NY: Routledge, pp 597–612.

Förster, T. (2013) On urbanity: creativity and emancipation in African urban life," in B. Obrist, V. Arlt, and E. Macamo (eds) *Living the city in Africa: processes of invention and intervention*. Zurich: Lit Verlag, pp 235–52.

Francis, R. and Chadwick, M. (2013) *Urban ecosystems: understanding the human environment*. London: Routledge.

Fraser, A. (2010) "Introduction: boom and bust on the Zambian Copperbelt," in A. Fraser and M. Larmer (eds) *Zambia, mining, and neoliberalism: boom and bust on the globalized Copperbelt*. New York, NY: Palgrave Macmillan, pp 1–30.

Fraser, A. and Larmer, M. (eds) (2010) *Zambia, mining, and neoliberalism: boom and bust on the globalized Copperbelt*. New York, NY: Palgrave Macmillan.

Fredericks, R. (2009) "Doing the dirty work: the cultural politics of garbage collection in Dakar, Senegal," unpublished PhD thesis, University of California, Berkeley, USA.

Fredericks, R. (2014) "'The old man is dead': Hip-Hop and the arts of citizenship of Senegalese youth," *Antipode*, 46(1): 130–48.

Fredericks, R. (2016) *Garbage citizenship: vibrant infrastructures of labor in Dakar, Senegal*. Athens, GA: University of Georgia Press.

Frederiksen, T. (2013) "Seeing the Copperbelt: science, mining and colonial power in Northern Rhodesia," *Geoforum*, 44: 271–81.

Freund, B. (2007) *The African city*. Cambridge: Cambridge University Press.

Gabriel, N. (2014) "Urban political ecology: environmental imaginary, governance, and the non-human," *Geography Compass*, 8(1): 38–48.

Gandy, M. (2008) "Cyborg urbanization: complexity and monstrosity in the contemporary city," *International Journal of Urban and Regional Research*, 29(1): 26–49.

Gatabaki-Kamau, R. and Karirah-Gitau, S. (2004) "Actors and interests: the development of an informal settlement in Nairobi, Kenya," in K. Hansen and M. Vaa (eds) *Reconsidering informality: perspectives from urban Africa*. Uppsala: Nordic Africa Institute, pp 158–75.

Gathanju, D. (2009) "Nairobi redraws its planning strategy," *Planning* (American Planning Association), July, pp 28–31.

Gendall, J. (2008) "Kibera public space project by Kounkuey design initiative: co-designing productive parks with the poorest of Kibera, Kenya," *Harvard Design Magazine*, 28: 67–9.

Gilbert, R., Stevenson, D., Girardet, H., and Stren, R. (eds) (1996) *Making cities work: role of local authorities in the urban environment*. London: Routledge.

Gilmer, B. (2014) *Political geographies of piracy: constructing threats and containing bodies in Somalia*. New York, NY: Palgrave Macmillan.

Gĩthĩnji, M. and Holmquist, F. (2012) "Reform and political impunity in Kenya: transparency without accountability," *African Studies Review*, 55: 53–74.

Githongo, J. (2010) "Fear and loathing in Nairobi: the challenge of reconciliation in Kenya," *Foreign Affairs*, 89: 2–9.

Glotfelty, C. and Fromm, H. (eds) (1996) *The ecocriticism reader: landmarks in literary ecology*. Athens, GA: University of Georgia Press.

GoDown Arts Centre and Kwani Trust (2009) *Kenya burning: Mgogoro baada ya uchaguzi 2007* [*The trouble after the 2007 election*]. Nairobi: The GoDown Arts Centre and Kwani Trust.

Gomba, O. (2013) "Niger Delta dystopia and environmental despoliation in Tanure Ojaide's Poetry," in O. Okuyade (ed) *Ecocritical literature: regreening African landscapes*. Lagos: African Heritage Press, pp 239–58.

Goodfellow, T. and Smith, A. (2013) "From urban catastrophe to 'model' city? Politics, security and development in post-conflict Kigali," *Urban Studies*, 50(15): 3185–202.

Gössling, S. (2001) "The consequences of tourism for sustainable water use on a tropical island: Zanzibar, Tanzania," *Journal of Environmental Management*, 61(2): 179–91.

Gössling, S. (2002a) "The political ecology of tourism in Zanzibar," in S. Gössling (ed) *Tourism and development in tropical islands: political ecology perspectives*. London: Edward Elgar.

Gössling, S. (2002b) "Human–environmental relations with tourism," *Annals of Tourism Research*, 29(4): 539–56.

Government of Kenya (2008a) *Nairobi metro 2030: a world class African metropolis*. Nairobi: Ministry of Nairobi Metropolitan Development, Republic of Kenya.

Government of Kenya (2008b) *Kenya vision 2030: a globally competitive and prosperous Kenya: first medium term plan (2008–2012)*. Nairobi: Office of the Prime Minister, Government of the Republic of Kenya.

Government of Kenya (2011) *Development of a spatial planning concept for Nairobi metropolitan region*. Nairobi: Ministry of Nairobi Metropolitan Development, Republic of Kenya.

Grant, R. (2009) *Globalizing city: the urban and economic transformation of Accra, Ghana*. Syracuse: Syracuse University Press.

Grant, R. (2015) *Africa: geographies of change*. Oxford and New York, NY: Oxford University Press.

Gray, J. (1963) "Zanzibar and the coastal belt, 1840–1884," in R. Oliver and G. Mathew (eds) *History of East Africa*. Oxford: Clarendon Press.

Green, L. (ed) (2013) *Contested ecologies: dialogues in the South on nature and knowledge.* Cape Town: HSRC Press.

Gridoux, M. (2012) "Trois questions á Khalifa Sall, maire de Dakar" ["Three questions for Khalifa Sall, Mayor of Dakar"], *African Business,* 25(December): 86.

Grove, R. (1995) *Green imperialism.* Cambridge: Cambridge University Press.

Gulyani, S., Bassett, E., and Talukdar, D. (2012) "Living conditions, rents, and their determinants in the slums of Nairobi and Dakar," *Land Economics,* 88: 251–74.

Gurney, K. (2014) "Cape Town: edge design," *Cityscapes,* 5: 34–49.

Gurney, K. (2015) "The conservationist: Luzann Isaacs manages a wetland park in a low-income urban area," *Cityscapes,* 6: 152–64.

Hake, A. (1977) *African metropolis: Nairobi's self-help city.* London: Sussex University Press.

Hall, T. and Hubbard, P. (1996) "The entrepreneurial city: new urban politics, new urban geographies?" *Progress in Human Geography,* 20: 153–74.

Hampwaye, G. (2005) "Decentralization and public service provision in Zambia: Lusaka's new solid waste management system," *Africa Insight,* 35(4): 80–9.

Hampwaye, G. and Rogerson, C. (2010) "Economic restructuring in the Zambian Copperbelt: local responses in Ndola," *Urban Forum,* 21(4): 387–403.

Hansen, K. (1997) *Keeping house in Lusaka.* New York, NY: Columbia University Press.

Harbeson, J. (2012) "Land and the quest for a democratic state in Kenya: bringing citizens back in," *African Studies Review,* 55: 15–30.

Hardoy, J., Mitlin, D., and Satterthwaite, D. (2001) *Environmental problems in an urbanizing world: finding solutions in cities in Africa, Asia and Latin America.* London: Earthscan.

Harrison, P. (2006) "On the edge of reason: planning and urban futures in Africa," *Urban Studies,* 43: 319–35.

Hart, G. (2010) "Redrawing the map of the world? Reflections on the *World development report 2009*," *Economic Geography,* 86(4): 341–50.

Harvey, D. (1996) *Justice, nature, and the geography of difference.* Oxford: Blackwell.

Harvey, D. (2012) *Rebel cities: from the right to the city to the urban revolution.* London: Verso.

Heynen, N., Kaika, M., and Swyngedouw, E. (eds) (2006) *In the nature of cities: urban political ecology and the politics of urban metabolism.* London: Routledge.

Hiemstra-van der Horst, G. and Hovorka, A. (2008) "Reassessing the 'energy ladder': household energy use in Maun, Botswana," *Energy Policy*, 36(9): 3333–44.

Hiemstra-van der Horst, G. and Hovorka, A. (2009) "Fuelwood: the 'other' renewable energy source for Africa?" *Biomass and Bioenergy*, 33(11): 1605–16.

Hodge, J. (2007) *Triumph of the expert: agrarian doctrines of development and legacies of British colonialism*. Athens, OH: Ohio University Press.

Home, R. (1997) *Of planting and planning: the making of British colonial cities*. London: Spon.

Honey, M. (1999) *Ecotourism and sustainable development: who owns paradise?* Washington, DC: Island Press.

Horton, M. (1996) *Shanga: the archaeology of a Muslim trading community on the coast of East Africa*. London: The British Institute in Eastern Africa.

Horton, M. and Middleton, J. (2000) *The Swahili: the social landscape of a mercantile society*. Oxford: Blackwell.

Hou, J., Spencer, B., Way, T., and Yocom, K. (eds) (2015) *Now urbanism: the future city is here*. New York, NY: Routledge.

Hovorka, A. (2006) "The No. 1 ladies' poultry farm: a feminist political ecology of urban agriculture in Botswana," *Gender, Place and Culture*, 13(3): 207–25.

Howden, D. (2013) "Terror in Westgate mall: the full story of the attacks that devastated Kenya," *The Guardian*, 4 October. Available at: http://www.theguardian.com/world/interactive/2013/oct/04/westgate-mall-attacks-kenya-terror

Huchzermeyer, M. (2011) *Tenement cities: from 19th century Berlin to 21st century Nairobi*. Trenton, NJ: Africa World Press.

Human Rights Watch (2008) *Law and reality: progress in judicial reform in Rwanda*. New York, NY: Human Rights Watch.

Hungerford, H. (2012) "Water, cities, and bodies: a relational understanding of Niamey, Niger," unpublished PhD thesis, Department of Geography, University of Kansas, USA.

Huxley, E. (1983) "Introduction," in *The night of the hyena: memoirs of Eric Aldhelm Torlogh Dutton* (on microfilm). Oxford: Rhodes House Library.

Imam, A., Mohammed, B., Wilson, D., and Cheeseman, C. (2008) "Solid waste management in Abuja, Nigeria," *Waste Management*, 28(2): 468–72.

Ingrams, W. (1931) *Zanzibar: its history and its peoples*. New York, NY: Barnes and Noble.

Ismael, S. (2015) *The Victoria Mxenge housing project: women building communities through social activism and informal learning*. Cape Town: UCT Press.

Jackson, P. (1989) *Maps of meaning: an introduction to cultural geography*. Winchester, MA: Unwin Hyman.

Jaeger, D. and Hackabay, J.D. (1986) "The garden city of Lusaka: urban agriculture," in G. Williams (ed) *Lusaka and its environs: a geographical study of a planned capital city in tropical Africa*. Lusaka: Zambia Geographical Association, pp 267–77.

James, R. (1961) *Lawns, trees and shrubs in Central Africa*. Cape Town: Purnell and Sons.

Janzen, J. (1978) *The quest for therapy in Lower Zaire*. Berkeley, CA: University of California Press.

Janzen, J. (1992) *Ngoma: discourses of healing in Central and Southern Africa*. Berkeley, CA: University of California Press.

Jonas, A., McCann, E., and Thomas, M. (2015) *Urban geography: a critical introduction*. Malden, MA: Wiley Blackwell.

Jones, O. and Cloke, P. (2002) *Tree cultures: the place of trees and trees in their place*. London: Berg.

Joseph, M. (2013) *Fluid New York: cosmopolitan urbanism and the green imagination*. Durham, NC: Duke University Press.

Juma, M. (2009) "African mediation of the Kenyan post-2007 election crisis," *Journal of Contemporary African Studies*, 27: 407–30.

Juma, S. (2014) Personal communications between author and Sheha Mjaja Juma, Department of Environment, Revolutionary Government of Zanzibar.

Jumbe, A. (2014) Personal communications between author and Aboud Jumbe, Department of Environment, Revolutionary Government of Zanzibar.

Kaberia, T. (2015) "Brutal police attack on pupils does not augur well for our rights and freedoms," *Daily Nation* (Nairobi), 20 January. Available at: http://www.nation.co.ke/oped/Opinion/-/440808/2596240/-/474xo8z/-/index.html

Kaika, M. (2005) *City of flows: modernity, nature and the city*. London: Routledge.

Kaika, M. and Swyngedouw, E. (2011) "The urbanization of nature: great promises, impasse, and new beginnings," in G. Bridge and S. Watson (eds) *The new companion to the city*. Oxford: Wiley-Blackwell, pp 96–107.

Kameri-Mbote, P. (2012) Author interview with Patricia Kameri-Mbote, Professor of Law, Strathmore University, Nairobi, 30 July.

Kanyinga, K. and Long, J. (2012) "The political economy of reforms in Kenya: the post-2007 election violence and a new constitution," *African Studies Review*, 55: 31–51.

Kapungwe, E. (2011) "Industrial land use and heavy metal contaminated wastewater used for irrigation in peri-urban Zambia," *Singapore Journal of Tropical Geography*, 32(1): 71–84.

Kapungwe, E. (2013) Personal communication with Evaristo Kapungwe, lecturer in geography, University of Zambia, Lusaka, 18 June.

Karani, P. and Jewasikiewitz, S. (2007) "Waste management and sustainable development in South Africa," *Environment, Development and Sustainability*, 9(2): 163–85.

Kassim, S. and Ali, M. (2006) "Solid waste collection by the private sector: households' perspective—findings from a study in Dar es Salaam City, Tanzania," *Habitat International*, 30(4): 769–80.

Katumanga, M. (2010) "A city under siege: formalised banditry and deconstruction of modes of accumulation in Nairobi, 1991–2004," in H. Charton-Bigot and D. Rodrigues-Torres (eds) *Nairobi today: the paradox of a fragmented city*. Dar es Salaam: Mkuki na Nyota Publishers, pp 327–49.

Katzschner, T. (2013) "Cape Flats nature: rethinking urban ecologies," in Lesley Green (ed) *Contested ecologies: dialogues in the South on nature and knowledge*. Cape Town: HSRC Press, pp 202–26.

Keil, R. (2003) "Progress report: urban political ecology," *Urban Geography*, 26: 640–51.

Keil, R. (2005) "Urban political ecology: a progress report," *Urban Geography*, 24: 723–38.

Keil, R. (2011) "Frontiers of urban political ecology," in M. Gandy (ed) *Urban constellations*. Berlin: jovis Verlag GmbH, pp 26–30.

Keil, R. and Ali, S.H. (2011) "The urban political pathology of emerging infectious disease in the age of the global city," in E. McCann and K. Ward (eds) *Mobile urbanism: cities and policymaking in the global age*. Minneapolis, MN: University of Minnesota Press, pp 123–45.

Keil, R. and Graham, S. (1998) "Reasserting nature: constructing urban environments after Fordism," in B. Braun and N. Castree (eds) *Remaking reality: nature at the millennium*. London: Routledge, pp 98–124.

Khale, S. and Worku, Z. (2013) "Factors that affect municipal service delivery in Gauteng and North West Provinces of South Africa," *African Journal of Science, Technology, Innovation and Development*, 5(1): 61–70.

Kiberenge, K. (2014) "Why 'city in the sun' is losing its shine," *Daily Nation*, 9 March. Available at: http://www.nation.co.ke/lifestyle (accessed 10 March 2014).

Killian, B. (2008) "The state and identity politics in Zanzibar: challenges to democratic consolidation in Tanzania," *African Identities*, 6(2): 99–125.

Kingoriah, G. (1983) "The causes of Nairobi's city structure," *Ekistics*, 301: 246–54.

Kingsley, P. (2013) "80 sexual assaults in one day—the other story of Tahrir Square," *The Guardian* (Manchester), 5 July. Available at: http://www.theguardian.com/world/2013/jul/05/egypt-women-rape-sexual-assault-tahrir-square (accessed 17 April 2015).

Kinuthia, M. (1992) "Slum clearance and the informal economy in Nairobi," *Journal of Modern African Studies*, 30: 221–36.

Kithakye, D. (2011) *Resettlement policy framework for Nairobi metropolitan services improvement project*. Nairobi: Ministry of Nairobi Metropolitan Development, Republic of Kenya.

Klopp, J. (2012) "Towards a political economy of transportation policy and practice in Nairobi," *Urban Forum*, 23: 1–21.

Kozain, R. (2013) "A brief history of throwing shit," *Chimurenga Chronic*, November 2013, p 3.

Kríbek, B., Mihaljevic, M., Sracek, O., Knesl, I., Ettler, V., and Nyambe, I. (2011) "The extent of arsenic and of metal uptake by aboveground tissues of *Pteris vittata* and *Cyperus involucratus* growing in copper- and cobalt-rich tailings of the Zambian Copperbelt," *Archives of Environmental Contamination and Toxicology*, 61(2): 228–42.

Kushner, J. (2013) "Income inequality: in Congo, a tale of two cities," Pulitzer Center on Crisis Reporting, 28 March. Available at: http://pulitzercenter.org/reporting/DRC-congo-kinshasa-income-inequality-a-tale-two-cities

Kusimba, C. (1999) *The rise and fall of Swahili states*. Walnut Creek, CA: AltaMira.

Kusimba, C., Kusimba, S., and Dussubieux, L. (2013) "Beyond the coastalscapes: preindustrial social and political networks in East Africa," *African Archeological Review*, 30(4): 399–426.

Larsen, K. (2005) *Where humans and spirits meet: the politics of rituals and identified spirits in Zanzibar*. New York, NY: Berghahn Books.

Larsen, K. (2014a) "Possessing spirits and bodily transformation in Zanzibar: reflections on ritual, performance, and aesthetics," *Journal of Ritual Studies*, 28(1): 15–29.

Larsen, K. (2014b) "Bodily selves: identity and shared realities among humans and spirits in Zanzibar," *Journal of Religion in Africa*, 44: 5–27.

Lauer, H. and Anyidoho, K. (eds) (2012) *Reclaiming the human sciences and humanities through African perspectives*. Accra, Ghana: Sub-Saharan Publishers.

Lawhon, M. (2012) "Relational power in the governance of a South African e-waste transition," *Environment and Planning A*, 44: 954–71.

Lawhon, M. (2013) "Situated, networked environmentalisms: a case for environmental theory from the South," *Geography Compass*, 7(2): 128–38.

Lawhon, M., Ernstson, H., and Silver, J. (2014) "Provincializing urban political ecology: towards a situated UPE through African urbanism," *Antipode*, 46(2): 497–516.

Lawhon, M., Silver, J., and Ernstson, H. (2015) "Politicizing urban ecologies: traveling theory as a postcolonial sensibility in African cities," unpublished working paper.

Lawson, V. (2010) "Reshaping economic geography? Producing spaces of inclusive development," *Economic Geography*, 86(4): 351–60.

LeBas, A. (2013) "Violence and urban order in Nairobi, Kenya and Lagos, Nigeria," *Studies in Comparative International Development*, 48: 240–62.

Liebs, V., Bikandu, B., Kanda, L., Lukoki, F., Schareika, N., and Fruth, B. (2013) "Signifying competence: herbalists in Kinshasa's urban context," in B. Obrist, V. Arlt, and E. Macamo (eds) *Living the city in Africa: processes of invention and intervention*. Zurich: Lit Verlag, pp 213–33.

Limo, E. (ed) (2011) *Metro bulletin*. Nairobi: Ministry of Nairobi Metropolitan Development, Republic of Kenya.

Livable Cities (2011) "Tahrir Square and the birth of democracy? Demonstrations on Tahrir Square," *Livable Cities*, 11 February. Available at: http://www.livablecities.org/articles/tahrir-square-and-birth-democracy (accessed 17 April 2015).

Loftus, A. (2012) *Everyday environmentalism: creating an urban political ecology*. Minneapolis, MN: University of Minnesota Press.

Louw, A. (2013) Author's focus group interview with Allah Louw, mechanic, resident of Djidah Thiaroye Kao, City of Pikine, Dakar, with Tom Hanlon, Alasse Elhadji, four US undergraduate students, and staff members of Partners Senegal, 9 January.

Maathai, W. (2006) *Unbowed: a memoir*. New York, NY: Anchor.

Mabandla, N. (2006) "The mist, the wind, and the two oceans," in S. Watson (ed) *Cape Town calling: a city imagined and the meanings of a place*. Johannesburg: Penguin, pp 184–96.

Macamo, E. (2013) "Living effervescence: the social in African urban settings," in B. Obrist, V. Arlt, and E. Macamo (eds) *Living the city in Africa: processes of invention and intervention.* Zurich: Lit Verlag, pp 291–7.

Macmillan, H. (1993) "The historiography of transition on the Zambian Copperbelt—another view," *Journal of Southern African Studies,* 19(4): 681–712.

Macmillan, H. (2012) "Mining, housing and welfare in South Africa and Zambia: an historical perspective," *Journal of Contemporary African Studies,* 30(4): 539–50.

Mamabolo, M. (2012) *Sauti! Moral and spiritual challenges facing 21st century Africa.* Braamfontein: Dalro and University of South Africa Press.

Manji, A. (2015) "Bulldozers, homes and highways: Nairobi and the right to the city," *Review of African Political Economy,* 42(2): 206–24.

Martinez-Alier, J. (2003) *The environmentalism of the poor: a study in ecological conflicts and valuation.* Northampton, MA: Edward Elgar.

Massaburi, D. (2015) Author's personal communication with Dr Didas Massaburi, Mayor of Dar es Salaam, Tanzania, 9 June, Berlin.

Matador (2013) Author's focus group interview with the rapper Matador at Africulturban, in Pikine West, City of Pikine, Dakar, with Tom Hanlon, Alasse Elhadji, four US undergraduate students, and staff members of Partners Senegal, 9 January.

Mawere, M. (2014a) *Culture, indigenous knowledge and development in Africa: reviving interconnections for sustainable development.* Bamenda, Cameroon: Langaa Research & Publishing Common Initiative Group.

Mawere, M. (2014b) *Environmental conservation though Ubuntu and other emerging perspectives.* Bamenda, Cameroon: Langaa Research & Publishing Common Initiative Group.

Mawere, M. and Mubaya, T. (eds) (2014) *African cultures, memory and space: living in the past presence in Zimbabwean heritage.* Bamenda, Cameroon: Langaa Research & Publishing Common Initiative Group.

Mbaye, M. (2013) Author focus group interview with Miriam Mbaye, Head of the Women's Association of Djidah Thiaroye Kao, with Tom Hanlon, Alasse Elhadji, four US undergraduate students, and staff members of Partners Senegal, 9 January, Pikine, Senegal.

Mbaye, J. (2014) "Hip hop politics: recognizing Southern complexity," in S. Parnell and S. Oldfield (eds) *The Routledge handbook on cities of the Global South.* London: Routledge, pp 396–412.

Mboya, J. (2014) "*Nai ni who? (Who is Nairobi?)*: collective urban vision development," in Centre for Fine Arts, Brussels (BOZAR) (eds) *Visionary urban Africa: built environment and cultural spaces for democracy.* Brussels: BOZAR, pp 66–71.

Mbuya, M. (2014) Author personal communication with Dar es Salaam's bicycle rights and environmental activist Mejah Mbuya, Hartford, CT, 5 April.

McGregor, J. (2005) "Crocodile crimes: people versus wildlife and the politics of postcolonial conservation on Lake Kariba, Zimbabwe," *Geoforum,* 36: 353–69.

Médard, C. (2010) "City planning in Nairobi: the stakes, the people, the sidetracking," in H. Charton-Bigot and D. Rodrigues-Torres (eds) *Nairobi today: the paradox of a fragmented city.* Dar es Salaam: Mkuki na Nyota Publishers, pp 25–60.

Melly, C. (2010) "Inside-out houses: urban belonging and imagined futures in Dakar, Senegal," *Comparative Studies in Society and History,* 52(1): 37–65.

Meyer, W. (2013) *The environmental advantages of cities: countering commonsense antiurbanism.* Cambridge: MIT Press.

Mihaljevic, M., Ettler, V., Šebek, O., Sracek, O., Kríbek, B., Kyncl, T., Majer, V., and Veselovský, F. (2011) "Lead isotopic and metallic pollution record in tree rings from the Copperbelt mining-smelting area, Zambia," *Water, Air, and Soil Pollution,* 216(1–4): 657–68.

Miller, C. (2012) "Development on the margins: Rwanda alternative grassroots economic policies," unpublished PhD dissertation, University of Kansas, USA.

Mitchell, J.C. (1956) *The Kalela dance: aspects of social relationships among urban Africans in Northern Rhodesia.* Manchester: Rhodes-Livingstone Institute.

Mohamed, S. (2015) Author personal communication with Salim Mohamed, co-founder, Carolina for Kibera (Nairobi), 9 March.

Moore, D. (1993) "Contesting terrain in Zimbabwe's Eastern Highlands: political ecology, ethnography, and peasant resource struggles," *Economic Geography,* 69(4): 380–401.

Moore, H. and Vaughan, M. (1994) *Cutting down trees: gender, nutrition and agricultural change in the Northern Province of Zambia, 1890–1990.* Portsmouth, NH: Heinemann.

Muchadenyika, D. (2015) "Slum upgrading and inclusive municipal governance in Harare, Zimbabwe: new perspectives for the urban poor," *Habitat International,* 48: 1–10.

Muema, R. (2012) Author interview with Rose Muema, Deputy Director, City Planning, City Council of Nairobi, 26 July.

References

Muhajir, M. (2011) "How planning works in an age of reform: land sustainability and housing development traditions in Zanzibar," unpublished doctoral dissertation, University of Kansas, USA.

Mulenga, A. (2013) "Two die in ZNS operation to remove squatters," *Saturday Post* (Lusaka), 15 June, p 4.

Murunga, G. (1999) "Urban violence in Kenya's transition to pluralist politics, 1982–1992," *Africa Development*, 24(1): 65–88.

Murunga, G. and Nasong'o, S. (2006) "Bent on self-destruction: the Kibaki regime in Kenya," *Journal of Contemporary African Studies*, 24: 1–28.

Mususa, P. (2012) "Mining, welfare and urbanisation: the wavering urban character of Zambia's Copperbelt," *Journal of Contemporary African Studies*, 30(4): 571–87.

Mwalimu, M.S. (2006) Author interview with Mwalimu S. Mwalimu, then Principle Secretary, Minister of Water, Energy, Construction and Lands, Revolutionary Government of Zanzibar, 22 June.

Mwelu, K. (2012) "A city's dilemma: settlement demolitions and evictions," *UIPNews* (Newsletter of the Centre for Urban Research and Innovations, Nairobi), January–June, pp 1–3.

Mwikya, K. (2013) "The politics of protest," *Chimurenga Chronic*, November, pp 24–5.

Myers, G. (1986) "Pastoralism and capitalism in Kenya: a spatial perspective on the articulation of modes of production," unpublished MA thesis, University of California, Los Angeles, USA.

Myers, G. (1999) "Political ecology and urbanization: Zanzibar's construction materials industry," *Journal of Modern African Studies*, 37(1): 83–108.

Myers, G. (2002a) "Colonial geography and masculinity in Eric Dutton's *Kenya Mountain*," *Gender, Place and Culture*, 9(1): 23–38.

Myers, G. (2002b) "Local communities and the new environmental planning: a case study from Zanzibar," *Area*, 34(2): 149–59.

Myers, G. (2003) *Verandahs of power: colonialism and space in urban Africa.* Syracuse, NY: Syracuse University Press.

Myers, G. (2005a) *Disposable cities: garbage, governance, and sustainable development in urban Africa.* Aldershot: Ashgate.

Myers, G. (2005b) "Place and humanistic African cultural geography: a Tanzanian case," *Journal of Cultural Geography*, 22(2): 1–26.

Myers, G. (2006) "The unauthorized city: late colonial Lusaka and post-colonial geography," *Singapore Journal of Tropical Geography*, 27(3): 289–308.

Myers, G. (2008) "Peri-urban land reform, political-economic reform, and urban political ecology in Zanzibar," *Urban Geography*, 29(3): 264–88.

Myers, G. (2009) "Naming and placing the other: power and the urban landscape in Zanzibar," in L. Berg and J. Vuolteenaho (eds) *Critical toponymies: the contested politics of place naming*. Farnham and Burlington, VT: Ashgate, pp 85–100.

Myers, G. (2010) "Social construction of peri-urban places and alternative planning in Zanzibar," *African Affairs*, 109(437): 575–95.

Myers, G. (2011) *African cities: alternative visions of urban theory and practice*. London: Zed Books.

Myers, G. (2014) "From expected to unexpected comparisons: changing the flows of ideas about cities in a post-colonial urban world," *Singapore Journal of Tropical Geography*, 35(1): 104–18.

Myers, G. (2015a) "Remaking the edges: surveillance and flows in sub-Saharan Africa's new suburbs," in A. Luescher and C. Loeb (eds) *The design of frontier spaces: control and ambiguity*. Aldershot: Ashgate.

Myers, G. (2015b) "A world-class city region? Envisioning the Nairobi of 2030," *American Behavioral Scientist*, published online 29 September, 59(3): 328-346.

Myers, G. (2016) "African ideas of the urban," in J. Hannigan and G. Richards (eds) *The handbook of new urban studies*. London: Sage.

Myers, G. and Muhajir, M.A. (2013) "'Wiped from the map of the world'? Zanzibar, critical geopolitics and language," *Geopolitics*, 18(3): 663–81.

Myers, G. and Subulwa, A. (2014) "Narrating Zambia from Lusaka and Mongu," unpublished paper presented at the annual meeting of the Association of American Geographers, 9 April, Tampa, FL.

Myers, G., Owusu, F., and Subulwa A. (2012) "Cities of sub-Saharan Africa," in S. Brunn, M. Hays-Mitchell, and D. Zeigler (eds) *Cities of the world* (5th edn). Lanham, MD: Rowman and Littlefield, pp 331–79.

Nahman, A. and Godfrey, L. (2010) "Economic instruments for solid waste management in South Africa: opportunities and constraints," *Resources, Conservation and Recycling*, 54(8): 521–31.

Nakayama, S., Ikenaka, Y., Hamada, K., Muzandu, K., Choongo, K., Yabe, J., Umemura, T., and Ishizuka, M. (2013) "Accumulation and biological effects of metals in wild rats in mining areas of Zambia," *Environmental Monitoring and Assessment*, 185(6): 4907–18.

Nchito, W. (2007) "Flood risk in unplanned settlements," *Environment and Urbanization*, 19(2): 539–51.

Nchito, W. (2013) Personal communication with Wilma Nchito, lecturer in geography, University of Zambia, 26 June, Lusaka.

Nchito, W. and Myers, G. (2004) "Four caveats for participatory solid waste management in Lusaka," *Urban Forum*, 15(2): 109–33.

Ndjio, B. (2006) "Douala: inventing life in an African necropolis," in M. Murray and G. Myers (eds) *Cities in contemporary Africa*. New York, NY: Palgrave Macmillan, pp 103–18.

Negi, R. (2013) "'You cannot make a camel drink water': capital, geo-history and contestations in the Zambian Copperbelt," *Geoforum*, 45: 240–7.

Negi, R. (2014) "'Solwezi mabanga': ambivalent developments on Zambia's new mining frontier," *Journal of Southern African Studies*, 40(5): 999–1013.

Nel, P. (2014) "African spirituality and space," in P. Post, P. Nel, and W. Van Beek (eds) *Sacred spaces and contested identities: space and ritual dynamics in Europe and Africa*. Trenton: Africa World Press, pp 279–300.

Neumann, R. (1998) *Imposing wilderness*. Berkeley and Los Angeles, CA: University of California Press.

Ngau, P. (2012) Personal communication with Peter Ngau, professor of urban planning, University of Nairobi, 21 July, Nairobi.

Ngau, P. (2013) *For town and country: a new approach to urban planning in Kenya*. Africa Research Institute, Policy Voices Paper Series. London: Africa Research Institute.

Niang, A. (2013) Personal communication with Abdoulaye Niang, Partners Senegal, Dakar, 4 January.

Niang, N. (2013) Author focus group interview with Ndeye Niang, women's NGO activist, Djidah Thiaroye Kao, with Tom Hanlon, Alasse Elhadji, four US undergraduate students, and staff members of Partners Senegal, 9 January, Pikine, Senegal.

Nixon, R. (2011a) *Slow violence and the environmentalism of the poor*. Cambridge: Harvard University Press.

Nixon, R. (2011b) "Slow violence, gender, and the environmentalism of the poor," in B. Caminero-Santangelo and G. Myers (eds) *Environment at the margins: literary and environmental studies in Africa*. Athens, OH: Ohio University Press, pp 257–85.

Njeru, J. (2006) "The urban political ecology of plastic bag waste problems in Nairobi, Kenya," *Geoforum*, 37: 1046–58.

Njeru, J. (2010) "Defying democratization and environmental protection in Kenya: the case of Karura Forest Reserve in Nairobi," *Political Geography*, 29(6): 333–42.

Njeru, J. (2012) "Mobilization and protest: the struggle to save Karura Forest in Nairobi, Kenya," *African Geographical Review*, 31(1): 17–32.

Njeru, J. (2013) "'Donor-driven' neoliberal reform processes and urban environmental change in Kenya: the case of Karura Forest in Nairobi," *Progress in Development Studies*, 13(1): 63–78.

Njeru, J., Johnston-Anumonwo, I., and Owuor, S. (2014) "Gender equity and commercialization of public toilet services in Nairobi, Kenya," in A. Oberhauser and I. Johnston-Anumonwo (eds) *Global perspectives on gender and space*. New York, NY: Routledge, pp 17–34.

Njoh, A. (2003) *Planning in contemporary Africa: the state, town planning and society in Cameroon*. Aldershot: Ashgate.

Njoh, A. (2012) *Urban planning and public health in Africa: historical, theoretical and practical dimensions of a continent's water and sanitation problematic*. Burlington, VT: Ashgate.

Njoh, A. (forthcoming) "The meta indigenous politico-administrative system, good governance and the modern republican state in Cameroon," *Journal of Asian and African Studies*.

Njoroge, M. (2009) "Interview with Kenyan architect Maranga Njoroge, by Berend van der Lans," *ArchiAfrika Newsletter*, September 2009, pp 2-3.

Nuttall, S. and Mbembe, A. (eds) (2008) *Johannesburg: the elusive metropolis*. Durham, NC: Duke University Press.

Nyirenda, M. (2013) Author interview with Gardens Department Director M. Nyirenda, Lusaka City Council, 11 July, with Angela Gray Subulwa and Mushebe Subulwa.

Nzeadibe, T. (2013) "Informal waste management in Africa: perspectives and lessons from Nigerian garbage geographies," *Geography Compass*, 7(10): 729–44.

Nzeadibe, T. and Mbah, P. (2015) "Beyond urban vulnerability: interrogating the social sustainability of a livelihood in the informal economy of Nigerian cities," *Review of African Political Economy*, 42(2): 279–98.

Obiechina, E. (1975) *Culture, tradition and society in the West African novel*. Cambridge: Cambridge University Press.

Obudho, R. (1997) "Nairobi: national capital and regional hub," in C. Rakodi (ed) *The urban challenge in Africa: growth and management of its large cities*. Tokyo: United Nations University, pp 292–335.

Odbert, C. and Mulligan, J. (2015) "The Kibera public space project: participation, integration, and networked change," in J. Hou, B. Spencer, T. Way, and K. Yocom (eds) *Now urbanism: the future city is here*. New York, NY: Routledge, pp 177–92.

Odongo, P. (2012) "Residents kill six lions in Kitengela," *Daily Nation* (Nairobi), 20 June. Available at: http://www.nation.co.ke/news/Residents-kill-six-lions-in-Kitengela/-/1056/1431358/-/12bujhgz/-/index.html

Odongo, P.T. (2012) Author interview with Patrick Tom Odongo, Director, City Planning, City Council of Nairobi, 26 July.

Odumusu, H. (2015) Author personal communication with H.E. Odumusu, Deputy Police Commissioner, Lagos, 9 March.

Oirere, S. (2012) "Nairobi commuter rail extension opens," *International Railway Journal*, 14 November.

Ojaide, T. (2013) "Forward," in O. Okuyade (ed) *Eco-critical literature: regreening African landscapes*. Lagos: African Heritage Press, pp v–viii.

Okolo, I. (2013) "Landscaping as a plot and character development medium in Ngugi wa Thiong'o's *Wizard of the crow*," in O. Okuyade (ed) *Eco-critical literature: regreening African landscapes*. Lagos: African Heritage Press, pp 15–30.

Okoyea, C. (2014) "An evaluation of the evolved African conception of the environment," *African Identities*, 12(2): 139–51.

Okurut, K. and Charles, K. (2014) "Household demand for sanitation improvements in low-income informal settlements: a case of East African cities," *Habitat International*, 44: 332–8.

Okuyade, O. (ed) (2013) *Eco-critical literature: regreening African landscapes*. New York, NY, and Lagos: Africa Heritage Press.

Olukoshi, A. and Nyamnjoh, F. (2011) "The postcolonial turn: an introduction," in R. Devisch and F. Nyamnjoh (eds) *The post-colonial turn: re-imagining anthropology and Africa*. Bemenda, Cameroon, and Leiden, Netherlands: Langaa Research Group and African Studies Centre, pp 1–27.

Oruka, O. and Juma, C. (1994) "Ecophilosophy and parental ethics," in O. Oruka (ed) *Philosophy, humanity and ecology: philosophy of nature and environmental ethics*. Nairobi: African Centre for Technology Studies.

Oteng-Ababio, M. (2010) "Private sector involvement in solid waste management in the Greater Accra Metropolitan Area in Ghana," *Waste Management & Research*, 28(4): 322–9.

Otiso, K. (2002) "Forced evictions in Kenyan cities," *Singapore Journal of Tropical Geography*, 23: 252–67.

Owuor, S. and Mbatia, T. (2012) "Nairobi," in S. Bekker and G. Therborn (eds) *Capital cities in Africa: power and powerlessness*. Cape Town: HSRC Press, pp 120–40.

Padfield, R. (2011) "Neoliberalism and the polarizing water geographies of the Zambian Copperbelt," *Waterlines*, 30(2): 150–64.

Painter, J. and Jeffrey, A. (2009) *Political Geography* (2nd edn). Los Angeles, CA: Sage.

Parnell, S. and Oldfield, S. (eds) (2014) *The Routledge handbook on cities of the Global South*. London and New York, NY: Routledge.

Parnell, S. and Pieterse, E. (eds) (2014) *Africa's urban revolution*. London: Zed Books.

Parnell, S. and Walawage, R. (2014) "Sub-Saharan African urbanization and global environmental change," in S. Parnell and E. Pieterse (eds) *Africa's urban revolution*. London: Zed Books, pp 35–59.

Parrot, L., Sotamenou, J., and Kamgnia Dia, B. (2009) "Municipal solid waste management in Africa: strategies and livelihoods in Yaounde, Cameroon," *Waste Management*, 29(2): 986–95.

Pearce, F.B. (1920) *Zanzibar: island metropolis of Eastern Africa*. London: MacMillan.

Pelling, M. (2003) "Toward a political ecology of urban environmental risk: the case of Guyana," in K. Zimmerer and T. Bassett (eds) *Political ecology: an integrative approach to geography and environment-development studies*. New York, NY: Guilford Press, pp 73–93.

Philifert, P. (2014) "Morocco 2011/2012: persistence of past urban policies or a new historical sequence for urban action," *Built Environment*, 40(1): 72–84.

Pieterse, E. (2008) *City futures: confronting the crisis of urban development*. London: Zed Books.

Pieterse, E. (2010) "Cityness and African urban development," *Urban Forum*, 21: 205–19.

Pieterse, E. (2013) "Introducing rogue urbanism," in E. Pieterse and A.M. Simone (eds) *Rogue urbanism: emergent African cities*. Cape Town: Jacana Media, pp 12–15.

Pieterse, E. (2014) "Filling the void: an agenda for tackling African urbanization," in S. Parnell and E. Pieterse (eds) *Africa's urban revolution*. London: Zed Books, pp 200–20.

Pieterse, E. and Parnell, S. (2014) "Africa's urban revolution in context," in S. Parnell and E. Pieterse (eds) *Africa's urban revolution*. London: Zed Books, pp 1–17.

Pieterse, E. and Simone, A.M. (2009) "Framing themes and questions for an engagement on African urbanism," unpublished paper available at African Centre for Cities, Cape Town: www.africancentreforcities.net.

Pieterse E. and Simone A. (eds) (2013) *Rogue urbanism: emergent African cities*. Cape Town: Jacana Media and African Centre for Cities.

Piggott, R. (1961) *A school geography of Zanzibar*. London: Macmillan.

Pile, S. (2005) *Real cities: modernity, space and the phantasmagorias of city life*. London: Sage.

Pinther, K., Förster, L., and Hanussek, C. (2012) "In Afropolis," in K. Pinther, L. Förster and C. Hanussek (eds) *Afropolis: city media art: Cairo Lagos Nairobi Kinshasa Johannesburg*. Cape Town: Jacana Media, pp 14–22.

Pirie, G. (2014) "Transport pressures in urban Africa: practices, policies, perspectives," in S. Parnell and E. Pieterse (eds) *Africa's urban revolution*. London: Zed Books, pp 133–47.

Pitt, B. and Boulle, T. (2010) *Growing together: thinking and practice of urban nature conservators*. Cape Town: South African National Biodiversity Institute and Cape Flats Nature.

Potts, D. (2004) "Regional urbanization and urban livelihoods in the context of globalization," in D. Potts and T. Bowyer-Bower (eds) *Eastern and Southern Africa: development challenges in a volatile region*. Harlow: Pearson Education, pp 328–68.

Potts, D. (2005) "Counter-urbanization on the Zambian Copperbelt? Interpretations and implications," *Urban Studies*, 42(4): 583–609.

Potts, D. (2006) "City life in Zimbabwe at a time of fear and loathing: urban planning, urban poverty, and Operation Murambatsvina," in M. Murray and G. Myers (eds) *Cities in contemporary Africa*. New York, NY: Palgrave MacMillan, pp 265–88.

Powdermaker, H. (1962) *Copper Town: changing Africa, the human situation on the Rhodesian Copperbelt*. New York, NY: Harper and Row.

Prashad, V. (2015) "Republic of Tahrir," *Frontline*, 3 April. Available at: http://www.frontline.in/world-affairs/republic-of-tahrir/article6993815.ece?homepage=true (accessed 22 April 2015).

Pullan, R. (1986) "The biogeography of Lusaka, with special reference to trees and shrubs," in G. Williams (ed) *Lusaka and its environs: a geographical study of a planned capital city in tropical Africa*. Lusaka: Zambia Geographical Association, pp 278–89.

Quayson, A. (2014) *Oxford Street, Accra: city life and the itineraries of transnationalism*. Durham, NC, and London: Duke University Press.

Rademacher, A. (2011) *Reigning the river: urban ecologies and political transformation in Kathmandu*. Durham, NC: Duke University Press.

Rakodi, C. (1986) "Colonial urban planning in Northern Rhodesia and its legacy," *Third World Planning*, Review 8: 193–218.

Rakodi, C. (2006) "Relationships of power and place: the social construction of African cities," *Geoforum*, 37(3): 312–17.

Rakodi, C. (2014) "Religion and social life in African cities," in S. Parnell and E. Pieterse (eds) *Africa's urban revolution*. London: Zed Books, pp 82–109.

Reyntjens, F. (2004) "Rwanda, ten years on: from genocide to dictatorship," *African Affairs*, 103(411): 177–210.

Rigg, J., Bebbington, A., Gough, K., Bryceson, D., Agergaard, J., Fold, N., and Tacoli, C. (2009) "The *World development report 2009* 'reshapes economic geography': geographical reflections," *Transactions of the Institute of British Geographers*, 34:128–36.

Rijal, H. (2014) Author personal communication with Hamza Rijal, Department of Environment, Revolutionary Government of Zanzibar.

Robbins, P. (2012) *Political ecology: a critical introduction* (2nd edn). Oxford: Wiley Blackwell.

Robert, S. (1991 [1951]) *Kusadikika* [*Land of make-believe*]. Dar es Salaam: Mkuki na Nyota Publishers.

Roberts, A. (1976) *A history of Zambia*. New York, NY: Africana Publishing.

Robins, S. (2006) "When shacks ain't chic! Planning for 'difference' in post-apartheid Cape Town," in S. Bekker and A. Leilde (eds) *Reflections on identity in four African cities*. Johannesburg: African Minds, pp 97–117.

Robinson, J. (2006) *Ordinary cities*. London: Routledge.

Robinson, J. (2011) "Cities in a world of cities: the comparative gesture," *International Journal of Urban and Regional Research*, 35(1): 1–23.

Robinson, J. (2013) "The urban now: theorising cities beyond the new," *European Journal of Cultural Studies*, 16(6): 659–77.

Robinson, J. (forthcoming) "Comparative urbanism: new geographies and cultures of theorising the urban," *International Journal of Urban and Regional Research*.

Robinson, J. and Parnell, S. (2011) "Traveling theory: embracing post-neoliberalism through Southern cities," in G. Bridge and S. Watson (eds) *The new Blackwell companion to the city*. Oxford: Wiley-Blackwell, pp 521–31.

Roy, A. (2009) "The 21st century metropolis: new geographies of theory," *Regional Studies*, 43(6): 819–30.

Sager, T. (2011) "Neo-liberal urban planning policies: a literature survey 1990–2010," *Progress in Planning*, 76: 147–99.

Salem, G. (1992) "Crise urbaine et contrôle social à Pikine: bornes-fontaines et clientélisme," *Politique Africaine*, 45: 21–38.

Salim, C. (2010) "Municipal solid waste management in Dar es Salaam city, Tanzania," *Waste Management*, 30(7): 1430–1.

Sall, J. (2013) Author's focus group interview with Jibril Sall, Director, Centre Leopold Senghor, Africulturban, in Pikine West, City of Pikine, Dakar, with Tom Hanlon, Alasse Elhadji, four US undergraduate students, and staff members of Partners Senegal, 9 January.

Samara, T.R. (2011) *Cape Town after apartheid: crime and governance in the divided city*. Minneapolis, MN: University of Minnesota Press.

Samatar, A., Lindberg, M., and Mahayni, B. (2010) "The dialectics of piracy in Somalia: the rich versus the poor," *Third World Quarterly*, 31(8): 1377–94.

Sampson, R. (1971) *So this was Lusaakas: the story of the capital of Zambia* (2nd edn). Ndola, Zambia: Mission Press.

Sandberg, L.A., Bardekjian, A., and Butt, S. (2015) *Urban forests, trees and greenspace: a political ecology perspective*. New York, NY: Routledge.

SARDC (Southern African Research and Documentation Centre) (1994) *State of the environment in Southern Africa*. Harare, Zimbabwe: SARDC.

Satterthwaite, D. (2014) "Urban poverty in low- and middle-income nations," in S. Parnell and S. Oldfield (eds) *The Routledge handbook on cities of the Global South*. London and New York, NY: Routledge, pp 569–85.

Schroeder, R. (1999) *Shady practices: agroforestry and gender politics in The Gambia*. Berkeley and Los Angeles, CA: University of California Press.

Schroeder, R. (2012) *Africa after apartheid: South Africa, race, and nation in Tanzania*. Bloomington, IN: Indiana University Press.

Scott, J. (1998) *Seeing like a state: how certain schemes to improve the human condition have failed*. New Haven, CT: Yale University Press.

Seburanga, J., Kaplin, B., Zhang, Q.-X., and Gatesire, T. (2014) "Amenity trees and green space structure in urban settlements of Kigali, Rwanda," *Urban Forestry and Urban Greening*, 13(1): 84–93.

Sembene, O. (1970) *God's bits of wood*. Garden City, NY: Anchor Books.

Shackleton, S., Chinyimba, A., Hebinck, P., Shackleton, C., and Kaoma, H. (2015) "Multiple benefits and values of trees in urban landscapes in two towns in northern South Africa," *Landscape and Urban Planning*, 136: 76–86.

Sheldon, K. (1996) "Urban African women: courtyards, markets, city streets," in K. Sheldon (ed) *Courtyards, markets, city streets: urban African women*. Boulder, CO: Westview, pp 3–27.

Shillington, L. (2012) "Urban political ecology in the Global South: everyday environmental struggles of home in Managua, Nicaragua," in T. Edensor and M. Jayne (eds) *Urban theory beyond the West: a world of cities*. London: Routledge, pp 295–310.

Shinn, J. (2015) "The rhetoric and reality of community empowerment in coastal conservation: a case study from Menai Bay Conservation Area, Tanzania," *African Geographical Review*, 34(2): 107–24.

Shirlow, P. (2009) "Representation," in C. Gallaher, C. Dahlmann, M. Gilmartin, A. Mountz, and P. Shirlow (eds) *Key concepts in political geography*. Los Angeles, CA: Sage, pp 308–18.

Sigauke, J., Chiwaura, H., and Mawere, M. (2014) "Connoisseurs of traditional medicine: the use and efficacy of traditional medicine in pregnant women's health care," in M. Mawere and T. Mubaya (eds) *African cultures, memory and space: living in the past presence in Zimbabwean heritage*. Bamenda, Cameroon: Langaa Research and Publishing Common Initiative Group, pp 111–34.

Simon, D. and Leck, H. (2014) "Urban dynamics and the challenges of global environmental change in the South," in S. Parnell and S. Oldfield (eds) *The Routledge handbook on cities of the Global South*. London and New York, NY: Routledge, pp 613–28.

Simone, A.M. (2004) *For the city yet to come: changing African life in four cities*. Durham, NC: Duke University Press.

Simone, A.M. (2010) *City life from Jakarta to Dakar: movements at the crossroads*. London: Routledge.

Simone, A.M. (2012) "No longer the subaltern: refiguring cities of the Global South," in T. Edensor and M. Jayne (eds) *Urban theory beyond the West: a world of cities*. London: Routledge, pp 31–46.

Simone, A.M. (2014) "Infrastructure, real economies and social transformation: assembling the components for regional urban development in Africa," in S. Parnell and E. Pieterse (eds) *Africa's urban revolution*. London: Zed Books, pp 221–36.

Slaymaker, W. (2001) "Ecoing the other(s): the call of global green and black African responses," *PMLA*, 116: 129–44.

Smit, W. (2015) "Transforming cities: analyzing the recontextualization of discourses of the urban in post-apartheid Cape Town," unpublished doctoral dissertation, University of Cape Town.

Smit, W. and Pieterse, E. (2014) "Decentralisation and institutional reconfiguration in urban Africa," in S. Parnell and E. Pieterse (eds) *Africa's urban revolution*. London: Zed Books, pp 148–66.

Soal, S. and Van Blerk, R. (2005) *Report to the Cape Flats Nature project coordinator*. Cape Town: Community Development Resource Agency.

Söderström, O. (2014) *Cities in relations: trajectories of urban development in Hanoi and Ouagadougou*. Malden, MA: Wiley Blackwell.

Sracek, O., Kribek, B., Mihaljevic, M., Majer, V., Veselovsky, F., Vencelides, Z., and Nyambe, I. (2012) "Mining-related contamination of surface water and sediments of the Kafue River drainage system in the Copperbelt district, Zambia: an example of a high neutralization capacity system," *Journal of Geochemical Exploration*, 112: 174–88.

Steck, J.-F., Didier, S., Morange, M., and Rubin, M. (2013) "Informality, public space and urban governance: an approach through street trading (Abdijan, Cape Town, Johannesburg, Lomé and Nairobi)," in S. Bekker and L. Fourchard (eds) *Governing cities in Africa*. Cape Town: HSRC Press, pp 145–68.

Stiles, D. (1992) "The ports of East Africa, the Comoros and Madagascar: their place in the Indian Ocean trade from 1–1500 AD," *Kenya Past and Present*, 24: 27–36.

Stoffberg, G., Van Rooyen, M., Van der Linde, M., and Groeneveld, H. (2010) "Carbon sequestration estimates of indigenous street trees in the city of Tshwane, South Africa," *Urban Forestry & Urban Greening*, 9: 9–14.

Sutton, J. (1990) *A thousand years of East Africa*. Nairobi: British Institute in Eastern Africa.

Swilling, M. (2006) "Sustainability and infrastructure planning in South Africa: a Cape Town case study," *Environment and Urbanization*, 18(1): 23–50.

Swilling, M. (2010) *Sustaining Cape Town: Imagining a livable city*. Stellenbosch: Sun Press and the Sustainability Institute.

Swilling, M. (2013) "Reconceptualising urbanism, ecology and networked infrastructure," in E. Pieterse and A.M. Simone (eds) *Rogue urbanism: emergent African cities*. Cape Town: Jacana Media and African Centre for Cities, pp 65–81.

Swilling, M. and Annecke, E. (2012) *Just transitions: explorations of sustainability in an unfair world*. Tokyo: United Nations University Press.

Swyngedouw, E. (1996) "The city as a hybrid: on nature, society, and cyborg urbanization," *Capitalism Nature Socialism*, 7(2): 65–80.

Swyngedouw, E. (2003) "Modernity and the production of the Spanish waterscape," in K. Zimmerer and T. Bassett (eds) *Political ecology: an integrative approach to geography and environment-development studies*. New York, NY: Guilford Press, pp 94–112.

Swyngedouw, E. (2005) "Governance innovation and the citizen: the Janus face of governance-beyond-the state," *Urban Studies*, 42(11): 1–16.

Swyngedouw, E. (2009a) "The antinomies of the post-political city—in search of a democratic politics of environmental production," *International Journal of Urban and Regional Research* 33(3): 601–20.

Swyngedouw, E. (2009b) "Circulations and metabolisms: (Hybrid) natures and (cyborg) cities," in D. White and C. Wilbert (eds), *Technonatures: Environments, technologies, spaces, and places in the twenty-first century*. Waterloo, Ontario: Wilfred Laurier University Press, pp 61–84.

Swyngedouw, E. (2011a) "H2O does not exist!? Retooling the Washington–Brussels consensus," paper presented to the Water and Sanitation Symposium, STEPS Centre, University of Sussex. Available at: https://www.youtube.com/watch?v=pQPak5tyHKg (accessed 17 April 2015).

Swyngedouw, E. (2011b) "Interrogating post-democracy: reclaiming egalitarian political spaces," *Political Geography*, 30: 370–80.

Swyngedouw, E. (2014) "Where is the political? Insurgent mobilisations and the incipient 'return of the political,'" *Space and Polity*, 18(2): 122–36.

Sy, A. (2015) Author personal communication with Amadou Sy, Director, Africa Growth Initiative, Brookings Institution, Washington, DC, 9 March.

Tait, J. (1997) *From self-help housing to sustainable settlement: capitalist development and urban planning in Lusaka, Zambia*. Brookfield, VT: Avebury.

Tangwa, G. (2010) *Elements of African bioethics in a Western frame*. Bamenda, Cameroon: Langaa Research and Publishing Common Initiative Group.

Tarimo, S. (2010) "Politicization of ethnic identities: the case of contemporary Africa," *Journal of Asian and African Studies*, 45: 297–308.

Tate, E. (2015) "Thomas Sankara and Burkina Faso's 'Black Spring,'" *The Bullet* (Socialist Project E-Bulletin 1078), 9 February. Available at: http://www.socialistproject.ca/bullet/1078.php

Thieme, T. (2010) "Youth, waste and work in Mathare: whose business and whose politics?" *Environment and Urbanization*, 22: 333–52.

Trefon, T. (2009) "Hinges and fringes: conceptualizing the peri-urban in Central Africa," in F. Locatelli and P. Nugent (eds) *African cities: competing claims on urban spaces*. Leiden: Brill, pp 15–36.

Trimingham, J.S. (1975) "The Arab geographers and the East African coast," in H.N. Chittick and R. Rotberg (eds) *East Africa and the Orient: cultural syntheses in pre-colonial times*. New York, NY, and London: Africana Publishing, pp 115–46.

Tsinda, A., Abbott, P., Pedley, S., Charles, K., Adogo, J., Okurut, K., and Chenoweth, J. (2013) "Challenges to achieving sustainable sanitation in informal settlements of Kigali, Rwanda," *International Journal of Environmental Research and Public Health*, 10(12): 6939–54.

Tukahirwa J., Mol, A., and Oosterveer, P. (2010) "Civil society participation in urban sanitation and solid waste management in Uganda," *Local Environment*, 15(1): 1–14.

Turner, V. (1968) *The drums of affliction: a study of religious processes among the Ndembu of Zambia*. Oxford: Clarendon Press.

Turok, I. (2013) "The resilience of South African cities a decade after local democracy," *Environment and Planning A*, 46(4): 749–69.

Turok, I. and Seelinger, L. (2013) "Averting a downward spiral: building resilience in informal urban settlements through adaptive governance," *Environment and Urbanization*, 26(1): 184–99.

UNEP (United Nations Environment Program) (2009) *Kenya: atlas of our changing environment*. Nairobi: UNEP.

UN Habitat (United Nations Habitat) (2010) *The state of African cities 2010: governance, inequality and urban land markets*. Nairobi: UN Habitat.

UN Habitat (2013a) *State of the world's cities 2012/13: prosperity of cities*. London and New York, NY: Routledge.

UN Habitat (2013b) *State of planning in Africa: an overview*. Nairobi: UN Habitat.

UN Habitat (2013c) *Unleashing the economic potential of agglomeration in African cities*. Nairobi: UN Habitat.

UN Habitat (2014) *State of African cities 2014: re-imagining sustainable urban transitions*. Nairobi: UN Habitat.

University of Nairobi (2012) *Approaches to informal settlement upgrading in East Africa*. Nairobi: University of Nairobi, School of the Built Environment, Centre for Urban Research and Innovations, Conference Proceedings.

Valette, E. and Philifert, P. (2014) "L'agriculture urbaine: Un impensé des politiques publiques marocaines?" *Géocarrefour*, 89(1/2): 75–83.

Van Alstine, J. and Afionis, S. (2013) "Community and company capacity: the challenge of resource-led development in Zambia's 'New Copperbelt,'" *Community Development Journal*, 48(3): 360–76.

Van Dijk, M.P., Etajak, S., Mwalwega, B., and Ssempebwa, J. (2014) "Financing sanitation and cost recovery in the slums of Dar es Salaam and Kampala," *Habitat International*, 43: 206–13.

Verniere, M. (1973) "Pikine, 'ville nouvelle' de Dakar, un cas de pseudo-urbanisation," *L'Espace Géographique*, 2: 107–26.

Vierke, U. and Siegert, N. (2013) "Urban memories and utopias: contemporary art in Luanda and Nairobi," in B. Obrist, V. Arlt, and E. Macamo (eds) *Living the city in Africa: processes of invention and intervention*. Zurich: Lit Verlag, pp 135–52.

Vital, A. (2008) "Toward an African ecocriticism: postcolonialism, ecology and *Life & times of Michael K.*," *Research in African Literatures*, 39(1): 87–106.

Vital, A. (2011) "Waste and postcolonial history: an ecocritical reading of J. M. Coetzee's *Age of iron*," in B. Caminero-Santangelo and G. Myers (eds) *Environment at the margins: literary and environmental studies in Africa*. Athens, OH: Ohio University Press, pp 185–212.

Vital, A. (2015) "Ecocriticism, globalized cities, and African narrative, with a focus on K. Sello Duiker's *Thirteen cents*," in S. Slovic, S. Rangarajan, and V. Sarveswaran (eds) *Ecocriticism of the Global South*. Lanham, MD: Lexington Books.

Vítková, M., Ettler, V., Hyks, J., Astrup, T., and Krībek, B. (2011) "Leaching of metals from copper smelter flue dust (Mufulira, Zambian Copperbelt)," *Applied Geochemistry*, 26: S263–66.

Von der Heyden, C. and New, M. (2004) "Groundwater pollution on the Zambian Copperbelt: deciphering the source and the risk," *Science of the Total Environment*, 327 (1–3): 17–30.

Wainaina, B. (2005) "How to write about Africa," *Granta*, 92: 92–5.

Waki Commission (2008) *Waki Commission of inquiry into the post-election violence following the December 2007 general election*. Nairobi: Government of Kenya.

Wanyoike, J. (2013) "Is urbanization in Africa a tool for prosperity or paucity?" Center for Urban Research and Innovations blog post. Available at: http://www.centreforurbaninnovations.org/ (accessed 9 March 2014).

Watson, V. (2003) "Conflicting rationalities: implications for planning theory and ethics," *Planning Theory and Practice*, 4(4): 395–408.

Watson, V. (2009a) "'The planned city sweeps the poor away …': urban planning and 21st century urbanization," *Progress in Planning*, 72: 151–93.

Watson, V. (2009b) "Seeing from the South: refocusing urban planning on the globe's central urban issues," *Urban Studies*, 46(11): 2259–75.

Wheeler, S. and Beatley, T. (eds) (2009) *The sustainable urban development reader* (2nd edn). London: Routledge.

Wheeler, S. and Beatley, T. (eds) (2014) *The sustainable urban development reader* (3rd edn). London: Routledge.

Whitaker, B. and Giersch, J. (2009) "Voting on a constitution: implications for democracy in Kenya," *Journal of Contemporary African Studies*, 27: 1–20.

White, L. (2000) *Speaking with vampires: rumor and history in colonial Africa*. Berkeley, CA: University of California Press.

White, L.T., Silberman, L., and Anderson, P. (1948) *Nairobi master plan for a colonial capitol*. London: HMSO.

Williams, R. (1973) *The country and the city*. Oxford: Oxford University Press.

Williams, R. (1976) *Keywords: a vocabulary of society and culture*. Oxford: Oxford University Press.

Williams, R. (1977) *Marxism and literature*. Oxford: Oxford University Press.

Williams, R. (1980) *Culture and materialism*. London: Verso.

Williams, R.O. (1949) *The useful and ornamental plants of Zanzibar and Pemba*. Zanzibar: Government of Zanzibar.

Wilson, T. (1982) "Spatial analysis and settlement patterns on the East African coast," *Paideuma*, 28: 202–19.

Wolf, T. (2009) "'Poll poison'? Politicians and polling in the 2007 Kenya election," *Journal of Contemporary African Studies*, 27: 279–304.

World Bank (2009) *World development report 2009: reshaping economic geography*. Washington, DC: World Bank.

Zambian Watchdog (2012) "PF plans to demolish Lusaka compounds now a reality," *Zambian watchdog*, 24 May. Available at: http://www.zambianwatchdog.com (accessed 18 October 2013).

ZATI (Zanzibar Association of Tourism Investors) (2014) "News," Zanzibar Association of Tourism Investors. Available at: http://www.zati.org/

Zimmerer, K. and Bassett, T. (2003a) "Approaching political ecology: society, nature and scale in human–environment studies," in K. Zimmerer and T. Bassett (eds) *Political ecology: an integrative approach to geography and environment-development studies*. New York, NY: Guilford Press, pp 1–25.

Zimmerer, K. and Bassett, T. (2003b) "Future directions in political ecology: nature–society fusions and scales of interaction," in K. Zimmerer and T. Bassett (eds) *Political ecology: an integrative approach to geography and environment-development studies*. New York, NY: Guilford Press, pp 274–95.

Index

Note: Page numbers in *italics* indicate tables and figures. Page numbers ending in the letter *g* refer to terms in the glossary.